Mountain Based

Paul Beedie

Mountain Based Adventure Tourism

Lifestyle Choice and Identity Formation

LAP LAMBERT Academic Publishing

Impressum/Imprint (nur für Deutschland/ only for Germany)
Bibliografische Information der Deutschen Nationalbibliothek: Die Deutsche Nationalbibliothek verzeichnet diese Publikation in der Deutschen Nationalbibliografie; detaillierte bibliografische Daten sind im Internet über http://dnb.d-nb.de abrufbar.
 Alle in diesem Buch genannten Marken und Produktnamen unterliegen warenzeichen-, marken- oder patentrechtlichem Schutz bzw. sind Warenzeichen oder eingetragene Warenzeichen der jeweiligen Inhaber. Die Wiedergabe von Marken, Produktnamen, Gebrauchsnamen, Handelsnamen, Warenbezeichnungen u.s.w. in diesem Werk berechtigt auch ohne besondere Kennzeichnung nicht zu der Annahme, dass solche Namen im Sinne der Warenzeichen- und Markenschutzgesetzgebung als frei zu betrachten wären und daher von jedermann benutzt werden dürften.

Coverbild: www.ingimage.com

Verlag: LAP LAMBERT Academic Publishing AG & Co. KG
Dudweiler Landstr. 99, 66123 Saarbrücken, Deutschland
Telefon +49 681 3720-310, Telefax +49 681 3720-3109
Email: info@lap-publishing.com

Herstellung in Deutschland:
Schaltungsdienst Lange o.H.G., Berlin
Books on Demand GmbH, Norderstedt
Reha GmbH, Saarbrücken
Amazon Distribution GmbH, Leipzig
ISBN: 978-3-8383-5043-1

Imprint (only for USA, GB)
Bibliographic information published by the Deutsche Nationalbibliothek: The Deutsche Nationalbibliothek lists this publication in the Deutsche Nationalbibliografie; detailed bibliographic data are available in the Internet at http://dnb.d-nb.de.
 Any brand names and product names mentioned in this book are subject to trademark, brand or patent protection and are trademarks or registered trademarks of their respective holders. The use of brand names, product names, common names, trade names, product descriptions etc. even without a particular marking in this works is in no way to be construed to mean that such names may be regarded as unrestricted in respect of trademark and brand protection legislation and could thus be used by anyone.

Cover image: www.ingimage.com

Publisher: LAP LAMBERT Academic Publishing AG & Co. KG
Dudweiler Landstr. 99, 66123 Saarbrücken, Germany
Phone +49 681 3720-310, Fax +49 681 3720-3109
Email: info@lap-publishing.com

Printed in the U.S.A.
Printed in the U.K. by (see last page)
ISBN: 978-3-8383-5043-1

Copyright © 2010 by the author and LAP LAMBERT Academic Publishing AG & Co. KG and licensors
All rights reserved. Saarbrücken 2010

Contents

Page	Section	Title

Chapter one: Introduction

Page	Section	Title
3		Introduction

Chapter two: Theoretical Framework

Page	Section	Title
17	2.1	Framing Mountaineering
22	2.2	Status, Legislators and Interpreters
30	2.3	Identity and Performance in Mountains
37	2.4	Summary

Chapter three: Research Design

Page	Section	Title
39	3.1	The Qualitative Research Paradigm
41	3.2	Qualitative Research and Tourism
42	3.3	An Emergent Research Design
45	3.4	A Journey into the Mountains
50	3.5	Research Design and the Tools of Data Collection
59	3.6	Fieldwork Details
63	3.7	Ethnographic Issues
66	3.8	Summary

Chapter four: The Cultural Reproduction of Mountains and Mountaineering

Page	Section	Title
68	4.1	Defining Mountains and Mountaineering
75	4.2	Romanticism and the Social Construction of Mountains
88	4.3	Building a Mountaineering Frame
97	4.4	Summary

Chapter five: The Body and Physical Capital

Page	Section	Title
99	5.1	Physical Capital
107	5.2	The Mountaineering Body
126	5.3	Summary

Chapter six: Clothing, Equipment and the Fashion of Mountaineering

Page	Section	Title
128	6.1	Fashion Systems
137	6.2	Technology, Equipment and Comfort
147	6.3	Cultural Capital and Distinction

| 152 | 6.4 | Summary |

Chapter seven: Measurement and Grading Systems

153	7.1	Mountaineering, Modernity and Measurement
156	7.2	Grading Systems, Capital and Mountaineering Careers
167	7.3	Munros and Munro Bagging
171	7.4	Maps Guidebooks and Magazines
175	7.5	Summary

Chapter eight: Performing in the Mountains

178	8.1	Introduction to Performing in the Mountains
179	8.2	Theorising Performance
182	8.3	Guides as Experts
187	8.4	Writing Scripts and Directing Performances
197	8.5	Guides at Work
203	8.6	Performance as Edgework
207	8.7	Summary

Chapter nine: Conclusions

| 209 | | Conclusions |

References

| 216 | | References |

Chapter one: Introduction

When I was eight years old I ran to the top of my first 'mountain', a hill somewhere in the Chilterns. When I was eighteen I was led up my first big 'mountain' roped ascent. The climb was Giants Crawl on Dow Crag, an imposing chunk of mountain overlooking Coniston in the Lake District. The first experience left me elated, the second too, but not before I had experienced great fear because, amongst other things, it was a long way down! I can recall my jagged and jittery movements high on this climb as I hugged the rock and followed the red and black rope onwards and upwards. I was hooked, and it was not many years later that I led my first extreme[1] rock climb. I can recall the names and grades of all the significant mountain ascents, walking and climbing, which I have completed in the last twenty-five years. Mountaineering has given me skills, knowledge and experiences that have made a major contribution to who I am. I have grown up with the mountains, I have climbed with many people, I have read mountaineering books and I have become a mountaineering instructor. People, places and the prevailing mountaineering culture have combined to construct who I am. This book is an exploration of 'being a mountaineer', and, as a mountaineering-researcher, I am located centrally to it.

Many years of reflection about mountaineering promoted an urge in me to find out and understand what 'it' is all about, as far as this might be possible. This book is a statement of where I currently stand in the ongoing process of understanding. It was that first climb on that big mountain crag that sowed the seed, because, I was doing something wild. I was curious to know what was round the next corner of the climb, and, eventually I became curious to know as much as possible, about wildness. Rothenberg (1995:xiii) articulates this idea in the following way:

> The idea of wildness has always been deeper than a place that exists because we place boundaries around it and call it a 'wilderness'. We love and fear the wild in all parts of our culture, and it exerts its power because of this.

Mountains are wild places in the way that Rothenberg uses the term. They are places of power, but, they are made so by people. I believe that people in mountains are exploring wild places but they are also exploring the idea of wildness. My fascination, therefore, in

---
[1] Climbing grades are explained in chapter seven.

not as simple as 'mountains', it is 'people in mountains'. Through history the relationship between people and mountains has rarely remained constant. My work as a mountaineering instructor, when I began this book, combined with a reflective dimension on wildness, and my personal walking and climbing, to identify an area of potential social research. I became curious about adventure tourism, an area of development, I thought, that appeared to be having an impact on the way people became mountaineers. I knew what social research was, but had little first hand experience of it. In the process of finding out more, gradually, some very broad ideas began to emerge with a focus that I became quite excited about. I had never undertaken a project of this scale and intensity before, so it became a little daunting. What follows is an account of how it all started, how it developed over a period of several years and the conclusions I have been able to draw. As with my first big climb on Dow Crag, I have reached a point of completion on the day. The ropes are now coiled and the glow of satisfaction remains. But, the climb was a beginning, and so is this book.

The aim of my study is to illuminate the relationship between identity, capital and social distinction in mountaineering in the context of consumer culture and adventure tourism. My emphasis is, therefore, on mountains. Mountains evoke ideas of adventure and appear to offer an opportunity to explore a 'natural' environment. However, mountains are socially constructed, and as such provide opportunities for the formation of identities. Mountains have historically been the preserve of people who 'know mountains', that is, have the knowledge and skills commensurate with exploratory endeavour in mountains. Such people might be thought of as mountaineers, a self-validating group created and sustained by its shared understanding of, and experience in, 'being a mountaineer'. Adventure holidays have, I would suggest, introduced new ways of 'being a mountaineer'. However, there is a potential tension broadly suggested by the agency-structure debate (Rojek 2000). The tension in this study emerges between what is 'natural' and what is socially constructed, and between freedom and constraint.

Mountains may appear to be 'natural', but historically there has been a process of change whereby 'meaning' has been inscribed on mountains through human activities. Such activities have been economic (e.g. farming), commercial (e.g. skiing) and social (e.g. mountain recreation). Such a process has 'en-cultured' mountains. When mountain holidays are organised and incorporate ideas of risk and challenge, the term adventure tourism appears in the literature (Christiansen 1990, Trauer 1999, Weber 2001). Adventure tourism may embrace established pursuits such as walking and climbing but a proliferation of activities has emerged to extend the possibilities embraced by the term 'mountain recreation'. This in turn has the potential to contest and even re-define the identity of 'mountaineer' by challenging the values held by the mountaineering tradition. Edensor (2000:95) expresses this point in his discussion of the 'appropriateness' of walking as recreation: "by espousing particular cultural values through their embodied practices, walkers acquire status among like-minded practitioners and assert these values to claim that their particular practices are 'appropriate' in a rural setting". Developing Edensor's point, it could be suggested that, the values projected by groups who identify strongly with the traditional pursuits (e.g. walking and climbing) contest mountain spaces with people who may espouse different values. Such groups might include those that practice activities such as mountain biking, orienteering, fell running, hang gliding, parachuting and white water rafting. All these activities (and many others) are embraced by the commercial possibilities of adventure tourism.

My focus is more specific in that I am particularly interested in people who buy holidays from companies that specialise in 'mountaineering', that is, walking-trekking, climbing and scrambling in mountains. Not only is mountaineering the background that I bring to this study through my own experiences, but it also opens up the possibilities of investigating a specific as opposed to a general effect of adventure tourism. The study is concerned, then, with two broadly defined groups, 'mountaineers' and 'adventure tourists'. These are by no means clear categories, indeed, ambivalence, "the possibility of assigning an object or an event to more than one category" (Bauman 1991:1) provides a key strand in the rationale outlined below. However, in order to demonstrate consistency and thereby help the discussion, 'mountaineer' is a term used to identify people who have knowledge, skills and experience that facilitate apparent 'freedom' from quotidian routine in urban life through climbing and walking. Mountaineers are most likely to operate independently when doing their activities. Adventure tourists buy adventure holidays and, therefore, are apparently 'constrained' though their dependency. The term 'client' is used to describe such people, who also seek freedom, but who have apparently chosen to let others decide how best they might achieve this.

As the project evolved it became clear that I was bringing together three areas of existing literature in a way that had not been attempted before. This synthesis of mountaineering literature, tourism literature and existing research into adventure tourism, defines the originality of my book. The following discussion expands on this point, and, thereby, sets out a rationale for what follows. Several factors influenced the proposed area of investigation and the research design. First, with some notable exceptions (Rothenberg 1995, Oelschlaeger 1991 who explore ideas of wilderness), mountaineering has not been extensively theorised. Despite a huge body of writing about mountaineering, explanatory theory is rare. The same point can be made in relation to adventure tourism, although there is evidence to suggest a heightened awareness that may well lead to an expanding literature of adventure tourism (Weber 2001, Hudson 2002). Second, of the limited empirical work that currently exists (Cloke & Perkins 1998a, 1998b, Weiler & Hall 1992, Cohen 1989, Binkhurst 1995, Allison et al. 1991), adventure tourism has hitherto been explored largely through the 'external' position of an 'impartial' researcher rather than the 'internal' perspective of a participant. It is only recently that the experience of clients has been acknowledged as a legitimate and important source of data (Weber 2001). As the following section will endeavour to show, existing theories of tourism emphasise structure and typologies and in doing so diminish the voice of the subjects at the expense of an ambition to provide 'completed' theories. A qualitative methodology, such as the one I have employed, and the position advocated by Weber (2001), is more likely to draw out the complexities of the real world settings in which mountain based adventure tourism operates.

This study was, therefore, conceived as qualitative and evolved as a broadly based methodology defined by the term ethnographic methods, or micro-ethnography (Wolcott 1990). The focus became the United Kingdom, (although I did travel to Spain with clients for one course), predominantly for practical reasons. Data collection tools came to include participant observation, interviews, telephone calls, written and oral feedback from transcripts, brochure and magazine analysis and any other opportunity to document the voice of clients. Sources of data included magazines such as High, Climber, On the Edge, Trail and The Great Outdoors and adventure company brochures. Videos were recognised as an important medium for showing climbers in action and television programmes such as

Wilderness Walks, and more recently Wild Climbs, (both transmitted by the BBC). I used these sources through my perspective as 'mountaineer' because they were related to the adventure holidays I accompanied. Thus, the emergent design followed the circumstances of the companies and the clients that provided data collection opportunities. For example, adventure tourism in mountains equates to a holiday lasting from a few days to, at most, a few weeks. Immersion in the field in the anthropological sense of a Whyte in Cornerville (1955), or Sands among collegiate athletes (1999) or even Edensor at the Taj Mahal (1998), does not compare when the 'world' is so temporary. Additionally, working with clients in mountains may be in low ratios. This tradition stems from the early days of Alpinism when a leisured and moneyed elite hired local guides to achieve mountaineering objectives (Bernstein 1989a, 1989b). This reflects important practical considerations of rope management in the more demanding forms of mountaineering, but does lead to small client groups at times. In summary, first, the rationale for this present study is based on a recognition of adventure tourism as an under researched area. Second, the adoption of a qualitative methodology is an attempt to present the voices of the groups under investigation.

It has been argued that 'ordinary' urban life and tourism have become less distinguishable, so that boundaries between these social worlds are no longer obvious (Ritzer & Liska 1997). It has also been shown, (Johnson & Edwards 1994), that a process of commodification has occurred in mountains generally, which has blurred the edges between mountaineering and tourism. Additionally, Beaumont (2002) has shown that mountaineering is more accessible to more people than ever before, primarily because of the courses and adventure holidays now available. It is from this body of knowledge that I have drawn the suggestion that adventure tourism has made a major contribution to democratising social access to mountaineering. Access, for the purpose of this study, is explained as follows. Access is not the changes that have resulted from globalisation, better communications and other developments, although this clearly has a part to play in stimulating and sustaining adventure tourist activity in hitherto remote corners of the world. Access, for my study, is more concerned with the social consequences of those changes, especially the ease with which people can now access the status and identity of 'mountaineer'. Adventure tourism has created an access gateway to mountaineering previously the domain of dedicated individuals who were prepared to spend years building the skills, experience and knowledge that has, hitherto, defined the identity of 'mountaineer'.

This process of democratisation has happened to British mountaineering before. The social elite epitomised by Hubank's (2001) Edwardian group in the Lake District was typically formed by educated, upper-middle class males and was representative of climbers of this era. The 1940s saw an insurgence of working class climbers into mountaineering in the Lake District (Birkett 1983), and particularly the Peak District where the Manchester based Rock and Ice Club played a prominent role in climbing and mountaineering developments (Gray 1979, Whillans & Omerod 1971). Curry (1994:4-9) suggests the politicisation of British Mountain spaces can be traced back to the mass trespass on Kinder in 1932. The momentum has been sustained so that the current changes are not only greater in scale than the working class 'revolution' that began in the 1930s, but the speed of change is faster. The British Mountaineering Council (BMC) suggest that climbing was the fastest growing adventure sport in the 1980s (BMC 1997), and that current BMC membership, a reflection of the number of British mountaineers, is above 55,000 for the first time (Summit 2002:3). The BMC Annual Report for 2001 states that the year was: "another growth year for membership which was 55,573 at year end" (BMC 2001:22). The report goes on to add: "there was also once again a sustained healthy growth in insurance sales" (BMC 2001:22). These figures show the popularity of climbing rather than a direct reflection of participation in adventure tourism, however, taken in alignment with Beamont (2002) it indicates a growing interest in mountaineering.

Mountains represent an environment that offers excitement, stimulation and potential adventure. This dislocation of self from ordinary everyday life to the extraordinary appears to provide a pleasurable experience that is central to tourism (Rojek 1997). Existing tourist theory purports to explain tourist behaviour in relation to 'mass tourism' (MacCannell 1976, Urry 1990, Rojek 1997) leaving the contemporary adventure tourist scene under researched. This is partly explained by the re-deployment of established tourism theory in new settings to which it may not be appropriately aligned. MacCannell's book (1976), for example, was extremely influential in shaping tourism research in the 1980s. He saw tourism as a search for authenticity missing from everyday life and developed Goffman's (1959) model of front and back regions, thereby, utilising a structured approach predicated on a uniformity of tourist ambition, interpretation and behaviour. There is no mention of mountains in MacCannell's book and rarely in the work that followed his approach. This point is illustrated by the work of Ritzer and Liska (1997). On one level, their theory of 'McDonaldisation' may have some merit in the way that it helps an understanding of packaged adventure holidays. However, as will be argued below, there are limitations.

Ritzer and Liska (1997) argue that the driving force of all social change is rationalisation and safety, the antithesis of the notion of adventure. They argue, (Ritzer & Liska 1997) that, as our ordinary lives are structured and, for the most part, undemanding, this leaves us unequipped to deal with extraordinary situations where we may need to be tolerant of inefficiency and the unpredictable. The net result is that we are attracted to packaged holiday formats because the product we are buying is usually clearly defined, including its cost. "Increasingly, our vacations are more and more like the rest of our lives" (Ritzer & Liska 1997:100). The package format reduces the unexpected, reduces the likelihood of both social and physical risks and ultimately reduces the effort involved in organising a holiday. Conversely it increases all aspects of safety, operates a subtle sense of (temporary) community through bringing together groups of like minded people and smoothes out any administrative or logistical problems. Packaging is the antithesis of the original concept of 'travail' or travel (Buzard 1993, Boorstin 1963). Thus, 'adventure' defined as 'uncertainty of outcome', (Miles & Priest 1999) becomes a point of debate. They argue (Ritzer and Liska 1997:101), "for many of those who desire to see the extraordinary, there is also a desire to have McDonaldized stops along the way, and to retreat to at the end of the day".

It has been suggested that all areas of life are subjected to rationalisation and civilising processes (Elias & Dunning 1986, Dunning 1996, Rojek 1995) and that the commodification and packaging of mountaineering is merely a manifestation of this (Johnson & Edwards 1994). Heywood (1994) has shown how climbers have traditionally been anarchic in their approach to their activities but that, today, there is growing evidence of conformity to standards (for example of safety through the use of bolted protection[2]) pervasive amidst other sports and activities. In particular, Heywood sees climbing as an

---

[2] Bolts are secure anchors placed in certain rock types, notably limestone in a UK setting, to provide protection for lead climbers. When a rope is clipped to a bolt with a carabiner, a strong alloy clip, a climber becomes physically more secure that might otherwise be the case.

opportunity for escape from a 'rationalised life-world'. However, through his discussion of the differences (or, I would contend, the similarities) between adventure climbing and sport climbing he shows how: "attempts to evade or resist rationalisation are becoming increasingly rationalised from within" (Heywood 1994:179). Mountaineers might be viewed as protectors of a valued tradition who resist an erosion of the idea of adventure through rationalisation. Similarly, clients might be carriers of rationalisation into mountains or seekers of a mountaineering identity.

The problem, as suggested by Ritzer & Liska (1997), is the fluidity of boundaries between normal life and tourism which brings the two formally distinct experiences closer together. In this respect, the shallowness of normal life is extended into vacation time promoting, in contradistinction to MacCannell (1976), a preference for inauthenticity. Cohen (1988) has already suggested in his critique of MacCannell that what might be considered to be 'authentic' is actually a dynamic concept, which Cohen (1988) calls 'emergent authenticity', that is, authenticity is socially constructed. Ritzer & Liska (1997) go further than this when they suggest that, because tourists are, "accustomed to the simulated dining experience at McDonald's [they will not want to] survive on nuts and berries picked on a walk through the woods" (Ritzer & Liska 1997:107). They argue, therefore, that, today, tourists actually search for inauthenticity. So, when Urry (1990) argues for tourism as an extraordinary experience, this may not apply to tourists who actively seek to minimise the differentiation of home and holiday life. Although mountaineering may be closer to the 'extraordinary' in the sense that Urry (1990) uses the term, (in so much as mountains offer an unpredictable and objectively dangerous environment), mountaineers have an ordered and rational approach to mountaineering. For example, bodies are trained for endurance and specific motility, and food intake approached scientifically; equipment and clothing has been specifically developed to assist comfort and mountaineering is measured and quantified. There could be, therefore, an undermining of the extraordinary as urban, civilised characteristics (by Western standards) move into mountains. Applying Ritzer and Liska (1997) suggests that, by the packaging of adventure, people become less equipped, through routine, to handle the unpredictable. Additionally, people are less tolerant of inefficiency, want to know exactly how much a holiday will cost and want a clear picture of the gains achievable through completing the holiday. However, a valid alternative perspective is that mountains are attractive because of their unpredictability. Mountaineering is adventurous and adventure in this context means engaging with risk so adventure becomes 'uncertainty of outcome' with meaningful consequences (Miles & Priest 1999, Mortlock 1973, 1984, Price 2000). This may be why many people see mountains as arenas for testing their limits. Mountaineering is an embodied experience encompassing a full range of sensory feedback, and there are risks involved. Clients have the opportunity to acquire practical skills (e.g. rope work and navigation), social skills (e.g. tolerance, patience and new perspectives) as well as the satisfaction of mountaineering achievements. Thus, it is too simplistic to suggest, as Ritzer and Liska (1997) do, that tourism can be reduced to a search for inauthenticity when mountain based adventure tourism retains elements of unpredictability, embodiment and risk taking. It may be that clients are seeking something more than everyday life, and this 'something' may be related to identity and their idea of an authentic self and all that this may mean to them socially.

A more realistic analysis is that packaging may well limit the scope clients might have to operate independently and thereby increases dependence upon guides. However, packaging is also a democratic facilitator in the way it opens up opportunities to explore mountains, environments that are far from predictable. The weather and terrain are two variables that can constantly change. The demands of mountaineering are far from being risk free, even with the technical expertise and knowledge available today. Although risk can be 'managed' so that aspects of real danger translate to perceived danger (Mortlock 1984), it remains omnipresent. There are real consequences for one's embodied experiences in mountains. Physically people become aware of their limitations. For example, legs tire when going up hill; feet may get blistered; people will shiver with cold when they stop to rest at the top of a climb; sweat might sting their eyes in the sunshine, while lips may crack and skin redden. Similarly, people might be blown off their feet by the wind, or graze an arm by sliding over a boulder. Or they may develop red weals in their shoulders from carrying rucksacks; or get sweaty palms and a dry throat as a result of the exposure of a traverse high on a steep mountain face, or need to empty their bowels half way up a rock climb. These are embodied responses very different from routine experiences. Emotionally people may move through complete tranquillity and oneness with mountain vistas to extreme fear and its resultant adrenaline rush. Thus, physical and emotional engagement in an adventure setting are likely to create a more extraordinary experience than Ritzer and Liska (1997) suggest. Tourism literature does not yet adequately theorise the adventure experience. One of the problems appears to be that the terms of reference for a study of mountain based adventure tourism are themselves open to interpretation.

Starting from a position that argues mountains are socially constructed, mountain space is seen to be political (Harvey 1989, 1993, Bender 1995) in that people will strive to define the space in relation to their own values, interpretations and understanding. The key terms of the context of this study are problematic to define as they will mean different things to different people. 'Adventure' is defined in terms of 'uncertainty of outcome'. However, this means that an undertaking that is an adventure for one person may not be for another, and may not be for the same person in a different place and at a different time. Thus, adventure is an idea, a state of mind and is subjective. It is difficult for a mountain guide to understand what level of emotional engagement is engendered in a client in any one setting and at any one time. It may also be problematic for a client to articulate the extent to which they might be 'having an adventure'. Conversely, clients taking part in an adventure holiday can define adventure in their own terms. However, because they are buying in the services of a company and its guides, clients may have their understanding of what is and is not an adventure defined for them.

Pursuing such a line of enquiry raises similar problems with other key terms. The descriptor 'mountain' is very broad, although certain criteria such as height, shape and covering (as in snow or rocky terrain for example) seem to apply. Mountains are understood as rugged places that attract bad weather and contain objective dangers, such as exposure to extreme elemental conditions and loose rock. Rugged refers to terrain and conjures images of rock outcrops, crags, gullies and precipitous cliffs. Mountains are a form of landscape that is often associated with the term 'wilderness'. In its purest atavistic state, wilderness is a landscape that has not been subjugated by human intervention, it is where people are not, or 'earth-sans-man' [sic] (Walter 1982). Mountain wilderness is a rapidly diminishing space and it is difficult to argue that wilderness exists in Britain. Mortlock (2001) argues that wilderness can not be found in the European Alps either, which is why his more recent exploratory walks and climbs have favoured the Pyrenees[3], an environment he finds 'wilder and less populated than the Alps', although he stops short

---

[3] The mountain range that straddles the French-Spanish border. It is 'wilder' than the Alps because, for example it has much less ski resort development and fewer settlements generally. Its mountains are not as high or spectacular as some of those in the Alps. See chapter four for further discussion.

of calling the Pyrenees 'wilderness'. There are similar problems with terms such as 'walking', 'trekking' and 'climbing'. Is it possible to be a climber without using ropes and harnesses for example? There are certainly examples in mountaineering literature of people who consider themselves climbers because they 'climb' mountains (Jerome 1979, Smith 1981) even though this means they walk to the top (as it is possible to do with almost all British mountains). Similarly the word 'trekking' has entered the language of mountaineering to mean an extended mountain journey, increasingly today connected symbolically to the use of trekking poles. Each of these terms can be de-constructed and shown to be representative of cultural meanings. These, in turn, reflect the values accorded them by different people. Mountaineers and adventure tourists, it is contended, will bring different degrees of understanding to mountains and may use this to negotiate social position and identity as mountaineers. In this way of thinking, the identity of mountaineer is a function of negotiation, a power struggle between mountaineers and adventure tourists.

Chaney suggests (1996:134):

> Modern tourism is selling a consumer good which is not so much a material good, although there may be incidental sales of tourist goods, but the use of places and facilities to generate extraordinary experiences. In consuming these goods the tourist is choosing to participate in a form of performance in which places are constituted for a variety of modes of appropriation.

There has always been a relationship between tourism and mountains. For example, coach journeys to spectacular waterfalls in the Alps can be traced back to the eighteenth century (Buzard 1993) and Thomas Cook's European 'tours', which began in the nineteenth century, incorporated Alpine itineraries (Brendon 1991). One result was a relatively spectacular growth in Alpine towns from which the most famous (or notorious) of Alpine peaks could be viewed. These included Chamonix, for Mont Blanc, Zermatt for the Matterhorn and Kleine Scheidegg for the Eiger (Poucher 1983). However, throughout such tourism development there remained differences between 'tourists' who came to gaze upon the sublime panoramas of the Alps and the mountaineers who climbed to the summits. The main distinguishing characteristic was the difference between gazing and physical engagement. Adventure tourism, then, is tourism in so much as it involves spatial mobility away from the ordinariness of everyday life towards the extraordinary or the exotic, but distinguishable within the broader context by its emphasis upon physical engagement. Thus, anyone who sets out to walk through or climb mountains has a level of engagement that is qualitatively different from the more superficial forms of tourist consumption encompassed by conceptualisations such as that of tourists as 'monitoring screens' (Crick 1989, Baudrillard 1985). Moving one's body by its own devices is a distinguishing characteristic of adventure tourism.

There is a great deal of discussion about definitions of tourism (Sharpley 1994:29-32), but fewer attempts to define adventure tourism. For purposes of discussion here, adventure tourism encompasses the following. First, adventure tourism has a focus that has a practical engagement. There is, therefore, a physical effort involved, to a greater or lesser extent, which from some perspectives is closer to work than holiday. Outdoor physical challenge, which may have positive image spin-offs like weight loss, physique development, sun tan and related stress reduction, may be influenced by cultural forces in late capitalist countries. Visser (1997:16) for example discusses the way cultural perspectives of tanned skin have changed throughout the twentieth century.

Second, adventure tourism is a business. Competition characterises the market and big companies have a tendency to dominate. Small, independent companies offering specific personalised itineraries such as White Peak Mountaineering find it difficult to compete with large international companies such as Explore, Himalayan Kingdoms and Exodus. The range and diversity of the holidays on offer from the bigger companies is enormous and included in such packages are both 'broad' and 'narrow' activities (Rubens 1999). The model for adventure recreation Rubens (1999) promotes sees adventure activities divided into two categories. 'Broad' activities sustain relatively low levels of excitement over long periods of time. Trekking to Everest would be an example, as mountain walking on a popular trail requires steady effort over many days. 'Narrow' activities offer adrenaline surging concentrations of excitement, which may last very short periods of time, One example is bungy jumping. An adventure holiday may encompass both, in various combinations. Both 'broad' and 'narrow' activities are provided by the bigger adventure tourism companies. Explore Worldwide (Brochure 1999), for example, include wildlife safaris in Tanzania, cultural touring in Vietnam, ethnic or tribal encounters in Borneo, sail-treks such as Philippines Island Adventure, hikes up Kilimanjaro, rafting down the

Zambezi, the Kimberley wilderness experience in Australia and Central Asia overland. Although my study does not have the international flavour outlined in the examples above, what becomes clear is how broadly based adventure tourism is. Mountain based itineraries are only one section of the activities on offer, although it should be noted that wild mountainous country does form the back-cloth to other adventure tourism activities such as mountain-biking, hang-gliding, white-water rafting and bungy jumping. One result of conflating tourism and mountain-adventure is that adventure tourists appear to need money more than mountaineering experience to participate.

As 'adventure' moves closer to 'tourism' so boundaries become hazy. The situation is exacerbated by the fact that many clients buying adventure packages are GRAMPIES (Christiansen, 1990), that is, people who are 'growing, retired, and moneyed, in good physical and emotional health'. The average age of clients who holiday with the company Exodus is now 41 years, and 77% of all Exodus clients are over 30 years old (Exodus Brochure 2000). The capital transfer equation, money for experience, is such that the more exotic and adventurous the holiday purchased the more this will cost. World-wide Journeys, another international company, have five day safaris on the Skeleton Coast of Namibia from £1820 per person (World-wide Journeys Brochure, 2001:30); Naturetrek offer 14 days in Canada with an itinerary called 'The Great Whales & Fall Migration' for £2795 per person (Birds magazine of the RSPB, winter 2000:25) and a journalistic estimate of the cost of climbing Mount Everest is £110,600 (Observer Magazine, 2000:7), although this is the cost for a group not an individual. Of this last total £46,700 is the cost of the permit required just to set foot on Everest, an example of the commodification of mountains. When clients are paying thousands of pounds for an adventure holiday their standard of living, and by implication their expectations of comfort, is likely to be high. Adventure tourist companies tread a careful line between selling adventure as an idea and delivering adventure as an experience.

In this introduction I have set out the purpose and rationale for this study. Additionally, I have introduced adventure tourism and mountaineering. In chapter two I set out a framework for my study. In chapter three I examine methodological issues and draw upon critique as a methodological tool in my discussion of the cultural reproduction of mountains and mountaineering in chapter four. In chapter five I examine the body as the site of inscribed physical capital. The discussion suggests body aesthetics and shaping through diet and training adhere to rules, first introduced in chapter four. Following this, in chapter six, the discussion examines ways that clothing and equipment are utilised to extend urban levels of comfort to mountains whilst also establishing visible credibility as a mountaineer. To support this, it is argued that capital accumulation requires mechanisms of measurement and such issues are discussed in chapter seven. As the discussion reaches a focus on the role of mountain guides, in chapter eight I explore the client-guide relationship. Chapter nine revisits the chapter summaries to draw conclusions.

Chapter two: Theoretical Framework

2.1 Framing Mountaineering

This chapter explores existing theoretical perspectives chosen to illuminate mountaineering identities in adventure tourism. I develop the idea that adventure tourism may represent a challenge to a mountaineer's reading of what 'mountaineering' is. Drawing upon Goffman's (1959) work, it could be argued that, being a mountaineer requires experience of the physical and social context of mountaineering so that other people can recognise and acknowledge the identity being performed. Such experience creates the potential for individuals to explore the physical and social world of mountaineering and is, therefore, about freedom. However, such an argument may not completely fit mountaineering. In order for individuals to put such freedom into practice, they need to adhere to points of performance that are generically recognised as being representative of that identity. Freedom does not exist without certain constraints. In the physical mountain world, for example, 'freedom' is constrained by practices that reflect an agenda of safety. So, when, for example, an idealistic youth called Chris McCandless set off into a remote area of Alaska without a map, and ultimately died there, (Krakauer 1996), his exploits were condemned as foolish and irrational by people who could not relate to the ideals of 'freedom' McCandless apparently pursued. In the social mountain world 'freedom' is constrained because 'being a mountaineer' means others must recognise a person as such. In practice this means using appropriate visual display (clothing, footwear and deportment for example), using Goffman's (1959) 'hints, cues and gestures' and talking a common 'language'. Thus, being a mountaineer means a person has 'freedom' to explore the physical and social worlds of mountaineering but to do so means adherence to an established set of rules and conventions that operate as constraints. Experience of mountaineering offers a frame of reference through which people can make sense of being a mountaineer. The following discussion explores how such a frame may have emerged.

Mountaineering as a sport developed in the latter half of the nineteenth century (Frison-Roche 1996) and, in its proponents' desire to 'conquer' mountains embraced elements of the modern world. Modernity as a distinctive pattern of social life (Chaney 1996) has a central concern with 'freedom' of the individual. This is primarily from the strictures of preindustrial society which was defined by constraints upon an individual's time (with no clear distinction between work and leisure), effort (in the form of labour), and knowledge of the world (in terms of travel). Such 'freedom' in a rational modern world facilitates a momentum towards an enlightened, informed and superior position so that selfhood is something we aspire towards and becomes, in the midst of our lives, an 'unfinished project' (Giddens 1990). Freedom appears to be a central concern of mountaineering. This is well illustrated by Gordon Stainforth writing about the Cuillin mountains of Skye (1994:109). Stainforth suggests that mountaineering allows people to 'open up' discoveries about themselves.

> An adventure, in its true sense, is something that comes to one; it is not an escape from anything. By opening ourselves up to all possibilities, we come to ourselves. I do not mean that we become egocentric; we simply come closer to finding or rediscovering our real selves. On a great day such as one can have in the Cuillin we emerge from our everyday shell, as the mountains come out of the clouds.

Stainforth suggests mountaineering is a liberating experience that draws its power from the idea of adventure in an extraordinary setting. Mountaineering as a sport has emerged from a context of modernity in so much as it is concerned with both freedom and control, in the latter instance: "submitting nature to the dominion of technological power" (Melucci 1996:42). From its origins in the nineteenth century, mountaineering appears to have offered a specific challenge to the modern world. The 'dominion' of nature in mountains remains an adventure and a finely balanced equation between challenge and control; this might be part of the appeal of mountaineering. Technology and mountaineering (as in ideas of conquest and regulation) are fundamentally linked and a history of the latter must be read as the powerful influence of the former. Miah illustrates this well (1999:4):

> Recent times have shown an unprecedented emergence and a greater plurality in the design, manufacturing and thus technology of mountaineering equipment. Fashion, performance and individuality in climbing and mountaineering are of the utmost importance. Such characteristics have been enabled by a mass consumer market, though even mass participation might also be symptomatic of what has become the modern, commercial and technologised [sic] mountain experience.

In order to make sense of an activity people need a 'context of understanding'. In the case of mountaineering this is established through discursive strands of history, through institutions, through guidebooks and manuals and through imagery in visual media such as brochures and calendars. Discourse is, "the production of 'things' by 'words'" (Sarup 1996:7). Crang (1998), adopting a broader interpretation, shows how representations and images are "constitutive of the world" (1998:190) and that verbal (talk and discussion) and non-verbal processes (such as pictures and images) impact on how we act and reproduce such ideas. Mountaineering is discursively defined by words and images. Bartlett (1993:3), for example, describes mountaineering as "intense life" but goes on to suggest that mountaineering may, "encourage reflection, perhaps suggesting new ideas about life and what it means, about our place in the world and how we should live" (1993:3). There is a strong educational undercurrent to the examples cited here. This is consistent with Gidden's (1990) idea of people as 'unfinished projects'. Moreover, such images of insight and self-advancement are not separate from an aesthetic discourse as 'education' pervades the literature of mountaineering. Bartlett, (1993) for example, discusses the writing of Francis William Bourdillon (1852-1921) whose poetry picked out 'moments of being' from his mountaineering experience. The picture in Bartlett's book (1993:6) depicts Bourdillon on the summit of the Matterhorn, a mountain of supreme aesthetic attraction as Wells (2001:7) reminds us:

> After Everest, the Matterhorn is probably the most famous mountain in the world. A 4,478m rock pyramid with an outline exhibiting a rough symmetry, it represents the very idealised picture of a mountain that a child might draw. As a consequence, its picturesque image adorns placemats, key fobs, biscuit tins and paper-weights and has even proved the inspiration for a well known brand of Swiss confectionary.

Words and images make an important contribution to the construction of a mountaineering frame. Mountains emerge as arenas for education (Mortlock 1984, 2001, Gair 1997), personal challenge and exploration (Fletcher 1967, Poucher 1964, Bartlett 1993, Bennet 1985), political contestation (Milburn 1997, Connor 1999), experience of the sublime (Smythe 1941 & 1946, Winthrop Young 1933), metaphors for life (Reid 1992, Maeder 1975) and places of spiritual enlightenment and catharsis (McCluhan 1996, Craig 1995). Such an understanding is taken for granted by mountaineers such as myself who have been 'educated' over an extended period of time. This represents a relatively stable and established mountaineering tradition.

In mountaineering, the frame relates to physical and the social components of that setting. In a physical sense, to 'know' the mountains equates to having spent time in them undertaking walking, scrambling and / or climbing activities. Through such immersion people are likely to become familiar with a variety of rugged terrain, for example, the difference between a maintained footpath and sliding across unconsolidated scree[4]. Similarly, people are likely to have experience of a variety of weather conditions ranging from sheltered valleys to exposed ridges where the wind will be much greater (because of fewer topographical features to ameliorate it) and the temperature will be lower (because of the atmospheric lapse rate whereby temperature decreases with altitude). Finally, experience of mountaineering is likely to lead to an appreciation of degrees of visibility depending upon the cloud level and variations in weather that can range from hot sunshine to blizzards. The unpredictability of mountains means that, in one sense, people can never really 'know' mountains, but can only draw upon similar experiences in order to formulate behaviour. Such experience of the physical is likely to lead to behaviour that is a common sense rational response to such conditions. For example, if the wind is strong people are likely to move away from exposed ridges, put on windproof jackets and take more care when moving across rugged terrain. The greater a person's depth and breadth of physical experience in mountains then the easier it becomes for that person to frame a response.

In a social sense, to 'know' the mountains is to have experience of time spent with other mountaineers. This is not restricted to mountains, although this is clearly the fundamental reference point, but encompasses peripheral spaces where mountaineers gather. These include club meeting rooms, pubs, equipment shops, mountain huts, slide presentations from adventure tourist companies and famous mountaineers, symposia and conferences. To spend time with mountaineers is to absorb patterns of behaviour relating to what to talk about, how to talk about it, how to dress and what mountaineering objectives one should aspire towards. Over time this imbues a process of inoculation that in turn will generate its own forms of behaviour. Behaviour is based on knowledge of how to 'perform' in the company of mountaineers. Goffman (1959:13) offers this perspective on such social interaction:

---

[4] Scree is unconsolidated rocks of all sizes. Scree results from processes of weathering in mountains and gravity operates to roll larger pieces further down the mountain. Scree collects on mountain slopes but is particularly common in gullies, which act as funnels through which these rocks will slide. Crossing them demands judgement, concentration and skill.

> When an individual enters the presence of others, they commonly seek to acquire information about him [sic] or to bring into play information about him already possessed. They will be interested in his general socio-economic status, his conception of self, his attitude towards them, his competence, his trust-worthiness etc. Although some of this information seems to be sought almost as an end in itself, there are usually quite practical reasons for acquiring it. Information about the individual helps to define the situation, enabling others to know in advance what he will expect of him. Informed in these ways, the others will know how best to act in order to call forth a desired response from him.

When Goffman suggests there are usually quite practical reasons for acquiring knowledge of other people, he is anticipating Bourdieu's (1986) theory of social distinction. When Goffman (op. cit.) says information helps to define the situation, he is defining what I have termed the 'frame' of a setting. A frame, then, is based on knowledge and experience and it helps people understand "how best to act in order to call forth a desired response" (Goffman op. cit.). My concern is with how people frame their behaviour in extraordinary places and social environments. Whilst I feel confident in claiming, following Goffman's (1959) analysis, that conversations, cues, hints and body language all play a part in how people become socialised, much of this is based on quotidian performances that Bourdieu (1986) would argue are often habitual. A frame for mountaineering may not be 'ordinary' for most people, who might find themselves in a mountain setting for which they have at best a limited frame, and at worst no frame at all. People, therefore, have the potential to be socially vulnerable in extraordinary settings, and this is particularly the case when the setting requires physical engagement, as in mountaineering. A mountaineering frame, such as my own, has been constructed from an extensive experience of mountain places and people. The frame that an adventure tourist brings to the adventure holiday setting may contain elements of a mountaineering frame to various degrees. However, it may also contain elements that might contest and challenge mountaineering tradition. Such contestation may not be a conscious 'attack' upon the traditional values of mountaineering but may be the result of a lack of experience of that setting, that is, a limited or non-existent frame. A person in such a position is likely to find, as Goffman (1959) suggests, the closest fit from their existing experience. A mountaineering frame is constructed around the systematic accumulation of experience gained from spending time in mountains and with other mountaineers. Following Jenkins (1996) it can be argued that mountaineers form a social group and define their own boundaries by defining the criteria by which one becomes 'a mountaineer'. Frames, then, may well intertwine the ordinary with the extraordinary, reflexive monitoring (as in time spent with a 'society' of mountaineers) with habitual non-reflexive norms (from the work place and family home for example) to significantly blur the edges of what it means to be a mountaineer.

The dependence of adventure tourists upon a packaged format staffed and organised by companies and the 'expert' mountain guides they employ suggests that such clients and potential clients may have limited frames of reference. It may equally suggest that, because it is a holiday, which is about pleasure and enjoyment, adventure tourists do not want the discomfort and stress of making all the arrangements for themselves. In either case, in order to negotiate unprecedented social situations, perhaps with limited knowledge and experience, such people, it is contended, will have a greater need of 'guidance'. This increases the likelihood of being guided by discursive conventions, cultural symbols, role models and images generated by the media. It is likely that each new generation (re)defines the present which, thereby, makes 'tradition' an ephemeral entity. Adventure tourism might challenge mountain tradition and, in turn, establish a re-definition or re-alignment of its codes and rules. What remains to be uncovered is the extent to which the mountaineering tradition may or may not be able to resist an influx of people who are not necessarily cognisant of the rules and conventions of mountaineering. Adventure tourism might, therefore, generate its own discursive agendas and practices. It is this interplay of freedom and constraint that is explored by Bauman (1987).

2.2 Status, Legislators and Interpreters

The subtitle of Bauman's (1987) book is, *Intellectuals: From Modern Legislators to Postmodern Interpreters*. Bauman critically examines what it has meant to be 'an intellectual' since the emergence of the term at the beginning of the modern age during the Enlightenment. The key points of relevance to the present study might be summarised through two related ideas. First, the category of 'intellectuals' was self determining and embraced a 'motley collection' (Bauman 1987:1) of artists, scientists and public figures. As a collective of social identity, intellectuals do not have an objective social boundary. At best it is suggested they set the parameters of the pool from which membership is drawn (Bauman 1987:2). Intellectuals are modernists, described as legislators who retain their

Bourdieu (1986, 1993) has developed a number of conceptual ideas and explored these in his theory of social distinction. Of particular note are 'habitus' and 'field', which can be broadly aligned to unconscious and conscious respectively, and 'capital' which broadly represents a currency of negotiation in the search for status. In his conclusion to *Distinction* (1986), Bourdieu suggests that the way individuals and groups project their properties and practices is integral to social reality. This book is concerned with social distinction and its central book concerns social class which, Bourdieu suggests, is as much about 'being-perceived' as it is about 'being'. The class focus offers alignment with Bauman's (1987) concepts of legislators and interpreters because both authors are concerned with social identity, which, as Jenkins (1996) explains is about belonging to a group and, at the same time, being different from others. At one level, for my study, Bourdieu's (1986) concern with class does not appear to be an important issue in an investigation of adventure tourism. This is because the discourses outlined above have combined with political challenges to a land owning hegemony in Britain, (notably in the Peak District in 1932, see Curry 1994 and Donnelly 1986 & 1993) to democratise access to British mountains. It is difficult to argue that mountaineering still retains the class allegiances that were characteristic of the origins of the sport in the nineteenth century. However, combining Bourdieu's concerns of class and distinction with Bauman's concepts of legislators and interpreters, it may be premature to ignore class issues. It may be more appropriate to avoid becoming embroiled in a detailed discussion of class issues, but to retain the possibility that empirical evidence may illuminate this idea as the book progresses. It has already been suggested that, as adventure tourism is relatively expensive, there may well be a close alignment between professional groups and a propensity to buy adventure holidays. A critical perspective on Bourdieu's (1986) work might be, therefore, that he allows the class issue to dominate his theory of social distinction at a time when 'class' per se is being replaced as a central concern of social identity by concepts such as 'lifestyle' (Chaney 1996). Nevertheless, Bourdieu is concerned with consumption, which he sees as the main mechanism for establishing distinction. Bourdieu's ideas are, therefore, important to explore for at least two reasons. First, it is a central concern of this present study to illuminate the relationship between adventure tourism and the tradition of mountaineering. Such a social identity concerns distinguishing oneself from non-mountaineers. Second, following a proliferation of practice commensurate with mechanisms such as commodification of mountains, such distinction is linked to the accumulation of capital, about which Bourdieu has a great deal to say. Three important conceptual ideas are 'capital', 'habitus' and 'field.'

Capital can take many forms. Mention has already been made of intellectual capital, which was used to mean gaining distinction through contributing to mountaineering literature. Intellectual capital is embraced by Bourdieu's broader definition of cultural capital. Bourdieu suggests (1986:12):

> Hidden behind the statistical relationships between educational capital or social origin and this or that type of knowledge or way of applying it, there are relationships between groups maintaining different and even antagonistic relations to culture, depending upon the conditions in which they acquired their cultural capital and the markets in which they can derive most profit from it.

Cultural capital is "acquired by means of a sort of withdrawal from economic necessity" (1986:54). But, such capital can be exchanged for economic gain. The cultural capital of mountain guides, for example, concerns their knowledge, skill and judgement. This can be exchanged for economic benefit, that is, clients pay for their services. Cultural capital includes physical capital and symbolic capital. Physical capital is the embodied manifestation of cultural capital, which, Bourdieu suggests (1986:70-71), operates as a 'sort of advance' that "enables the newcomer to start acquiring the basic elements of the legitimate culture". Symbolic capital is about acquiring a "reputation for competence" (1986:291) and an "image of respectability" (1986:291). Cultural capital, and its subdivisions, becomes the currency of distinction. The greatest currency is held by the 'legitimate culture', and, by inference, the least is held by those who have yet to acquire such cultural capital. Such a conceptualisation aligns closely with Bauman's (1987) model of interpreters and legislators: it is the latter who have the greatest cultural capital. However, implicit in Bourdieu's (1986) definition of cultural capital is the idea that the value of cultural capital in the "market" has much to do with the "conditions" under which a person has "acquired their cultural capital" (op.cit.) Bourdieu is suggesting that the process of cultural capital accumulation is important enough to generate the potential for "antagonistic relations to culture" (op.cit.) Such a position clearly reflects the potential juxtaposition of old and new set out by Bauman (1987). However, although the accumulation of cultural capital can be conscious, Bourdieu suggests that everyone is a product of a culture that, in turn, is responsible for inculcating a set of practices that are absorbed unconsciously, that is, people operate unconsciously through habit(s). Bourdieu (1986, 1993) uses the term habitus to describe this process.

Habitus (Bourdieu 1986, 1993) is a concept that is useful to explore how forms of behaviour are generated in different social settings. Bourdieu (1993:5) formally defines habitus as the system of:

> Durable, transposable dispositions, structured structures predisposed to function as structuring structures, that is, as principles which generate and organise practices and representations that can be objectively adapted to their outcomes without presupposing a conscious aiming at ends or an express mastery of the operations necessary in order to attain them. Objectively 'regulated' and 'regular' without being in any way the product of obedience to rules, they can be collectively orchestrated without being the product of the organising action of a conductor.

Rojek sees habitus as an "imprinted generative schema" (Rojek 1995:67). By this he means a propelling force in a system of social conduct. People act and react in specific situations in a manner that is not always calculated and is not about consciously following rules. These dispositions are inculcated in childhood and become a second sense. Bourdieu (1993) suggests they are 'durable' and will last a lifetime; they are 'transposable' in that they can generate practices in multiple settings (or 'fields'). Moreover, they are 'structured structures' in that they incorporate the social conditions of the inculcation environment. Thus, Bourdieu is able to argue in *Distinction* (1986) for class habitus by showing how working class habits generate common preferences across a range of cultural practices. Habitus is, therefore, literally our habitual way of doing things. It operates at different levels to determine everyday enactments, like the way we walk, and more deeply rooted ideas such as how we respond to issues of gender, race and sporting propensity. Habitus is closely related to the concept of distinction (Bourdieu 1986). Distinction, Rojek suggests (1995:68), is the social evaluation of habitus and a key element of identity construction.

People do not act in a vacuum but operate within social situations. In Bourdieu's terminology (1986, 1993) such social contexts are 'fields'. A field is a socially structured space, relatively autonomous yet possessing its own rules and regulated by the people within it. The concept of a field is dynamic in that changes in people's positions will change the structures of the field. Two crucial ideas encompassed by this concept are that interests and resources at stake in the field are not necessarily material and that competition between people operating in the field is not necessarily based on conscious forms of behaviour. Social fields, Bourdieu argues, (1986, 1993), operate through a system of power which is based on forms of cultural capital. A field is a structured system of social positions in which the system defines the experience for the people in it. The distribution of cultural capital determines the structure of the field at any given moment:

> Struggle is a dominant feature of fields as agents use 'strategies' to preserve or improve their occupancy of positions relative to the defining capital of the field (Jarvie and Maguire 1994:194).

Cultural capital has a number of elements and is measured in different ways. For example, academic capital is gauged by degrees accumulated and publications accredited. Symbolic capital is about prestige and celebrity. For example, in mountaineering Sir Edmund Hillary (most famous for being the first person to stand on the summit of Everest), a bee-keeper from New Zealand, has considerable symbolic capital in recognition of his achievements. Physical capital concerns the body as a bearer of symbolic value. According to Shilling (1993:127-128):

> The production of physical capital refers to the development of bodies in ways which are recognised as possessing value in social fields, while the conversion of physical capital refers to the translation of bodily participation in work, leisure and other fields into different forms of capital. Physical capital is most usually converted into economic capital (money goods and services), cultural capital (for example, education) and social capital (social networks which enable reciprocal calls to be made on the goods and services of its members).

The body is the site of physical capital and this is located partly through habitual patterns. Williams and Bendelow (1998:49-50) explore the idea of bodily hexis, that is the way that corporeal techniques are embodied and performed in a habitual, unreflexive way. Body techniques, they argue, are 'technical' in that they take a specific form of movement. They are 'traditional' in that they have to be learnt through education or training and they are 'efficient' in that they serve a definite purpose. Bodily hexis is a concept of embodied habitus developed by Bourdieu (1977:94) and defined as:

> Political mythology realised, em-bodied, turned into permanent dispositions, a durable manner of standing, speaking and thereby of feeling and thinking, principles which are placed beyond the conscious use of the mind.

This is not to suggest that the agency of conscious reflective behaviour is subsumed within a plethora of habitual embodied practices, but rather that this is a part of the bigger picture of the accumulation of physical capital that combines everyday habitual patterns of behaviour with conscious reflective norms. In this respect bodily hexis and disposition contribute to distinction and, therefore, identity-status.

Mountaineering might be considered as a field and mountaineering activities as having the potential for cultural capital accumulation. The mountaineering field is subject to internal changes and, therefore, is subject to legislative controls. Such legislation is manifest in the rules and codes of mountaineering. Mountaineers such as Bartlett (1993) know the rules of mountaineering because they are written down in instruction manuals such as Langmuir (1995), Fyffe and Peters (1990) and in Summit magazine, the official publication of the British Mountaineering Council (BMC). Such protocol has helped create an 'established' perspective on what mountaineering is. This perspective has gained credence through longevity and is self regulating in so much as there are institutionalised structures such as clubs, journals and meetings for discussion and debate on issues ranging from climbing ethics to walking access, guidebooks, climbing styles and mechanisms for reporting developments such as new routes. It is this perspective that is adhered to by Bartlett and others who perpetuate discourses that sustain an 'established' view of what it means to be a mountaineer. This becomes a frame of reference for those who have, or who aspire towards accumulating, the cultural capital of mountaineering. Such cultural capital is located in the acquisition of the skills and knowledge of mountaineering, and acquired through physical endeavour in mountains. For Bourdieu, culture is incorporated bodily. Jarvie and Maguire (1994: 189-190) suggest that a 'deeply embodied habitus' leads to a 'feel for the game', in this case, the 'game' of mountaineering (Tejada-Flores 1978). In other words, being with other members of a community means that lessons are absorbed about manners, customs, style and deportment. These will continue to operate unconsciously, that is through habitus, and reflexively. Reflexive means that social processes are partly constituted through the ways they are identified, enacted and responded to (Chaney 1996:6). To 'perform' is to display cultural capital in ways that construct distinction.

Understanding mountaineering through Bourdieu's (1986) concept of a field is a strong starting point. However, whilst it is useful to theorise how positions are achieved and maintained in the field, this raises the question of how 'the field' responds to attempts from 'outsiders' to enter the field. The growth of adventure tourism outlined in chapter one may be challenging the established trajectories of cultural capital acquisition. Self-reliance and independent operation through exercising judgement, and engaging in decision making are the hallmarks of an experienced mountaineer. These are not necessarily requirements for a person who is buying a mountaineering adventure holiday. A fundamental difference between an established and experienced mountaineer and a less experienced 'newcomer' such as an adventure company client entering the field is the level of inculcation possible over the very different time scales involved. Arguably, established mountaineers are likely to understand the rules of the field and, through practice, to have absorbed habitual forms of behaviour through prolonged immersion in mountains. Less experienced 'interpreters', it may be contended, are more likely to bring habitual patterns of behaviour from other aspects of their lives to the mountain setting.

2.3 Identity & Performance in Mountains

The metaphor of performance endures from Goffman's (1959) work and has been developed in the analysis of contemporary tourist settings (Edensor 1998, 2001). Goffman's concerns with the micro-sociology of everyday settings have not only established a template for exploring the significance of performance but also have a richness that informs contemporary theorising on ideas of social hierarchy, dominance and control and symbols. It is these two aspects of his work that have relevance to this book. Williams and Bendelow (1998:60-61) draw parallels between Goffman and Bourdieu when they discuss the way symbols, for Goffman, (for example of class status) have 'organic moorings' in the body and serve as a restrictive mechanism to enhance and preserve prestige. This is a similar idea to Bourdieu's notions of habitus and physical capital. Because a field is conceived as a dynamic social space, whereby positions are determined by cultural capital, identity becomes negotiable.

With particular reference to culture, Jenkins (1996) argues that identity formation results from, "the internal-external dialectic of identification" (Jenkins 1996:20). His starting point is defining what is meant by identity. The term has two distinct meanings, identical or sameness and distinctiveness that assumes continuity over time. Thus, the term suggests both similarity and difference (Jenkins 1996:3). Identity does not just happen, it must be established thereby suggesting that we must identify with something or someone. In the context of social relations this implies a degree of reflexivity (Giddens 1991, Melucci 1996). Jenkins suggests that the reflexive nature of social relations creates social identity which is about meaning. Furthermore, he continues, because meanings are innovated, agreed and shared in the social world, identity becomes negotiable to a certain extent. He goes on to argue that we have a plurality of roles or identities, and that these are constantly being revised. Jenkins (1996) argues that all social activity is a process of stabilisation in so much as the dynamic component of identity formation, combined with the multiple roles demanded by everyday life, can lead to social disorientation and self-confusion. Identity, then, emerges as a central concern in the social world. Melucci (1996) argues that the security afforded by a stable sense of identity slows down the flow of information, which confuses the identity issue, thereby creating a sense of social cohesion. Identity gives the social world meaning. The diversity of images which invade everyday lives via a multitude of media are creating new potential identities all the time, and it is not too difficult to understand how terminology such as 'escape' and 'search for identity' enters tourism literature (Rojek 1993, Cohen & Taylor 1992). Mountains are symbols of stability (Bernbaum 1997, Jerome 1979, Craig 1995, McLuhan 1996, Hart 1968) and have been socially constructed as escape locations, a discussion developed in chapter four.

Jenkins (1996) argues that the two poles that define what identity is, similarity and difference, can be related to the individual and the collective. The individual is about personal identity and how we are different from others and the collective is about social identity emphasising a sense of belonging. Jenkins (1996) argues that the individually unique and the collectively shared are similar, not different. They are merely expressions of the two poles of our understanding of what constitutes identity. From this stance Jenkins develops his basic argument as follows. Individual identity has no meaning in isolation from the social world of other people. Individuals are unique but selfhood is socially constructed. The self is essentially an ongoing synthesis of (internal) self-definition and (external) definitions of oneself offered by others. This is how his internal-external dialectic emerges (Jenkins 1996:20). This validation of identity through the presentation of self in a social setting clearly stems from Goffman (1959). The extent to which a performed identity is accepted or rejected is a function of how well one has understood the rules of deportment (e.g. gesture and body language), display (e.g. clothing and insignia) and communication (particularly language) in that setting. The idea of collective social identities fits well with the established view of mountaineering outlined above. Jenkins says, collective identities are located within territory or regions and, "since bodies always occupy territories, the individual and the collective are to some extent superimposed" (Jenkins 1996:27).

Melucci (1996) deepens the theory. He suggests identity is a paradox whereby any individual identity, "presupposes a degree of equality and reciprocity" (Melucci 1996:30). He extends Jenkins' (1996) argument by introducing the concept of vectors. Melucci (1996) suggests identity is subject to a system of vectors in tension. These vectors constantly seek to establish an equilibrium between ourselves and others in terms of recognition (Melucci 1996:34). Melucci (1996) is in alignment with Bourdieu (1986) when he suggests identity takes the form of a field which is constantly subjected to internal and external shifts, "with its borders changing in accordance with the varying intensity and direction of the forces that constitute it" (Melucci 1996:34). Being on holiday, for example, will change the directional impact of these vectors and account for behaviour that is different from everyday life. The temporary nature of some social settings is not prominent in Bourdieu's (1986) theory of social distinction. The holiday setting is one example of a temporary social world. According to Melucci (1996), the inheritance of modernity is, "our need and duty to exist as individuals" (Melucci 1996:42), yet people have become 'nomads of the present', that is, people no longer have definitive identities. People transmit and receive unprecedented quantities of information, which necessitates a response, and the rhythm of change: "accelerates at an immense pace" (Melucci 1996:43) in the search for anchors to stabilise identity. There is a suggestion here that people aspire towards a sense of stability encompassed by 'being seen' as part of a collective social identity. The argument has been made hitherto that adventure tourists may aspire towards the social identity of 'mountaineer'. However, there may be other attractions for those clients who buy mountaineering holidays. Bourdieu (1986) says habitus is structured, transposable and durable which suggests, for the field of mountaineering, a sense of continuity and perhaps stability for those who have established positions within it. However, this does not necessarily follow for newcomers for whom mountaineering activities might be a much more temporary and intermittent set of experiences.

Melucci (1996:46-47), therefore, uses the concept of 'field' slightly differently from Bourdieu (1986) but they agree that this concept has a dynamic component. Melucci (1996) argues for identity as a process rather than an essential metaphysical being so that identity emerges as, "a dynamic system defined by recognisable opportunities and constraints" (Melucci 1996:47). The process is regulated by constraints that open and close. Identity is the negotiation of such constraints, literally one's 'responsibility' meaning responding for and responding to. Maintaining identity boundaries is, therefore, about people's ability to respond in any one setting (Melucci 1996:46-49). Identity, then, according to both Jenkins (1996) and Melucci (1996) is a process and not a static phenomenon. Furthermore, Melucci (1996) develops the concept of responsibility as crucial to this process. Goffman (1959) suggests that, when facing other people in a social setting we perform as actors, responding to hints, cues and gestures in order to gain knowledge (and therefore advantage) to enhance our performance. Such a metaphor presupposes a script that defines how we should behave in a particular setting. Even when the social setting is new, Goffman suggests: "the individual will already have a fair idea of what modesty, deference, or righteous indignation looks like, and can make a pass at playing these bits when necessary" (1959:79). He goes on to suggest that social experience provides tools to improvise if necessary. The strength of such an argument lies in the intimation that identity is not a material thing but rather a pattern of appropriate conduct. Goffman's (1959) model thus becomes seminal in understanding identity as social negotiation. He argues that most aspects of the way we engage in everyday living are layered. We behave in certain ways depending upon where we are and who we are interacting with. Behaviour, therefore, varies with environment and audience. In the performance metaphor people become actors, social space becomes a stage and the enactment therein results from learning the rules.

Goffman (1959) says we learn who we are in the perceived definitions of others. This is especially true in face to face encounters and when the social interaction involves significant others. The setting becomes the frame, and the relevant script enables people to perform consistently based on their previous performance by the rules of that setting; this is what is happening on the surface. At a deeper level, Goffman (1959) links the symbolic to personal advancement. In his discussion of notions of performance for example, he suggests the enactment aims to find out about the other. Implicit in his work is the idea that knowledge is power. 'Knowing' about others enables social positioning and is thus about commonality, difference and status, or, put another way, Bourdieu's (1986) notions of capital and position. Identity, then, is socially constructed. Rojek's (1995:2) articulation of social construction is stated thus:

> In other words, even at the high point of modernity there was an ambiguity about leisure experience. At its most basic level the ambiguity relates to the age-old conflict between agency and structure. In pursuing our various projects of freedom we realise that our concept of freedom is itself socially constructed and therefore carries with it particular constraints and limits.

The key point here concerns social construction. Rojek argues (1993, 1995), that in leisure people are subjected to constraints and structures in the same way that they are in other areas of their lives. Behaviour in a leisure setting is determined by rules in the same way that other areas of people's lives are regulated. Modernity becomes "a grid which is imposed upon life" (Rojek 1995:59). The 'voluntary contract' by which this grid operates is sustained by power or 'carceral networks' (Rojek 1995:59). Carceral networks are webs of control that simultaneously empower and regulate behaviour. Legislators, it could be argued, operate carceral networks. Rojek's carceral networks, as they might operate in mountaineering, can be related to Bourdieu's (1986) concept of cultural capital because they are dependent upon knowledge, skill and expertise. Legislators can control mountaineering discourse in ways that consolidate their own position. One of the most powerful 'constraints' that mountaineering-legislators operate is an agenda of safe practice. This has emerged as part of a much broader theory of civilising processes (Elias & Dunning 1986). The following section sets out the rational position of 'civilisation' in relation to mountaineering. It is suggested that, although mountaineering is a part of leisure, its practice does have real (life enhancing and life threatening) consequences. The purpose is to demonstrate the importance that an articulation of the 'seriousness' of mountaineering has to the power operated by legislators, as this, in turn, is likely to provide constraints upon the potential interpretations of 'being a mountaineer' negotiated by adventure tourist clientele.

Civilising processes (Elias & Dunning 1986) support a legislative agenda by creating a discourse of safety and thereby empowering the carceral networks operating in the field. Civilising processes operate at two levels, that of our individual bodies (as in bodily cleanliness and discipline) and that of social organisation (as in making life safer and more comfortable). Dunning (1996), drawing on Elias's theorising on manners, deportment, bodily control and discipline, suggests that mimetic or play activities de-routinize body and limbs leading to increased motility and pleasure through movement. His argument is that routines can lead to ontological security but emotional starvation. Dunning refers to sport and leisure as offering opportunities for "...controlled de-controlling of emotional controls" (1996:196). Some activities offer greater scope for such "...civilised arousal" (1996:196) than others; mountaineering, arguably, falls into this category. So, according to Dunning, a certain emotional starvation accounts for the contemporary interest in exciting leisure pursuits that generate tension (Dunning 1996:195-196). Tension leads to vitality, which in turn redresses the emotional imbalance encouraged by the civilising constraints of rules and regulations (Dunning 1996:197). But mountains are not immune from 'civilising processes' and do contain a framework of safety. Applying Edensor's work (1998, 2001), mountains become spaces where the 'enclavic' characteristics of form and structure (footpath construction, sign-posts, fencing off dangerous features, managing landscapes) are seen gradually to be replacing the 'heterogeneous' characteristics of free expression, exploration, self-reliance and improvisation. I can draw upon my own experiences of rock climbing to provide an example of how the civilising processes operate. Climbing pioneers tied a hemp rope around their waists and, when leading up a route, protected themselves by looping slings over projections of rock and, because the rope ran through a carabiner[5] and was fed out by the stationary second climber, such rope management provided rudimentary protection (Frison-Roche 1996). Today, the same principle applies (although ropes are stronger and lighter and climbers wear padded harnesses) but some rock climbs are protected by in-situ bolts. These are still linked to the rope via a carabiner but are

---

[5] A carabiner is an alloy metal clip through which a rope can be passed (to create a 'running belay') or into which a knot can be tied to anchor climbers to a rock face when they are not actually moving upwards ('belay'). Carabiners are carried on climbs and utilised to safeguard climbers. Climbing with ropes and carabiners is therefore less dangerous than climbing without them.

clearly much stronger than rope slings, more reliable in holding falls and, together with more sophisticated running belays used in adventure climbing which includes camming[6] devices, make climbing a 'safer' proposition. There are many other manifestations of safety in mountains. The idea that an adventurous sport such as climbing should be made 'safer' is consistent with one central thrust of civilisation, the idea of rational order.

Drawing upon my own mountaineering experiences of being led and leading in mountains, I contend that mountains are where some people actively seek recreation in anticipation of being placed in circumstances of emotional and physical stress. Pursuing this argument, it appears likely that people who choose to go mountaineering are resisting the 'civilising process' (Elias & Dunning 1986) and, therefore, exercising a practical articulation of freedom because mountaineering retains the potential for 'civilised arousal'[7]. Mountaineer-legislators do go to great lengths to retain the central ingredient of adventure in the sport. This is especially the case for British mountaineers. Reasons for this might include the depth of tradition that exists in Britain, for example, Haskett-Smith as the 'Father of rock-climbing' (Birkett 1983) and British dominance in exploratory Alpine climbing in the nineteenth century (Frison-Roche 1996). A review of popular mountaineering literature over the latter part of the twentieth century shows vehement resistance from legislators to developments that might reduce the adventurous element of the sport (Wilson, 1978, Perrin 1983). Perpetrators of such developments might be thought of as interpreters and they include, in the examples below, national park authorities, entrepreneurial interests, and climbers who have learnt to climb in an era of climbing walls. Examples include marker posts on the summit plateau of Ben Nevis, footpath construction on Snowdon, helicopter flights over Skye (High 1999a) and the ongoing bolt debate which currently distinguishes sport climbing (using bolted protection) and adventure climbing, using protection placed by the lead climber (Heywood 1994, Lewis 2000). However, as subsequent chapters will show, mountaineering contains elements of planning, reporting, institutional structure, measurement and applied science, all of which are essentially rational. Moreover, knowledge of these elements of mountaineering are constituents of cultural capital so that, for example, being able to use a Silva Type 4 compass to navigate

---

[6] Camming devices, such as the 'Friends' manufactured by the company Wild Country, have spring loaded cams that can be placed in hitherto un-protectable flared cracks that will not hold a conventional piece of climbing hardware. More protection of this kind makes climbing 'safer'.

[7] I believe that the key to understanding mountaineering lies in an appreciation of the ongoing tension between freedom and constraint. Mountaineering is simultaneously subject to the rational consequences of civilisation whilst vehemently resisting developments that undermine the idea of adventure in mountains.

in poor visibility is a point of distinction. Not being able to use a compass raises the possibilities of becoming lost and the subsequent mobilisation of rescue parties and its attendant agendas of the need to operate safely in the seriousness of mountains. The sensible way to achieve a balance between the heightened emotions achieved by mountaineering and safe practice in the mountains is to engage experts (instructors and guides). This is the principle upon which adventure tourism operates. The safety context, therefore, becomes a powerful tool to be used in ways that are likely to consolidate the legislative position against potential interpretations of 'being a mountaineer' introduced by people who have limited cultural capital in mountaineering.

2.4 Summary

Mountaineering is socially constructed, that is, people make sense of it in relation to a broadly accepted understanding of what the activities entail and the identity of 'mountaineer'. This chapter began with an exploration of 'framing' mountaineering. It has been argued that a mountaineering discourse is the essence of the mountaineering tradition responsible for such framing. This tradition, in turn, provides the cultural capital available in the field of mountaineering. Following Bourdieu (1986), 'taste' in this context is about creating distinction by accumulating cultural capital, itself determined by the mountaineering tradition. Cultural capital might be viewed as a currency to be used in the negotiation of identity. Cultural capital is an amalgam of different forms of capital but of particular importance to an investigation of mountaineering identity are symbolic capital and physical capital. The former is important because mountains are powerful symbols which, when consumed, convey prestige and status. The latter is important because 'to mountaineer' involves physical engagement, a process that inscribes itself on the body.

Mountaineering might be conceived as a social field with a variety of people such as guides, climbers, hikers, clients, writers, photographers and adventure company directors all manoeuvring for a position that might reflect distinctiveness. This may yet prove to be an oversimplification of a social world that may be difficult to reduce to one field. However, the concept of 'field', which is about social identity through collective understanding, and the concept of 'frame', which has more to do with individual identity and is based upon personal experience, remain important. So too does a theoretical perspective that suggests identity is constructed through a combination of reflexive and habitual performance on a series of stages that broadly represent mountain spaces. There are many different spaces in which it is possible to practice being a mountaineer. These include national parks, equipment shops, climbing walls, local crags, audio-video presentations, mountaineering huts and pubs in mountain areas. It may well be that adventure tourism is an example of a fragmentation of mountaineering. It is possible, following Bauman (1987), to conceive a tension between defenders of the mountaineering tradition (legislators) and the range of newcomers to mountains (interpreters) who have the potential to re-define what being a mountaineer means. This is, however, to assume that clients who buy adventure holidays seek to become mountaineers. It may be that many of them have a much broader interpretation of the gains to be made through their mountaineering aspirations. Rather than concentrating on the collection of the cultural capital of mountaineering per se, they may be interested in new friendships, play, getting fit, feeling healthy and seeing the world for example. The contentions presented here are, first, that mountaineering is defined by a tradition, second, that clients have to become mountaineers to various degrees, and third, that clients buy into a climate of dependency when they purchase an adventure holiday. Subsequent chapters explore these contentions by using the conceptual ideas outlined in this chapter. The following chapter explores the methodology of data collection.

Chapter three: Research Design

3.1 The Qualitative Research Paradigm

This chapter explains the practices of 'doing the fieldwork' as I experienced them. This means that the account set out here, including the interpretation of the data, embraces my own political perspectives, social relationships in the field and epistemological position. Qualitative methodology has rejected the dominant positivist model of research because this fails to capture the true nature of social settings (Hammersley and Atkinson 1995). The qualitative approach uses unstructured forms of data collection such as interviews, observations and verbal descriptions as opposed to quantitative measurement and statistical analysis. The aim is to recognise the centrality of the human agent in the construction of meaning in the social world. Such an approach firmly locates this study in the interpretive [sic] paradigm (Sparkes 1992). The purpose of qualitative research is to understand: "a particular social situation, event, role, group or interaction" (Creswell 1994:161). Moreover, a key component of such research is immersion in the everyday setting of the group to be studied. This means that: "the researcher enters the informant's world and, through ongoing interaction, seeks the informant's perspectives and meanings" (Creswell 1994:161). Sparkes (1992:25) summarises:

Interpretive [sic] researchers believe that while the natural science approach with its positivistic assumptions may be appropriate for the study of the physical world they are not appropriate for the study of the social world which they see as having very different characteristics.

Interpretive researchers see the world through a series of frames which have emerged from their own empirical experience, hence: "all facts are value laden and many constructions are possible" (Sparkes 1992:26).

Qualitative research designs emerge in a number of different ways (Creswell 1994:146), and may have different characteristics. My project, whilst clearly located in the interpretive paradigm and, therefore, encompassing qualitative assumptions, does have some distinctive features. For example, the project is based upon many of the assumptions outlined by Creswell (1994:162). These include, research in a natural setting, the researcher as the primary instrument of data collection, data reporting through the participant's words and a concern with the processes of the setting. Additionally, the assumptions include the utilisation of tacit knowledge and the acknowledgement that, as in Goffman's (1959) micro sociology, verification, whereby the researcher seeks a true representation of the subject's world, replaces validity as a way of checking 'truthfulness'. However, although the central premise of reporting on ways that participants make sense of their world remains, unlike some qualitative designs, this project has been given a sense of theoretical direction by the period of reading before the fieldwork. Through this precedent the aim of illuminating identity through uncovering the rules influencing behaviour has emerged. Additionally, as the researcher for this project and a qualified instructor-guide, I bring an established mountaineering frame to this setting and, therefore, my own values have a significant bearing on the research design.

So, as part of its paradigmatic position, my project has developed a methodology that is broadly ethnographic (Burgess 1984, Cresswell 1994, Hammersley 1992, Kellehear 1993, Spradley & Mann 1975, Whyte 1955). I have spent most of my life recreating in mountains, something that has developed my interest in adventure. Adventure, because it is a state of mind, is transferable across social circumstances. Undertaking this research project has become an adventure for me. Part of this interest was directed towards finding out about how interpretive researchers operated. Anthropology, the discipline commonly associated with enthographic work, has moved from 'original' wilderness (remote islands, jungle), which is diminishing rapidly, to the 'new' wilderness (Light 1995:195) of social deprivation in urban areas. This latter generic area of investigation includes slum areas (Whyte 1955), bars (Spradley & Mann 1975), working class housing estates (Jenkins 1984) and football ('hooligan') supporters (Hughson 1996). Whilst I was more interested in mountains than such environments, these studies highlighted research design issues. For example, accessibility to a subject group in order to engage in participant observation is a key issue. Furthermore, existing studies may be as much determined by how accessible a group is, and what strategies the researcher may have for becoming a participant, as by the more general concerns of illuminating the social mechanisms behind less well understood social groups. "The ideas grow up in part out of our immersion in the data and out of the whole process of living" (Whyte 1955:280). The following section argues that existing approaches to a study of tourism, the closest fit to adventure tourism in terms of existing studies, have, generally speaking, failed to illuminate how tourist behaviour might be understood. This is because research studies that emphasise designs based upon the qualitative paradigm are under represented in the literature.

3.2 Qualitative Research and Tourism

In order to achieve the aim of the book, that is, to illuminate the relationship between identity, capital and social distinction in mountaineering in the context of consumer culture and adventure tourism, I used critique as a method. The following points offer a critical position on tourism research methods. First, surveys, questionnaires and brochure analysis dominate existing methodologies in tourism (Buck 1977, Cloke & Perkins 1998a, Dann, 1996, Dilley 1986, Loker-Murphy 1995, Selwyn, 1996, Weiler & Hall 1992). There is always a place for statistical data in any scientific investigation, because facts set the research in the empirical world. However, there is a danger that, when used exclusively, an unbalanced perspective is presented. Such methodologies also favour the articulate and the educated above other sections of society. Harrison (1991) demonstrated that this was clearly the case when she investigated attitudes to the British countryside. She set up group 'seminars' for people from working class backgrounds, ethnic minorities and other people living in inner city areas. Her results challenged existing attitudes to the countryside that had been projected by land-owners and planning authorities. More recently the work of Le Sage (2000) provides further support for qualitative methods. She presents empirical evidence drawn from a series of in depth semi-structured interviews that uncovered significant differences in attitudes to the countryside between ethnic minorities and white middle class Bedfordians. According to Le Sage's findings, and contrary to a commonly held perception that ethnic minorities have no interest in countryside recreation, both Afro-Caribbean and Pakistani families enjoy a variety of rural recreations including picnics and walks in the countryside. The existing literature and empirical work on this subject had generalised about the attitudes of 'people of colour' (Le Sage 2000:1) to the countryside. Reflection on such findings demonstrates the value of qualitative methods.

Second, our way of thinking about sport, leisure and tourism is dominated by 'homo clausus' thinking (Dunning 1996:191). Dunning argues that, hitherto, sociology has not taken physical activity seriously enough. Clearly the sport of mountaineering is one of the most physically demanding sports that currently exist: it is also one of the most intriguing and, at times, most misunderstood, particularly by non-participants. Mountains have a cultural heritage that extends much further back than modern times. Mountaineering literature commonly has an implicit agenda that purports to 'explain' the sport by reaching a wider audience than mountaineers. For journalistic and artistic accounts the results seem to have great popular appeal. Academic accounts (Mitchell 1983 is an example), in contrast, are limited. I have failed to locate any ethnographic investigations concerning mountaineering or mountain based adventure tourism, although Weber (2001), at least establishes the principle of using qualitative methodologies to construct studies of adventure tourism. Weber argues that such methodologies are more likely to illuminate the subjective nature of adventure by letting the 'voices' of the participants come through.

A third and related consideration is a tendency to theorise tourist behaviour from a structuralist perspective. MacCannell (1976) is the most obvious example, and his work has been very influential in this area. More recently Edensor (1998) has challenged MacCannell's approach by arguing that tourism is a continually changing set of processes rather than a structured set of social characteristics. Urry's work (1990, 1995) has also been influential in theorising tourism. However, by conceptualising the tourist experience via 'the gaze' (1990) he has accelerated academic debate into the realms of post-tourism without due regard for what might be happening on the periphery of mainstream tourism. Urry, like MacCannell before him, implies that, as we are all tourists, we are all subjected to a process of universalisation and superficiality. Gazing upon mountains (as in a coach tour through Scotland) and actually climbing mountains are two very different experiences. The former experience has been explored in theoretical terms as part of mass tourism. However, although the coach tour and a mountaineering holiday are both experiential, the mountaineering experience is concerned with the actor-participant encountering the actual terrain of the mountains rather than viewing mountains from the warm confines of a coach.

3.3 An Emergent Research Design

Having suggested that using ethnographic methods is an appropriate way of investigating the idea of what it means to be a mountaineer, this section draws upon the framework provided by Hammersley and Atkinson's (1995) *Ethnography: Principles in Practice*. Hammersley and Atkinson (1995:1) define ethnography as referring to a set of methods:

> In its most characteristic form it involves the ethnographer participating, overtly or covertly, in people's daily lives for an extended period of time, watching what happens, listening to what is said, asking questions – in fact, collecting whatever data are available to throw light on the issues that are the focus of the research.

Ethnography, according to Hammersley and Atkinson (1995), must provide a critical and reflective account of the research process: the researcher is a part of the world of study. My position as an experienced 'hands on' mountaineer and instructor during my fieldwork positioned me as a key player in the adventure tourist experience. Hammersley and Atkinson suggest (1995:21-22) that:

> By including our own role within the research focus, and perhaps even systematically exploiting our participation in the settings under study as researchers, we can produce accounts of the social world and justify them without placing reliance on futile appeals to empiricism, of either positivist or naturalist varieties.

I undertook five periods of field work, with each lasting between three and eight days in the period between the summer of 1998 and the summer of 1999. I recall an initial feeling of helplessness, brought on by my inexperience of data collection using ethnographic methods. When I met my first group of clients, at the start of the first of those five trips, I had only a limited, mostly theoretical idea about how to proceed. In fact, my field notes from that first day suggest a rising panic as I was introduced to each of the clients of a sort that I rarely experience when actually guiding in the mountains. Although experienced as a mountaineer, I was a novice researcher. The feeling of vulnerability I had that first day may be similar to that of a client who might be a novice mountaineer. If this is the case, for different reasons, we may all have been feeling insecure about our social positions. However, I also recorded how relatively quickly my 'immersion' in the field was achieved. The most obvious manifestation of this was the growing confidence I gained over those initial days in knowing what to observe, when and how to contribute to dialogue (or back off) and how to lead (or be led by) the clients in ways that retained the 'naturalness' of the setting. In this respect the project was undergoing an emergent design.

An emergent design also includes the extent to which secondary data and existing theory are woven in to an evolving project. Hammersley and Atkinson (1995) suggest it is rare and perhaps foolish to go into a primary data collecting arena unprepared. The origins of all research are in 'foreshadowed problems' (1995:24-19). That is, an articulation of the ideas that informed the conception of the research project. 'Foreshadowed problems' can be developed from a life experience idea, social theory, an unprecedented research opportunity or, most commonly a literature survey. All of these played a part in my own emergent project, the results of which have been set out in chapter two. This point is well made by Hammersley and Atkinson (1995:29):

> Exploring the components and implications of a general foreshadowed problem with the help of whatever secondary literature is available is certainly a wise first step. Relevant here are not only research monographs and journal articles but also official reports, journalistic exposés, autobiographies, diaries, and 'non-fiction' novels. There comes a point, however, when little more progress can be made without beginning the collection of primary data – though reflection and the use of secondary literature should of course continue beyond that point.

Thus, secondary sources of data support the initial design and continue to do so as fieldwork begins, and after it has finished. This is consistent with my own experiences because, being a mountaineer myself, I am interested in any literature, TV programme, magazines or videos that have a bearing upon mountaineering. A further point of structure, the fact that I undertook five different courses of fieldwork, also increases the likelihood of using secondary data in an ongoing 'supportive' capacity. The suggestion is, therefore, that some preparatory work is useful but that the period of primary data collection still needs a fluid and flexible approach because it is through this data that the original findings will emerge. Unlike a positivist approach, an ethnographic design is fluid. However, although a theoretical framework for this study emerged from the period of literature review and secondary data collection that preceded the fieldwork, themes were not identified before the fieldwork began. Rather, these emerged from the inter-linked data collection, analysis and interpretation phases. The following section details the journey through which the methodology for this study emerged.

3.4 A Journey Into The Mountains

Many factors have influenced the design of this study. These include significant others, background reading and practicalities of entering the field. People who have influenced the design of this project are too numerous to mention in detail. They include my own mountaineering heroes whose achievements I sought to emulate, those who taught me to climb and many colleagues and advisers. Collectively, these people have both fired my imagination and directed the resultant energies. Throughout my life I have soaked up books about adventure and progressed to mountaineers accounts of their climbing lives. With maturity I have moved into academic areas in order to more clearly understand the world of mountaineering in general and the challenges presented to this world by adventure tourism in particular. So, I became interested in adventure tourism in mountain areas, and realised that I could readily draw upon an extensive personal library and knowledge of mountaineering literature accumulated over many years of reading.

I am an experienced mountaineer. The significance of such an identity is considerable for me. My early experiences as an apprentice in the Lake District began in the summer of 1976. Although only a student myself, I quickly recognised two things. One was that I felt excited and alive when in mountains; I enjoyed the adventurous possibilities that existed and I wanted to explore mountains in a similar way to Eric Shipton[8]. The second was that being a mountaineer could be used to impress people. I now understand this twofold motivation to be about the self and the social, that is, I was cognisant of the status-identity issue in mountaineering from very early in my career, although I may not have understood it or even acknowledged it in the way that I do now. I learnt a great deal from my formative years about how to climb and use specialist equipment. I noticed the attention that climbers gained when they arrived back at base wearing rucksacks and carrying ropes. I experimented with poses and positioning gleaned from the instructors I was 'working' with. I was taught respect for mountains, to 'take nothing but photographs and to leave nothing

---

[8] Eric Shipton, one of the most famous exploratory mountaineers of his era (the 1930s through to the 1960s) was an early hero of mine. An older friend of mine that I was at university with had actually had dinner with 'the great man' in Edinburgh, a point of 'distinction' that raised my friend's status enormously with people who knew of Shipton's fame. I used a quotation from Shipton's first autobiography (Upon That Mountain 1943) for a dissertation I wrote during my PGCE year at UCNW Bangor. Shipton's second autobiography, That Untravelled World appeared in 1969, both published by Hodder & Stoughton. Peter Steele's insightful biography Eric Shipton: Everest and Beyond was published by Constable in 1998.

but footprints', an adage drawn from the British Mountaineering Council's (BMC) publication about conservation 'Tread Lightly' (BMC 1997). I logged my mountaineering ascents and climbs. In short, I have been 'constructed' by the mountaineering world of people and places I move within. The values of this world have became my own as I have sought to position myself by gaining qualifications and bending first my education, and then my professional teaching career around adventure education. I value physical challenges, I place a value on the conservation of mountain environments and I believe that mountain adventures are educational in the broadest sense of the term. I see mountains as places to escape to from the towns where I have lived and I enjoy the sense of freedom that I feel out in the wind, rain, sun and snow. I gain enormous satisfaction from 'looking after' myself, and others, in this challenging environment. It is very satisfying to be comfortable in adversity. I enjoy living 'on the edge' whereby my skills and equipment are engaged and tested by mountaineering, but I am not reckless. I have a considered approach to mountaineering based on a confidence drawn from many years of experience and I retain a great *enthusiasm* for mountains. I have served my apprenticeship. I am a traditionalist in that I 'learnt' the values of mountaineering from others and, I am a 'legislator', as all guides and instructors must be. I hope, however, I might be thought of as a 'reflective-legislator' in so much as I am genuinely interested in how 'being a mountaineer' today might be 'interpreted'. It is this background of experience and values that I have brought to this study.

Practicalities, particularly for a single, zero funded ethnographer, become important pragmatic components of research design. From the time that the idea of using an adventure tourist company as a 'gateway' to a subject group emerged, before I had even written my research proposal, I began the practical exploration of its possibilities. Atkinson (cited in Hammersley and Atkinson 1995:34) suggests 'gatekeepers' are: "actors with control over key sources and avenues of opportunity". Gatekeepers are significant others in the field of mountaineering and they hold positions that enable them to control specific social mobility into and out of the field. The gatekeepers I had to negotiate with were the directors of adventure tourist companies. Establishing a route into the world of adventure tourism required me to negotiate my own potential position through such gatekeepers. I started three related activities. First, I put myself on the mailing lists for a dozen or so different adventure tourist companies operating in mountain areas and have received brochures and newsletters ever since. Second, I began to attend slide show presentations by several of these companies and third, I introduced myself as a prospective leader or co-leader of one of a company's expeditions or treks either personally, at the slide shows, or more formally by letter or e-mail communication. In one case I actually applied for a specific post and was interviewed. My rationale was simple: I was not looking for a job but I was looking for an opportunity to interact with (and by definition observe) adventure tourists in mountains. I chose a focus of the Himalayas, specifically Nepal, a country that I had read extensively about but never actually visited. I had undertaken an independent mountaineering expedition to the Karakoram Mountains[9] in Northern Pakistan in 1990. I was one of a team of four. We made a first ascent of a minor peak but, more importantly met people who were involved in adventure tourism, in particular a liaison official from Hoper in the Hunza valley and a group of clients with a guide in Gilgit. This experience led me to reflect upon the attractions of the Himalayas as an adventure tourist destination.

My plan evolved into a strategy. This was to trade my mountaineering experience in leadership, including the status of my qualifications[10] as a mountaineering instructor, for the opportunity to be a part of a trek or expedition that would give prolonged contact with a group of adventure tourists in the mountains. In addition, a company that 'sponsored' me in this way would have direct access to my fieldwork results, something that I felt could impact on the way the company targeted and provided for their clientele. The very practical considerations of limited finances determined this initial strategy. I could not afford to buy myself onto a trek or expedition as a member of the group. This remains the case despite extensive attempts to gain funds through various grant aid agencies and travel scholarships. Overall, I made little progress with this strategy, although I gained an insight into the administrative and personnel structures of a variety of adventure tourist companies. This was enlightening but did not take me any closer to accessing a group of adventure tourists in the mountains.

A number of factors led me to a redefinition of my access strategy. The greatest limitation to my case for 'working' for a company was my lack of local knowledge in Nepal. This proved to be far more disabling to my cause than the impetus I felt I could offer with twenty

---
[9] The Karakoram Mountains are a part of the Greater Himalayas and include several 8000m. peaks including K2 the second highest mountain in the world. We climbed an minor peak in the Rakaposhi massif north of Gilgit.
[10] I hold the Mountain Instructors Certificate or MIC and I have been a member of the Association of Mountaineering Instructors (AMI) since its beginnings in the mid 1980s.

years experience of leading groups in mountains throughout the world. Additionally, qualifications do not seem important when a company is operating in non-industrialised countries such as Nepal. I had inadvertently raised an issue about 'being a mountaineer' before I had even undertaken any fieldwork. I had discovered that mountaineering qualifications are only one aspect of credibility as a mountaineer. There is a clear suggestion from my experiences of negotiating with gatekeepers that specific knowledge of a mountain area was more important than qualifications. This was pointed out to me, politely, by the director of Himalayan Kingdoms (HK) with whom I spent a pleasant but ultimately unproductive hour. I approached this man directly as previous efforts with other companies left me in dialogue with middle managers at best and with polite written refusals at worst. A further factor operating against me was the proposed ethnographic methodology itself. It is difficult to be convincing about research outcomes when potential findings are difficult to predict and when they might be of more academic than commercial interest.

So, despite having identified key gatekeepers to my proposed research area, I failed in my primary access strategy. Hammersley and Atkinson (1995:66-67) suggest that a failure to make progress towards access may well be because of a perceived threat to the social ordering of the setting posed by an investigative researcher. It is not unusual, they suggest, for the most interesting research questions to target the most sensitive issues. This can lead, in turn, to a cautious response to overtures from someone like myself. My field notes reflecting upon this early period of negotiations with gatekeepers are illuminating in the way that they explore why I failed to make progress with access at this stage:

> I had a long wait before being ushered into SB's office [in the Bristol based company Himalayan Kingdoms (HK)]. This made me more nervous and I mentally went through my 'sales pitch' the essential ingredients of which were 'I'm an experienced mountaineer, can I come to work on one of your treks so that I can do some research?' Everyone seemed friendly during my wait on the worn out sofa. I was offered coffee and had plenty of time to survey the old, slightly tatty open planned room, complete with flickering computer screens, telephones, desks piled with paper and loads of maps on the wall, some with drawing pins in and notes attached. It felt a warm and welcoming, and exciting place to be – adventure oozed from the walls and faces of the people working there. SB was finishing a conversation with a client (first name terms I noted) as I entered his big office. He

excused the fact that he had to eat his lunch (a French stick sandwich) while he listened to me. The nerves made me talk too fast, but what I was trying to do was anticipate the HK agenda so I could project myself in the right way. SB was polite and asked some questions about my experience before subtly directing me towards the cheapest of the HK holidays in Nepal as the most useful option to facilitate my proposed research. His concerns were for extending his clientele which ultimately, as far as I could see, would have more tangible use to him than a researcher whose 'business' might impact the social balance of a group in ways that were not easy to predict and which may not be to the benefit of HK.

As a variation on the theme of such a direct approach, I actually applied for a job as trekking leader with the London based company Terra Firma (TF) and was asked to an interview. My field notes again:

Using my A-Z of London I successfully navigated myself to the terraced house south of Victoria which is the London base for Terra Firma. A young couple, whose business it was, (the directors) made me as comfortable as they could amongst the buckets of plaster and stripped but unvarnished floorboards in an open planned office-front room in a house that was clearly undergoing a major renovation. I was less nervous than my Bristol experience because I had a clearer picture of what was wanted and B and her partner seemed genuinely impressed by my credentials. (Or were they just being polite?) It quickly became apparent that I could not work in Nepal over the periods that they wanted me – a problem that I had not fully appreciated in my preliminary planning. But I did learn a lot today about the way TF operates, particularly about targeting clientele with careful brochure structuring. I felt inspired and enthused by the dialogue and, once my 'employment' became a non-issue, the tension went out of the setting. Thereafter, we each set about learning as much as possible about our respective interests (me of their company, them of my mountaineering background and technical expertise).

This interview experience was inconclusive about whether knowledge of Nepal would be an issue in employment. Trips to London and Bristol did advance the research design by giving me greater insights into the companies and how they work. However, I was no closer to accessing clients in the field. I considered the fall back option of travelling to Nepal independently and simply travelling amongst adventure tourist groups who would be moving through the mountains in the popular post-monsoon season of October to December. In this respect I could observe adventure tourists in the field without committing myself to one group. This approach would thereby model itself on Douglas's exploratory journey described in his book *Chomolungma Sings the Blues* (Douglas 1997). In this book Douglas circumnavigates the Everest massif and describes the people, Western and indigenous, of the region and the places he travels through. His book is well written and readable but it remains a journalistic account. The lack of academic rigour in his book is an observation that my proposed fall back option would also lay itself open to such a criticism when clearly our two target audiences, the armchair traveller and the informed academic respectively, are very different. This realisation made me feel uncomfortable with this option, something that has been confirmed by discussions with various colleagues and advisers. Such a research strategy would not be systematic and in-depth participant observation.

The question of the role that the researcher might adopt remained problematic. To be an impartial observer of adventure tourists from outside a group, I reasoned, was unlikely to produce data beyond the superficial. It is clearly important to be a part of the social construction of a group by being within it, one of its members. The key development in this stage of the project was that I became more realistic about the practicalities of access. Two points of reflection moved this agenda forward. The first of these was that I had had more success with gatekeepers when I projected myself as an instructor first and a researcher second. The research agenda was less important to the companies than the potential of a quality 'leader' who came without a quality wage bill attached. The second was that I broadened my hitherto narrow perspective on the Himalayas as a research location. I had discovered through my 'foreshadowing' preliminary research of brochures in particular that there was a great deal happening in adventure tourism in British and European mountains. Using contacts established through my membership of AMI (the Association of Mountaineering Instructors), and embracing this reflective position, I began to make progress. I gained access to two Sheffield based adventure tourist companies (Foundry Mountain Activities, (FMA) and Himalayan Kingdoms Expeditions, (HKE), now Jagged Globe (JG). I subsequently found it relatively easy to make arrangements for 'working' with groups of clients from these companies in locations such as Scotland, the Lake District, the Peak District and the Picos de Europa in Northern Spain.

3.5 The Research Design and the Tools of Data Collection

Having created an opportunity to enter the field, the next stage was to develop the qualitative methodology. Creswell (1994:1-2) defines qualitative study as:

An inquiry process of understanding a social or human problem, based on building a complex, holistic picture, formed with words, reporting detailed views of informants and conducted in a natural setting.

Practical limitations with fieldwork, partly driven by the temporal dimensions of the holiday format shaped the research. Participating in people's lives involves watching what happens, listening to what is said and asking questions (Hammersley and Atkinson 1995). The assumptions underlying this approach are consistent with those set out by Creswell (1994) for qualitative research, so that reality is as seen by the participants. Two interrelated approaches are used to collect data, observations and interviews. As Hammersley and Atkinson (1995) suggest, using two methods is a way of each informing the other. For example, points of behaviour observed in the mountain setting (written up in field notes) can be explored more fully in an indoor setting through an interview format (when the dialogue can be recorded and the data transcribed). The following section explores participant observation and interviews in more detail and, weaves together the research context noted by Hammersley and Atkinson (1995) with my own emergent design. This is followed by details of the five blocks of fieldwork.

Hammersley and Atkinson (1995) propose that there are three major dimensions along which internal sampling occurs: time, people and context. I found the temporal dimension an interesting one that raised important questions about self-organisation. For example, day and night activities are not clear cut in the mountains when alpine starts to a day can occur from midnight onwards and a day of activity might extend to twenty-four hours. This is clearly shown by the start of the Foundry Mountain Activities (FMA) trip to the Picos de Europa in September from 17th – 22nd 1998. I arrived at Arenas de Cabrales with my two clients on the afternoon of day one and was joined by a second guide and two more clients later that night. At 3 a.m. on the morning of day two we left the valley hotel in complete darkness and drove to the start of the walk required to reach our mountain, Naranjo de Bulnes (2519m.). We ascended to a point of spectacular aspect by dawn and moved on to the base of our climb. By the end of the afternoon we stood on the summit and spent the next three hours descending to the hut which was to be our base. It was now 9 p.m. on the evening of day two and it had been dark for more than an hour. Valley to summit to hut had taken 18 hours, during which there was little respite from the physical demands required in achieving the objective. A further example of the extent to which temporal patterns become distorted and anything but 'normal' can be drawn from the second FMA trip to Skye that I worked on. This took place from the $18^{th} - 26^{th}$ June 1999. Days five and six from this seven day itinerary had been set aside for me to take one of the clients on a continuous crossing of the Cuillin Ridge from south to north[11]. As the full group were on the ridge on day five, the client and myself did the day of planned activity and then, as the others set off to return to the valley, we stayed up on the ridge and made our way to Gars Bheinn, the southernmost summit. We began our crossing of the ridge, normally a two day expedition, at 3 p.m. on the afternoon of day five in glorious sunshine. A combination of latitude, season and good weather enabled us to continue to climb until 11 p.m. that night when it began to get a little dark. We then shivered through a cold bivouac (sitting in our rucksacks on a ledge above An Dorus, a point of access to the ridge between the summits of Sgurr a' Ghreadaidh and Sgurr a' Mhadaidh) until it became light at around 3.30 a.m. on day six and we could continue on our way. Despite a sea mist that made navigation of the most technically demanding section of the ridge tricky, we were on the summit of Sgurr nan Gillean, the northernmost summit, by 9 a.m. on day six. The full traverse was completed in 18 hours, which included an 'overnight' stop. Time, as shown through these examples becomes distorted, compressed and extended. Here the ethnographer is, in principle, in play all day and, sometimes all night too. There is no question of selecting which 'events' to participate in as there is often only one happening. As a mountaineering ethnographer I became deeply and intensively involved in such elements of the adventure holiday, which made for concentrated periods of participation but created problems such as a lack of personal space for reflecting on the participation and writing up field notes.

Thus, isolated personal space was difficult to locate at times. Unlike with Whyte (1955), who had a room in Cornerville that provided a private base for his operations, in mountains there is no obvious place to write up notes. Engaging in participant observation in the mountains demands a certain flexible approach to temporal structuring and an imaginative use of space for those times when the researcher might have the chance to reflect on a period of data collection. Such temporal and spatial distortions promoted questions of how and when to record information as there are clearly practical considerations of having the time and space to write things down. None of this was obvious to me when I started the

---

[11] Sgurr nan Eag at the southern end of the ridge is 924m. Thereafter, moving north, the ridge undulates to a high point of 993m. at Sgurr Alasdair and finishes at Sgurr nan Gillean 965m. in the north.

project, however, the holiday format of the fieldwork did have advantages. One of these is that, despite some periods of very intense mountaineering activity, busy periods would often be followed by 'rest' days. This was certainly the case following the ascent of Naranjo de Bulnes outlined above. Moreover, over a period of a year (1998-1999) I undertook five periods of fieldwork, each with different sets of clients and using four different mountain areas (I was able to go to Skye twice). This meant that I could learn from my experiences of one trip before embarking on the next. Additionally I could (and did) interweave fieldwork in mountains with post-trip interviews, usually at a location of the client's choosing, thereby supporting the data collection process in ways suggested by Hammersley and Atkinson (1995). A variety of approaches are therefore needed to actually collect data, particularly when it comes to writing it down. Each circumstance is different and adaptability seems the key. For example, in the Lake District I had my own room in a custom built centre but on the first Skye trip I shared a communal bunk in a bothy[12].

What emerges from the fieldwork is a narrative that is drawn from engagement in a social world with constantly shifting spatial and temporal parameters within the bigger context of place and time for the holiday. So, when McNeill (1990:83) suggests that qualitative research should be 'validated' so that "the subjects of the research accept it as a true account of their way of life", what he really means is that it should be verified. Even in the case of verification, through cross referencing interviews with observations and sending back interview transcripts to the clients to add comments, this can only happen at the descriptive level. The participant's perceptions of why they behave as they do may not be consistent with social theorising.

To achieve the objectives of the research, observations are required to be 'well rounded' (Hammersley and Atkinson 1995). The practicalities of applying such a strategy meant that I actively sought time with clients in all social settings encountered in the adventure holiday format. These included the mountains but also the minibus, the bothy, the pub the climbing shop and the hostel. It is through such a strategy that issues and concepts emerge to set

---

[12] A bothy is a large hut with basic amenities for sleeping, washing and eating. Generally cheap, functional and located in or close to popular mountain areas it becomes a social intersection for walkers and climbers 'passing through' an area. The one we used on the first Skye course had one huge communal bed into which people roll, side by side, wrapped up in their sleeping bags.

the context for the observations. Following the writing of field notes and reflection upon these, such observations may begin to fit a pattern and inform the emergent project design by providing a focus for future observations. This can be illustrated by an extract from my field notes for the Lake District trip when, as it was a particularly wet and windy week, the issue of comfort in adversity arose and manifested itself through an emerging theme of clothing and equipment:

> The following morning, when sorting out kit for a scrambling day Peter strapped the rope to his rucksack, without consulting the others. Peter's rucksack had straps designed to hold either crampons or a rope. He knew what to use these straps for. None of the group challenged his desire to carry the rope, so he was politely ignored. Most were preoccupied. As we sat in the spacious hallway that forms the 'wet' area of the centre (where the rules say boots must be left). There was a certain reluctance to move out of the Centre as it was clearly raining heavily, with strong winds driving rain against the doors. A lone voice broke the quiet with: "Well, this is what we have all this bad weather kit for". The discussion that followed reflected what people were wearing today and the extent to which this kit would allow them to feel comfortable when out on the hills, especially as we intended to get into some exposed and rocky situations. The group were still experimenting with layering systems and indeed different shell garments. The reality that this kit would be tested to the full today was in everyone's mind and dominated the conversations. Wally was wearing a ventile cagoule that he had purchased after reading Rannulph Fiennes' account of crossing Antarctica. Paul, the policeman, was wearing a red gore-tex cagoule with matching over-trousers, purchased because this make came out with a high star rating as reported in Trail magazine. Peter was lacing up his gaiters rather self consciously, aware that he was the only member of the group wearing them. Perhaps he was unsure whether he was trend setting or passé. Michael wore his usual Rohan cotton shirt and trousers, it was the blue outfit today. His brown outfit had got wet yesterday. Over this he wore a substantial North Face cagoule. I checked that each member was carrying the appropriate spare kit and food. We stepped out into the rain. Twenty rapid strides got us to the minibus and some early relief. There was not much conversation during the drive away from the valley. Each individual was hugging their rucksack and, if like myself, probably trying not to think about the rain that was bouncing off the windows.

Writing these field notes made me aware that ideas of comfort and how this might influence behaviour was emerging as a framework for future observations: Hammersley and Atkinson (1995) suggest that the researcher should resist the temptation to see, hear and participate in everything that goes on. They also emphasise the need to be systematic and disciplined in writing up field notes. This was an erratic procedure for me. It was often the case that I had intense periods of activity when it was virtually impossible to write down anything, followed by quieter phases when, if I was lucky, I was able to retreat to a back region of sorts (Goffman 1959), and write-up without interruption. This was the case in the

Lake District when I had my own room, and on the penultimate night my own tent on a windswept fell-side, but was not the case on Skye where such writing up had to take place in the communal areas. In the Picos de Europa my back region was an isolated boulder overlooking the hut. However, writing things down helped the identification of categories and concepts in the field. The research process thus represented a continuous movement between emerging interpretations of reality and empirical observations. The main tools of participant observation were, for me, the human senses, particularly sight and hearing. However, I did take photographs and some of these shots have acted as durable data that I have been able to take away from the setting and use to further develop the ideas emerging from the fieldwork.

The three main points in considering interview and other verbal data are, who to ask, how to ask and how to analyse (Hammersley and Atkinson 1995). Drawing upon the work of Lofland (1976) and Spradley (1970), Hammersley and Atkinson 1995:50-51) provide a framework which begins to address these problems. Hammersley and Atkinson (1995) suggest that, in a socially homogenous group, an adequate representation will normally require some sampling. This was certainly the case with my study whereby the pool of potential subjects over the five blocks of fieldwork included twenty-five clients and nine guides. So, rather than attempting to observe and / or interview everyone, key actors, particularly gatekeepers need to be identified. Hammersley and Atkinson (1995:50) suggest 'member-identified categories' or observer-identified categories'. In the early stages of ethnographic research the former category tends to dominate as the researcher is, in my experience, still being strongly guided by the members of the social setting as the design is more embryonic. In the later periods of fieldwork I was clearer about who I wanted to interview. Moreover, as the field notes accumulated I was also clearer about what questions I wanted to ask. Following Hammersley and Atkinson's (1995) call for representation, I was careful to sample as full a range of clients as possible. Of the twenty-five clients, the age range covered 22 to 60 years, four were female and these were part of the scrambling and walking courses; the climbing courses were all male. There were no ethnic minorities and all subjects were professional people or skilled workers with the majority being in managerial positions. (Occupations ranged from accountant, lawyer, merchant banker, teacher, and company director to architect, interior designer and computer programmer. There were several students on one course, a forester, two policemen, an exhaust fitter and one social worker. Several subjects were aged 50+ and retired). The fieldwork covered walking, scrambling and climbing activities.

The process of interviewee selection was, therefore, a considered response to the subject pool and formed an important component of the development of analytical ideas. Despite what Hammersley and Atkinson (1995) claim to be a common problem to ethnographers, the gatekeepers to the client-world of my project had little influence over who was selected for interview. This is because, once in the field, I was generally at the same starting point in terms of relationship development with the clients as the gatekeepers themselves. I could therefore produce my own sample, although I did allow myself to be guided by a process of 'member identified categories' to a greater extend in the early stages of my work. Here I am alluding to the sub-groups that Hammersley and Atkinson (1995) suggest can form in some situations. This was most noticeable for me in the Lake District where the group was large and I can only claim to have been a participant observer for the clients I worked with closely on the mountains. In the Centre sub-groups did form but these did not appear to be related to mountaineering credibility as far as I could see. I also exerted further structural control by making a clear distinction between the fieldwork and the interview process by allowing a temporal and spatial separation from the field. My fieldwork data collection did involve dialogue, discussions and conversations that provided verbal data, but I recorded these as field notes with some verbatim statements and did not treat them as formal interviews. I saw such data as signposts towards areas of potential analysis and, therefore, a starting point for future exploration. However, in a field setting the researcher has to be prepared to adapt to unexpected developments that may provide excellent data collection opportunities.

The unpredictability of ethnographic design is illustrated by an opportunity that arose in a bar in Arenas de Cabrales. A small group of us that mixed two guides and clients were celebrating our successful series of climbs on Naranjo de Bulnes when two guides from the adventure tourism company Exodus, plus a large group of their trekking clientele came in to the same bar. The notes that I was able to write up (on the flight home the following day) picked up on a number of fascinating observations and dialogue. Both groups were in a 'celebratory' mood having successfully completed their respective itineraries and behaviour was loud, demonstrative and, for the males, bawdy. The guides from the two groups mingled and discussed 'guiding matters'. The 'trekkers' from Exodus and the 'climbers' from FMA stayed physically separated but within earshot of the 'banter' that reflected the mountaineering achievements of each group. Then, one somewhat drunk and emboldened male trekker came over to the climbers I was with and offered to buy some drinks. On the strength of the response (the details of which I missed) he proceeded to pick a fight with the perpetrator of the response, also a male, who then fuelled the flames by asking if the trekker's invitation to 'go outside – now!' was a subterfuge for a proposed sexual encounter. The potentially volatile situation was quickly re-stabilised by one of the Exodus guides gently leading his client away and 'normal' banter resumed. One reading of this unexpected encounter between two groups of clients with different companies, is that the juxtaposition of people on adventure holidays brings to the surface interpretations of walking and climbing as 'hierarchy' in the field of mountaineering. It was clear to me that the gestures, deportment and use of specialist language from the climbers was designed to set them apart from the trekkers. In other words, different activities are invested with different levels of symbolic capital. This encounter was not part of my strategic planning but nevertheless provided me with some powerful data, reflection upon which has in turn contributed to the analytical phase of this study. This was the only time social confrontation of this kind was evident over the five periods of my fieldwork but it raised the identity issue, in this case climbers-walkers, so that I was able to explore this further when I sat down with my interviewees.

The difficulty of writing during the mountain activity periods has already been discussed. I reasoned that both clients and guides as potential interviewees and myself as researcher would benefit from a period of reflection on the experiences that I was keen to talk about. I took care to allow the interviewee to select the venue for the interview to maximise the opportunity of creating a relaxed setting (Hammersley and Atkinson 1995). Through a process of contacting the interviewee and explaining my intentions ('to listen much more than to talk myself, and I have no hidden agendas'), I explained that I would use a small tape recorder with their consent so that I could transcribe our dialogue at some later date. I completed twelve post-holiday interviews ranging from the shortest at forty-five minutes to the longest at two and a half hours. The time scale of the interviews was generated as much by the real life circumstances of the clients, such as working hours, as the propensity they had to talk about their experiences. This generated about 60,000 words of transcripts. The context where people talked to me was important because they may well behave, act or elicit different responses depending on where they are. Being conscious that I had to fit my interviews into the working lives of the clients I had no preconceptions about where the interview took place although people's own homes usually provided the most favourable conditions because they were quiet, distraction free and made the interviewee feel relaxed. However, at various times I found myself interviewing in a pub, a pizza restaurant, a wine bar in Islington and an elevated office in Central London. From this latter vantage point, the client Hugh, and myself were able to discuss the similarities of the skyscraper landscape of Central London and the mountains of the Picos de Europa[13]. This was an instance of the setting influencing the points of reflection informing the dialogue. We were both 'taken back' to the mountains, something that facilitated discussion about what happened there. This example also illustrates how each interview was conducted. I had drafted a series of questions, which were constructed around themes and issues emerging from reflection upon the empirical observations. This strategy allowed me to explore the issues that I deemed pertinent but, by allowing the interview to be relaxed and to a large degree client driven, I did not close down any avenues that emerged during the interview. Thus, I did not move on to new questions until the existing topic had 'dried up' and, additionally, some questions were improvised depending upon the detail of the dialogue emerging. A good example of such a dialogue is presented in chapter six. This example shows how I became involved in a section of dialogue about climbing walls with Chris, who was a client with FMA's Picos de Europa course, which provided some interesting data about dress codes for climbers. The questions I constructed the interviews around are set out in the table below. I generally asked the same questions to guides and clients.

Post Fieldwork Interview Questions
When were you last in the mountains? How often do you go? Where do you go? What do you do?
What mountaineering activities do you most often do?
What do you want to do next?

---

[13] In his book 'The ordinary Route' the accomplished essayist, educator, guide book writer and mountain climber Harold Drasdo makes a similar comparison when he suggests that Cathedrals and other distinctive buildings in urban areas can inspire the same awe and aesthetic sensibilities as mountains.

What do you recall about our FMA-HKE-JG-WE holiday?
What did you enjoy the most? What did you enjoy the least?
What do you think makes a person a mountaineer?
What mountains are you attracted to? How do you learn about these mountains?
Do you think of yourself as a tourist?
Is there a difference between climbers and walkers?
What did you expect to achieve by signing up for the holiday? Did you achieve this?
Were there other things that gave you pleasure-satisfaction about what we did?
Do you feel comfortable in mountains?
How much specialist clothing and equipment do you have of your own?
Will you buy more specialist clothing and / or equipment in the future?
To what extent did the mountaineering holiday contrast with your normal life?

In this way, as I discovered, the interviewer can effect semi-structured interviews and retain a degree of control around the research agenda (Bryman 1988, Hammersley and Atkinson 1995). Thus, participant observation in the field led to a more formal interview setting for selected clients and together these two methods contributed data that was subjected to ongoing analysis to illuminate the research focus of this project. The following sections deals first with the fieldwork details and then with some broader ethnographic issues before the final section summarises the chapter and points the way forward as the narrative unfolds.

3.6 Fieldwork Details

This section gives precise details of the fieldwork I undertook, the clients and guides on each course, accommodation and any other key points relevant to the later chapters. I also indicate which clients and guides were interviewed, that is, sat down with me and undertook a taped dialogue. Other clients and guides are cited verbatim in later chapters but these did not necessarily sit down with me in this manner. At the start of each course / holiday I declared my research interests and gained client and guide consent to use direct citations of dialogue for the purposes of this book. This point is discussed further in the next section. I have changed clients' first names. The adventure company names remain.[14] I also use the term 'course' throughout this book because I feel more comfortable with a term that reflects the role I played, that is, of a mountain guide-researcher. Additionally, the term 'course' or 'expedition' is used consistently in the brochures of the companies I undertook my fieldwork with, namely Foundry Mountain Activities, Wilderness Expertise and Jagged Globe. This is an interesting point of discussion to which I shall return, but here I wish to set out the details of the fieldwork. I worked on five courses / holidays. The clients were paying for a holiday, a term I do use occasionally because it is aligned to the theme of freedom. Later chapters will show that the opposition of 'freedom' and 'constraint' become important to the evolving discussion.

Fieldwork Details	
Dates:	August 17th – 25th 1998
Company-Organisation:	Foundry Mountain Activities
Mountains:	Cuillin Ridge, Skye
Accommodation:	Croft Bunkhouse, Portnalong.
Clients:	Leanne (interviewed 16.9.98); Jim (interviewed 20.10.98); Anthony (interviewed 20.10.98).
Guides:	PB, Tim (interviewed 18.11.98), Ben.

---

[14] I have used different (first) names for the clients to protect individual identities although, having contacted all the adventure companies I worked with, each seemed perfectly happy to allow me to promote them directly. The overall intention and hope is that the reader begins to 'see' both the clients and the places that we visited as the later chapters extend the narrative and the discussion.

Points of Information: A week of mixed weather. Notable ascent of Pinnacle Ridge of Sgurr Nan Gillean. Failed attempt at full traverse of the Ridge but exciting bivouac in Coir' a Ghrunnda. Predominantly a walking and scrambling course.

Dates: September 2nd – 9th 1998

Company-Organisation: Wilderness Expertise / Birmingham & Warwick University

Mountains: Central Lake District

Accommodation: Priestly Centre, Torver

Clients: Pam, Peter, Wally, George, Michael (there were others but I had limited contact with these as they were based primarily with the other guides).

Guides: PB, Mike, Craig, Danny (interviewed 19.11.98)

Points of Information: A wet and windy week. One night under canvas otherwise based in the comfortable custom built centre. Predominantly a walking and scrambling course.

Dates: September 17th – 22nd 1998

Company-Organisation: Foundry Mountain Activities

Mountains: The Picos de Europa, Northern Spain

Accommodation: Hotel in Arenas de Cabrales & mountain hut under Naranjo de Bulnes.

Clients: Chris (interviewed 1.12.98), Dave (interviewed 10.11.98), Tom (interviewed 8.12.98), Hugh (interviewed 4.11.98).

Guides: PB, Tim

| Points of Information: | The sun shone! The first mountain day was exceptionally long but it was followed by a rest day. This was the only exclusively climbing course in the fieldwork. |

Dates:	November 15th – 17th 1998
Company-Organisation:	Himalayan Kingdom Expeditions – Jagged Globe[15]
Mountains:	The Peak District
Accommodation:	Hotel, Hope
Clients:	Mike, Paul (interviewed 29.11.98), Jayne, Adrienne, John.
Guides:	PB, Chris, Richard.
Points of Information:	A weekend of walking and checking equipment with plenty of social interaction. Purely walking but in anticipation of Andean mountaineering.

Dates:	June 18th – 26th 1999
Company-Organisation:	Foundry Mountain Activities
Mountains:	Cuillin Ridge, Skye.
Accommodation:	Portree hostel & local hotel.
Clients:	Bruce, Peter, Derek, Brendan, Lee, Robert, Anthony (again), Vaughn.
Guides:	PB, Tim, Gary.
Points of Information:	Advertised and sold as a 'Cuillin Summits' course, not a traverse of the Ridge as had been the case in the previous year. The aim was to ascend

---

[15] Himalayan Kingdoms, which formerly had two branches (Himalayan Kingdoms Trekking & Himalayan Kingdoms Expeditions), re-organised itself into two companies at about this time. My contact has been with the expeditions company, now firmly established as Jagged Globe. The clients I worked with in the Peak District were on a 'familiarisation' weekend organised as training before they were to depart for some Andean mountaineering in Equador. My finances did not stretch to joining them in South America.

all the Cuillin Munros[16], including the most difficult Munro, The Inaccessible Pinnacle. Anthony and myself completed the north-south traverse of all the summits in dry conditions. We made use of a cache of water set out on the ridge in the previous year. This was predominantly a walking and scrambling course with the occasional foray into climbing activities.

3.7 Ethnographic Issues

A number of issues arose that had a bearing on both the way the data was collected and the way it was analysed. Some of these, such as time management in a mountaineering setting, have been alluded to and discussed already, but others need to be aired. Some issues, prominent in the literature such as avoiding 'going native' (McNeill 1990, Bryman 1988, Hammersley and Atkinson 1995) were non-issues for me as I was already a mountaineer and the only thing the clients had in common was they had all paid for an adventure holiday in the mountains. Much more pertinent to my research design were the interrelated issues of impression management, establishing relationships and sustaining a dual position of researcher and mountaineering instructor. Following the guidelines set out by Hammersley and Atkinson (1995), it helped that I looked like a mountaineer in the way I dressed and my general deportment. Furthermore, I did not expect social relations to bond into a deep rapport at the first meeting; this happened in most cases over a number of days and was the result of immersion in mountains and other spaces. It was noticeable, for example, that the group bonded much faster on the first Skye trip because there was no escape from each other – there were no back regions – we cooked in one room, ate and talked in another and slept in the third. The bothy only had three rooms. On the second Skye course some of the clients did not even stay in the hostel where the bulk of the group were based as they were prepared to pay more for an up-market hotel. On this course establishing social relationships took longer. Hence, when Hammersley and Atkinson (1995) suggest that a researcher can ease the pressure of the research agenda by spending time in the setting engaged in activities other than data collection, this

[16] See chapter seven for an extended discussion of Munros, that is, Scottish mountains over 3000 feet.

presupposes that opportunities to 'escape' exist. My experience may have been different from other settings but I rarely, if ever, shut off from observations and data gathering potential in the field. This, I believe, actually reduced the problem of sustaining a dual position of researcher and instructor-guide because my own behaviour was consistent and I was able to establish continuity in my relationships with clients. There is, however, an important area of identity and 'field position' that emerged from the issues related to impression management and the relationship between guide and client. This is explored in some detail in chapter eight and draws strongly upon theoretical work from Goffman (1959) and Edensor (1998) when alluding to the work of the guide as a 'performance' and thus a key component of impression management.

My role in the five blocks of fieldwork that I completed was managed so that I was an instructor-guide first and a social researcher second. However, this role was not fixed and the realisation of my own performance necessitated a flexible approach. Hammersley and Atkinson (1995) suggest it is possible to distinguish between the 'complete participant', 'participant as observer', 'observer as participant' and 'complete observer'. In general terms it was impossible for me to be anything other than a complete participant when we were engaged in mountain activities. However, in other settings, the pub for example, I could be more withdrawn with an inclination towards observation. The reality is, therefore, fluid, in my experience, depending upon the setting and the nature of the 'activities'. A further issue that is best understood in terms of fluidity concerns access. Specifically, this concerns the extent to which a researcher reveals their data collecting activities to their subjects. There are practical and ethical considerations for being either overt or covert when undertaking participant observation. The design of this study follows the sequence of engagement in participant observation set out by McNeill (1990) and endorsed by others such as Burgess (1984) and Hammersley & Atkinson (1995) which raises an ethical question for the researcher. The arguments for and against whether to be overt or covert about one's research agenda have been well aired (Kellehear 1993, Creswell 1994:165). However, Henderson (1991) suggests that, rather than taking overt and covert as two discrete categories, the two positions should be seen as extremes on a continuum. Her argument is that the researcher's position can not be fixed because circumstances change by time, place and group (Henderson 1991:62). This is clearly the case for my own project. The ethical issues surrounding the debate can not, however, be ignored. For ethical and practical reasons I chose to declare my research interests to the clients I worked amongst.

My standard declaration was that I was writing a book about adventure tourism and, in order to gain a clear insight into what this entailed, I wanted to spend time with clients in the mountains. This strategy maximised my data collection potential because I developed good relationships with most clients during their mountain holiday experience(s). The clients, in turn, seemed to accept, and even enjoy, the fact that someone was taking a keen interest in their mountain activities. Such a positive social rapport made it easier to arrange the follow-up interviews. These clients were clearly fully engaged with the data collection process; for example they all gave me permission to use a Dictaphone to record our dialogue. For some of these interviewees I sustained this dialogue by asking for feedback from the transcribed interviews and followed up annotated notes with 'phone calls. Clients in turn would occasionally contact me and ask for advice about future mountaineering projects they had in mind, and in one case one client, Anthony, returned for a subsequent Skye trip and I worked with him for a second time in the Cuillin mountains.

The framework for analysis involves data transformation via three aspects as set out by Creswell (1994:152-157). That is, description, analysis and interpretation of the 'sociation' (Hetherington 1996) sharing group. This is the broad framework that is followed in the empirical chapters. Although Creswell (1994), drawing upon the work of Wolcott (1990) suggests description should involve "presenting information in chronological order" (Creswell 1994:152) this has not necessarily happened in this project. This is because each block of fieldwork further refined the research by allowing time for reflection and analysis to be interwoven with empirical data collection. Whilst this may have mitigated against a descriptive chronology, it remains consistent with the second main thrust of Creswell's (1994) framework, namely the principle of 'progressive focusing'. In this respect, data is presented in the later chapters as an examination of applicability of this setting to theories set out in chapter two. Creswell (1994:152) suggests analysis: "is a sorting procedure...This involves highlighting specific material introduced in the descriptive phase or displaying findings through tables, charts, diagrams and figures". By searching the data for 'patterned regularities', he suggests, a thematic analysis became possible which can then be related to larger theoretical frameworks. Such a process reaches its logical conclusion in Creswell's (1994) third aspect, the interpretation of data. Here again, in my project, recourse can be made to the theories introduced in chapter two. Emergent themes from the fieldwork were re-examined in relation to data and points of analysis drawn out in relation to the theory.

Thus, I have suggested that my research methodology has much in common with a contemporary perspective upon ethnography. There are, however, some discordant points, generated by practical, methodological and empirical issues, which have been illuminated by the preceding discussion. This has made some aspects harder to achieve, but others easier to achieve than in comparable designs. An example of the latter is the ease with which it was always possible to leave the field (Hammersley and Atkinson 1995). The subject group(s) of adventure tourist clientele came together for a set period of time, in a holiday format that had distinct temporal and spatial boundaries, (as in, for example, 'The Cuillin Summits: seven days on Skye', FMA brochure 2000) and which upon completion of the itinerary disbanded. In this respect there was always a known start and finish to each period of fieldwork so 'leaving the field' was an expected part of the experience. The field consisted of a heterogeneous mix of people who became a temporary social group[17], united through the adventure they had signed up for. When the adventure was over, the field disintegrated and fragmented. Much of the rest of this book is concerned with the continuities, rather than the discontinuities, which can be illuminated through data analysis.

3.8 Summary

This chapter critically examines the project from its inception towards the presentation of findings. The focus for each of the empirical chapters represents a theme that has emerged from data analysis. This is then examined in relation to the theories outlined in chapter two. The initial ideas emerging from the pre-fieldwork period were shaped by personal experience and methodological issues to establish the design that has been outlined in this chapter. Data from the fieldwork were recorded in notebooks and points needing clarification and / or development were highlighted to produce a focus for

---

[17] Hetherington (1996) refers to such temporary or transitory groups as 'sociations'. This conceptualisation could well be a useful tool for future research into adventure tourism.

subsequent fieldwork observations or questions that could be followed up at the time of the interviews. What emerges in the remainder of this book is, therefore, my interpretation of the impact of adventure tourism on the field of mountaineering. This has been constructed around my own values and interpretations of the data and presented in relation to existing theoretical perspectives. The next chapter examines the way that mountain spaces have been socially constructed with particular reference to the fieldwork areas. This seems important because the clients have expectations of their holiday that have been generated by broad cultural forces. The chapter on physicality is important because the embodied character of adventure tourism distinguishes it from other aspects of tourism. Clothing and equipment emerged as important themes because they relate to identity through display. Measurement, a theme that has emerged from the literature of modernity, seems to be important to clients. Finally, the chapter on the guide returns the focus to one of the primary mechanisms of cultural reinforcement that of the presentation of self as a mountaineer. The next chapter examines the cultural reproduction of mountains.

Chapter four: The Cultural Reproduction of Mountains and Mountaineering

4.1 Defining Mountains & Mountaineering

Mountains, as with all space (Cosgrove & Daniels 1988, Shields 1991, Aitchison, Macleod & Shaw 2000, Bender 1995), are socially constructed. Change is part of the present, but 'interpretation' of landscape is 'in the eye of the beholder' (Meinig 1979). In this chapter I will explore ways that mountains and mountaineering have been constructed through a mountaineering tradition to acquire symbolic capital. The distinctive position of mountaineer, which some adventure tourists may aspire towards, is aligned to understanding and accumulating such symbolic capital. Being a mountaineer involves a way of 'seeing' that is framed by more broadly accepted cultural definitions of mountains and mountaineering, and in particular, understanding the rules through which the symbolic capital becomes meaningful in social distinction.

A mountain is a space open to interpretation. A person's interpretation of what constitutes a mountain changes with experience. Reid for example (1992:181-4), in his autobiographical essay Landscape of the Settled Heart describes how his understanding of topography changed over time. The 'mountain' of his boyhood, a mound behind his house, was seen as exactly that when he revisited his 'home' location when in his forties. There are at least three different perspectives of British mountains, represented by landowners, residents and mountaineers. A landowner such as the National Trust might see the mountains as an environment in need of conservation. This perspective may be at odds with a resident farmer whose concerns are essentially economic. A mountaineer, by contrast might see only 'the freedom of the hills' to walk and climb and may resent limitations on this 'right' presented by other interests. For example, Jim Perrin's essay Black Earth, Black Light (1986:55-59) is a mountaineer's reaction to an aesthetic infringement on a favourite mountain, in this case a 'road' bulldozed into a remote area. Mountains accommodate roadside climbing crags and remote trekking peaks, documented long-distance footpaths and spectacular features such as waterfalls, ski resorts, areas of farmland and politically delineated areas such as Areas of Outstanding Natural Beauty. Such a range of managed and 'natural' spaces, large and small, populated and unpopulated areas, with varied degrees of access, combine with an increasing diversity of recreational activities to provide an environment rich in exploratory potential. People take different things from their explorations, and thus offer the possibilities of multiple interpretations of 'meanings'.

Mountaineering involves travelling or progressing up, down and through mountains. Bartlett (1993), although subtitling his book 'The Reason We Climb', offers no definition of mountaineering as such, but implies that climbing "those prodigious lumps of stone" (1993:1) is the essence of the experience. He goes on to say: "Nature has provided us with a variety of excresences [sic], from the hills of England to the 8000 metre peaks of the Himalaya. Mountaineering simply means our efforts to get up them under our own steam" (1993:1). To drive through such a region, or to take a helicopter, or to take a cable car to a summit is to miss the obvious point of physical engagement. Whilst such essentially passive forms of engagement can certainly be considered as recreation, as in the way tourists might absorb the view of the Matterhorn from the town of Zermatt (Walter 1982), they may not be considered to be mountaineering. Being a mountaineer is determined by rules commensurate with mountaineering tradition. One rule, for example, is that using a helicopter is wrong; it is akin to putting an escalator up the mountain (Suits 1980:84-87). Yet helicopters and aeroplanes are used to facilitate achieving mountaineering objectives. Bush pilots fly mountaineers into remote areas in North America, particularly the Denali region of Alaska (Mills 1961). Companies such as Jagged Globe (JG) make full use of such access. Mike, a client with JG, described how he had been guided to the top of Denali, descended safely but then had to wait ten days for the weather to clear long enough for the bush pilot to fly in and pick up his group. He told me, with a wry smile, that he was late back to work. Access of the type that compresses the time needed to make a mountain ascent is becoming more common. Nepal now has 27 STOL airstrips (Short Take-off & Landing) vastly improving access to remote areas (Choegyal 1997:121). This example indicates how boundaries do shift, often as a result of a demand for a more concentrated experience whereby the more tedious elements of a mountaineering expedition can be eliminated, or at least reduced, by using flights to move people closer to remote mountains more quickly.

So, mountain and mountaineering are terms that may be interpreted differently by different people but the 'meanings' of these terms are culturally embedded. Harvey (1989:204) suggests: "neither time nor space can be assigned objective meanings independently of material processes, and that it is only through investigation of the latter that we can properly ground our concepts of the former". Thus, objective conceptions of time and space are created through material practices and processes that reproduce social life (Harvey 1989, 1993). This leads Harvey (1989:239) to conclude that: "spatial and temporal practices are never neutral in social affairs". The central thrust of Harvey's argument is that, when space and time are connected to money social practices become defined by commodity production. Thus, there is always social struggle because capital is not distributed evenly. In his discussion of the postmodern condition Harvey (1989:283-307) sets out a series of defining characteristics of postmodernity. These include the mobilisation of mass fashion markets that inform recreational activities and generate lifestyles; an emphasis upon the "virtues of instantaneity" (1989:286); volatile market forces which constantly construct new signs and imagery; ephemerality of issues of identity and the collapse, or at least fluidity, of spatial boundaries and differentiations. This leads, Harvey (1989) argues, to a central paradox which elevates the importance of capital in the defining space because places are likely to be differentiated in ways attractive to capital (1989:296). Place bound identities, as in being a mountaineer for example, become more difficult when historical continuity is threatened by these characteristics of postmodernity. Harvey summarises (1989:302):

> Place-identity, in this collage of superimposed spatial images that implode upon us, becomes an important issue, because everyone occupies a space of individuation (a body, a room, a home, a shaping community, a nation), and how we individuate ourselves shapes identity.

The suggestion here is, that place bound identity is important because such a development rests upon the notion of tradition. There is a certain irony, noted by Harvey (1989:303) that tradition is now often preserved through the commodification process. Tradition in mountaineering has been encapsulated in many ways, but one prominent form has been the mountain exhibition. Bill Murray, a prominent Scottish mountaineer and writer in the 1940s and 1950s, in his introduction to Humble's seminal ([1952] 1986) guidebook to the Cuillin Mountains of Skye, describes a ground breaking initiative in formulating 'correct' mountain behaviour. What is significant about Humble's exhibition is that he took it out of the mountains and into cities. Murray explains (cited Humble 1986:xviii):

[Humble] pioneered the Duff Memorial Mountain Safety Exhibition, 'Adventure in Safety', held in Glasgow in 1968, and subsequently in London, Edinburgh, Aberdeen and Fort William. It became a permanent, transportable exhibition, which showed great numbers of hill walkers how best to enjoy mountains.

The key point is that there has been, and arguably still is, a discourse that people need to be shown 'how best to enjoy mountains', an intimation that an appropriate set of behaviours defines what it means to be a mountaineer. Bauman's (1987:5) argument that legislators operate a 'meta-professional authority' is supported by the evidence here. The 'authority' being legislated for is how to enjoy mountains. In this example, experienced mountaineers, such as Humble, set out the appropriate behaviours for mountaineering. Moreover, here is clear evidence that such a discourse of safe practice is not restricted to mountains because he took his exhibition into cities. The legislative authority is drawn from 'being experienced' in mountaineering. This, in turn, suggests that 'experience' is cultural capital (Bourdieu 1986). Humble's exhibition was a manifestation of his experience, that is, a display of his cultural capital. Through his exhibition he was operating a legislative control over people who might be interested in mountaineering, but perceived themselves to be less experienced than Humble. Humble was distinguishing himself, and in doing so building his identity as mountaineer.

Although Humble's concern was essentially the safe enjoyment of mountains, his 'roadshow' established an approach that has been adopted by all the large adventure tourist companies operating in Britain today. Such shows are usually developed around slides or other audio-visual forms of presentation. The social construction of mountain spaces is, thereby, increasingly occurring outside the mountains themselves, supporting Harvey's view of fluid boundaries between spaces. Evidence for such a claim can be found in a number of examples. First, from March 15th – 17th 2002 The Outdoor Show, "the greatest line-up of outdoor kit and inspiration ever" (www.theoutdoorsshow.co.uk) took place at Birmingham's National Exhibition Centre. This was a mixture of trade show, conference and activity displays. Most adventure tourism companies were represented, a significant example of mountaineering ideas being constructed in an urban setting. Second, the British Mountaineering Council (BMC) provided an Alpine Lectures series (www.thebmc.co.uk) at Manchester, Penrith, Nottingham, London, Bath and Exeter throughout March 2002. This series was sponsored by Sheffield based Jagged Globe, a prominent adventure company providing guided ascents of mountains all over the world. Summit magazine says of this series: "whether you are a novice or a hardened alpinist [sic] there is always more to learn" (Summit 2002:7). The agenda here is safe practice in the mountains but it is also noted that people might "spot new adventures" (Summit 2002:7). The series is presented by British mountain guides and the suggestion is that people can learn from the experience of the lecturers and, by implication, be guided into visiting areas that are recommended by the verbal and visual presentations of these guides. This is an example of the way that certain mountains are given cultural meaning and a symbolic status through promotion by significant others – and it is happening in the cities. Finally, there is now a Munro Society (www.munrosociety.org.uk) for the 3000 completers [sic] of the summits. Vowles (2002) suggests "The Munro Society has been formed to represent their interests in access and conservation and be a powerful voice for experienced mountaineers" (memorandum to the Association of Mountaineering Instructors from anne@fachwen.org.) The Society is based at Perth, Scotland, and it is clearly aimed at 'experienced mountaineers'. To be a member of the Munro Society is to have distinction. It could be argued that this is a strategy of experienced mountaineers to preserve their distinctiveness because it is an exclusive 'club'. So, The Outdoor Show is responsible for a democratisation of access to mountaineering but the understanding that people who go to the show is being constructed by a legislative position that 'controls' the distribution of the cultural capital of mountaineering, particularly the symbolic capital of certain mountains. This is further developed by the lecture series, which sets out a discourse of safety that restricts 'freedom' to those people with the appropriate experience and skills. The Munro Society is clearly an exclusive group drawing upon the symbolic value of their 'completed' [sic] experience, thus illustrating Harvey's point that "how we individuate ourselves shapes identity"(op. cit.)

The exhibition momentum, begun by Humble, has been continued today at the new Rheged centre (www.mountain-exhibition.co.uk). This has been created by the British Mountain Heritage Trust and is now fully open (Wells 2001). Sponsored by the mountaineering equipment manufacturers Helly Hansen, the exhibition displays: "a journey through British mountaineering history" (Wells 2001:121). It brings together archive film, artefacts and photography, mountain art, a film about Everest and commentary from famous British mountaineers. This may be the strongest initiative yet aimed at celebrating and therefore conserving, or (re)producing a mountaineering tradition. Places are constructed through specific images so that they are differentiated by degrees of capital invested in them and by their capacity to construct some limited sense of identity: "in the midst of a collage of imploding spatialities" (Harvey 1989:304). The idea of wearing mountain clothing in cities, for example, moves the spatial location of mountain-identity construction away from the mountains themselves. This increased 'accessibility' to mountaineering fits Harvey's (1989) analysis and illustrates the 'paradox of commodification' as a mode of conserving heritage. In other words, in conserving a legislative position through a permanent exhibition, mountaineering is simultaneously opening up the fluidity of its boundaries thereby encouraging plurality of interpretation and spatial mobility in the expression of mountaineering identity. Nevertheless, as the exhibition clearly shows, the 'traditional' view of mountaineering has emerged from a set of readings of the social world that have a Romantic aesthetic as a central discourse.

The Romantics valued wild mountains for aesthetic reasons and because the 'wildness' led to sensory arousal through embodied experiences that were considered 'real' or authentic when set against the de-sensitising proclivity of urban life. Mountains came to represent 'wildness' symbolically in nature. It is Urry's contention (1995:174) that:

> Reading nature is ...something that is learned; and the learning process varies greatly between different societies and between different social groups within any society.

It is mountaineers who set the rules for their own 'society'. People have learnt to 'read' mountains in ways consistent with the values of Romanticism. Pre-dating Romanticism mountains were considered to be the home of demons and dragons (Fleming 2000). Consider Evelyn's view from 1726 published in his 'Sacred Theory of the Earth' which was typical of how mountains were viewed at this time:

> Tis prodigious to see and to consider of what Extent these heaps of Stones and Rubbish are!...in what Confusion do they lie? They have neither Form nor Beauty, nor Shape nor Order....There is nothing in Nature more shapeless and ill-figured than an old Rock or a Mountain....I fancy, if we have seen the Mountains, when they were new born and raw...the Fractions and Confusions of them would have appeared very ghastly and frightful (cited in Bernbaum 1997:121, capitals in the original).

The Romantics re-defined wild places in cultural terms so that mountains which Evelyn had suggested were 'ghastly and frightful' in 1726 become "landscapes of aesthetic evaluation" (Urry 1995:195) by the middle of the nineteenth century. The consumption of certain landscapes became an indicator of taste and, therefore, became part of social distinction.

Hills, mountains and moors have, from a Romantic perspective, long been seen as places to escape to from the perceived constrictions and complexities of urban life. The example from Dave set out below offers evidence of the extent to which some adventure tourists seem to have absorbed this central idea. According to a Romantic view of nature, mountains appear to offer an escape environment, the attraction of a simpler way of life, a chance to exercise and feel alive, experience purity and literally re-create oneself. Such a set of experiences appears to operate in a realm of freedom - mountains, in a Western culture, have become symbolic of freedom and represent to many a 'real' way of living. This is borne out in my actual conversations with adventure tourists. Dave, one of the Foundry Mountain Activities (FMA) clients from the Picos de Europa course, said:

> I feel like I belong out there much more than I do here. The wind might be blowing, it might be raining and horrible but I don't mind. When I'm in the city I've got this pilot light burning and in the mountains the whole thing comes on and I feel really alive. All week when I am here I wish that I could be out in the countryside, not even in the mountains but just outside the city.

Here Dave is clearly showing that, although ideas of mountaineering might be symbolically represented in city spaces, the 'real' experience can only be found outside the city so that his 'boiler can come alive'. Dave's emphasis is upon the dampening effect that city life can have on sensory experience. It is possible that just being outside the city can 'fire up his boiler'. However, his chosen source of sensory stimulation is mountains, in which he perceives a 'freedom'. Here is evidence of a resistance to civilising processes (Elias & Dunning 1986) but the idea of freedom has become socially constructed because Dave believes he can only 'be alive' in mountains. The immersion in mountains experienced by pioneers who were literally exploring un-trodden ground is projected as our contemporary mountaineering experience of freedom, but such 'exploration' is now controlled by cultural definitions of what a mountain is, where the 'best' mountains are and how one should approach and climb such mountains. Such ideas are reinforced by initiatives such as the Rheged Centre. The following section explores ways that mountains are given cultural meanings.

4.2 Romanticism and The Social Construction of Mountains

Mountains are the archetypal wilderness space. Wilderness as defined socially has its origins in pre-modern times during the agricultural revolution of about 10,000 years ago (Short 1991:5). Wilderness can be understood through distinctions of cultivated and uncultivated land, savage and settled people and domesticated and wild animals. Until the Middle Ages, civilisation was deemed to have advanced in relation to the clearing of forests, cultivation of the soil and the conversion of wild landscape into human settlement. Thus, "uncultivated land meant uncultivated men [sic]" (Thomas 1984:15). Thomas concentrates on England and argues that between 1500 and 1800 a whole series of changes occurred in the way people at all social levels perceived and classified the natural world. Reading nature became, and continues to be, a learned response that varies with social groups and through time and by location (Urry 1995).

There was no concept of wilderness until civilisation evolved to the point of urbanisation. Everywhere was wilderness until towns became established and offered a civilised alternative. But, fuelled by the Romantic Movement of the eighteenth and nineteenth centuries, the appeal of the wild natural environment increased. Wilderness and wild both appear in the literature, often without a clear differentiation. Wilderness is about place, wild is about the values aligned to such a place. 'Wild nature' is a Romantic idea that concerns a way of becoming sensually alive, as Dave does when he goes into mountains. Wild is about resisting civilising processes, which bring order and control and, therefore, operate to reduce the excitement of adventure. The Romantics aligned their 'authentic' selves to wild nature and constructed mountains, particularly those in the Lake District, as wild places that offset the civilising momentum commensurate with urban life. Towns and cities became places that constrained human potential whereas mountains came to be thought of as places of freedom in which a person could discover an authentic self.

Pre-dating Romanticism, in the West, with the emergence of towns, nature came to be seen as a realm of unfreedom and hostility, an arena that needed to be controlled (Macnaghten & Urry 1998:7-15). This is the classical view of wilderness (Short 1991), and it is this position that is opposed by Romanticism. In the same way that modernity separated the mind and the body, so nature and society became dichotomised, an ideological position that led to exploitation and degradation of land and an estrangement from the natural world (Macnaghten & Urry 1998). The term nature has taken on multiple meanings (for example, primitive or original existence, the physical as opposed to the human environment and rural as opposed to urban) so that our understanding of the term has led to changing interpretations (1998:8). Macnaghten & Urry (1998) argue that the way that nature was made singular and abstract provides key insights into how people saw themselves and their place in the world. It was the Enlightenment that began a process of transformation which effectively separated and abstracted nature from humanity. The new sciences of the sixteenth and seventeenth centuries brought the study of nature into a series of laws, cases and conventions discoverable through positivist rules of inquiry. Creation was now seen in mathematical and geometrical terms. However, a critical position emerged in response to the Enlightenment. This became broadly identified with Romanticism.

It was Jean Jaques Rousseau, 1712-1778, who became one of the founding proponents of Romanticism. The Romantic tradition substituted aesthetic for utilitarian standards (Macnaghten & Urry 1998). This alternative view of the natural world stemmed partly from the life sciences, an arena where mechanical doctrines had not totally supplanted sensory qualities. In essence, from the Romantic view, nature was seen to be too complex to be understood by positivist laws. This interest in natural history occurred at a time when many people were experiencing the turmoil of industrialisation in the form of smog filled factories, poor housing, the destruction of countryside, and growing disease. These aspects resulted from a massive interference with nature and they were easy to see as 'unnatural'. However, it was much harder to articulate a coherent 'natural' alternative. The critical position of the Romantics attempted to construct such a case (Macnaghten & Urry

1998:12). In doing so, however, it became necessary to distance oneself spatially from the excesses of capitalism epitomised in the urban setting of late eighteenth and nineteenth centuries. Shields (1991), notes the attractions of beaches in this liminality, but clearly mountains are a good example.

Anderson (1970) uses the emergence of Romanticism to explain the origins of mountaineering. He claims the existence of an adventure instinct in humans and calls this the Ulysses factor. This is a difficult claim to substantiate, however, Anderson does link mountaineering and Romanticism. Anderson's argument is that mountaineering began as a response to the diminishing possibilities of exploration of the physical world. This response, for Anderson, is an 'implosion' of his 'adventure instinct'. The result is that mountaineering becomes self-exploration, and adventure a personalised and subjective idea. Anderson (1970) identifies the importance of the Romantics in influencing such a development, and is, therefore, consistent with other sources (see for example Macnaghten & Urry 1998, Urry 1995, Bernstein 1989a) in the way he acknowledges the relationship between mountaineering and Romanticism. Anderson (1970:66-67) argues that the new Romantic tradition of aesthetic appreciation met a human need left by the diminishing returns possible from physical exploration. He goes on to explain that it was the Romantic poets, who epitomised and ultimately publicised this tradition. By writing about nature in the way that they did they were seeing a new relationship between the social and the natural worlds. Anderson argues that the result was a new philosophical basis that enabled people to continue to 'explore'. One physical expression of this new philosophy was the emergence of the sport of mountaineering (Anderson 1970, Frison-Roche 1996, Bernstein 1989a). As long as the activity was an 'exploration' to the participant, and it contained an element of the satisfaction of curiosity through physical endeavour, then it met the defining criteria for the Ulysses factor. The activity, Anderson argues, becomes an end in itself. Mountaineering, which began with the pursuit of scientific data amidst the glaciers of the Alps and the Andes (Frison-Roche 1996), could now be enjoyed as an end in its own right, even as play (Stephen [1894] 1936). Mountaineering became a way of experiencing 'nature'.

Romantics sought to construct peripheral social spaces such as mountains as symbols of a rapidly diminishing natural world. The mechanism through which they did this was reactive not proactive and is broadly defined by the term conservation. Starting with an initiative that evolved from the work of John Muir (1992) and other 'environmentalists' in North America, a political momentum to establish national parks was created. This movement has had a strong bearing on the construction and management of wild places throughout the developed world. But in Britain, because of the density of the population and the relative dearth of wilderness, control and management of wild mountain spaces has been a highly contested, and, therefore, a political issue. This has been the case from the time that the Romantics first 'discovered' the Lake District to the present day (Donnelly, 1986, 1993, Milburn 1997).

For 'romantics', that is, people who subscribe to the values of Romanticism, wild places have become symbolic of a lost innocence. The wilderness stood for insight and ultimately redemption and universal truth (Short 1991:10). Here it is possible to find the origins of the educational discourse informing mountaineering today. It is also possible to see the importance of conservation to the mountaineering tradition. Education about mountains embraces an understanding of their aesthetic appeal and being educated means to understand the British Mountaineering Council motif of Tread Lightly, namely 'take nothing but photographs, leave nothing but footprints' (BMC 1997). Leanne, an FMA client who came on the first Skye course, and no stranger to world travel, had this to say about her own experiences of adventure:

> I do like to get away from a lot of people. It's a lot more beautiful. I do get a lot more from places that are not accessible and that are away from lots of people – these are special places. In the rainforests of Vietnam part of our trekking there had no Western impacts or influences. To me you can't get a better place in this world than somewhere that has not been affected by outside influences. So I do get a lot more from places like Vietnam. I do like to get off the sign-posted tracks. I have learnt so much about myself in these situations.

An aesthetic discourse is articulated through terms like 'beauty', enlightenment through remote places seemingly immune from 'outside influences' and learning through such experiences comes through very strongly. My analysis of Leanne's statement thus identifies the close affinity she has with the essence of Romanticism. Today, Romanticism has replaced the classical position as the dominant perspective[18] (Short 1991, Rothenberg 1995).

One of the clients, Tom, responded to his first experiences of the Picos de Europa mountains in this way, recognising that the use of helicopters was inappropriate to fully absorbing a mountain aesthetic:

> The walk to the foot of the climb was absolutely an integral part of the experience. The dawn and that great sight when you first see Naranjo de Bulnes, orange in the early sun. It is a fantastic valley, something you don't actually realise until you walk down again. What a lovely valley, with that mixed Alpine cum English vegetation and scenery. It's quite odd with all that bracken and heather, fantastic.

Excursive ideas of walking emerge here as 'an integral part of the experience'. The aesthetics of the orange sunrise are also articulated. There is also a hint of heightened senses in noting the 'odd...bracken and heather'.

The Romantic vision remains escapist, which is an idea underlying Leanne's preference for being away from 'outside influences', and is most easily achieved in geographically marginal zones. Visiting such areas is what adventure tourism provides for and clients show this in what they say about being in mountains. Dave, whose 'pilot light' fires up when he is in the mountains so that he 'really comes alive', and Leanne who likes 'special places' illustrate a romantic allegiance.

'Authentic' nature, in the Romantic tradition, is exclusive of people. Walter (1982) calls this 'earth-sans-man' [sic]. Images are projected, via guidebooks for example, that represent that space symbolically. Leanne and Dave are romantic in that they have had their understanding of mountains constructed through culture. Leanne had struggled on our ascent of Gars-bheinn, the southernmost summit of the Cuillin Ridge and our starting point for a proposed full traverse. But when we did gather as a group on the summit, the cloud that had enveloped us, and the rest of the Ridge, cleared momentarily to reveal a full

---

[18] The reasons for this are likely to be complex and beyond the remit of this book to discuss at this juncture.

panorama of all eleven Munros. This lasted a tantalising twenty seconds before the cloud rolled back. It was the only time we saw the Ridge in its entirety all week. Leanne was transfixed by the view, visibly moved but said nothing. Her rucksack was at her feet, she had one foot on it, and, resting one arm on her raised thigh, she gazed away from the group across at the emerging panorama. Later, during our interview, Leanne openly discussed this specific moment and said:

> Different mountains give different things but a constant is the awe I feel because they are so much more powerful than us.

Awe of wild places is a value of Romanticism and here, Leanne's 'reverence' for what we momentarily saw was evidenced by her reaction. Leanne's deportment was particularly noticeable but she was not alone as Tim and Ben as guides and Anthony and Tom as clients all took on similar poses. Guidebooks contain images of people in mountains absorbed by the scenery and rarely, if ever, looking at the camera. The poses adopted by the group in that short period were like the pictures in books. No one said a word, each person went 'inside' themselves for that mini period of 'awe'. Moreover, certain types of scenery appear to be valued above others. Barthes (1973) makes this point in his essay *The Blue Guide* (1973:74). The way this guide book series is written about France and Spain reinforces a Romantic vision of those countries. Scenery, Barthes argues, is defined by the picturesque (mountains and gorges for example) and certain types of scenery (steep and craggy for example) are mentioned at the expense of plains and plateaux. Similarly, the Blue Guide vision eliminates the human life of the country, or at best reduces people to stereotypes. I have identified similar patterns in the Baddeley guide to the Lake District (1884) and the more recent Wainwright series (1955-1966) for the same area. I selected these guides because they offer detailed accounts of the Lake District, one of my fieldwork areas, and they demonstrate that the values of Romanticism remain intact across time. The Lake District was an important place for Romantics. Wordsworth, for example, lived there and wrote some of his most enduring poetry about the area (de Selincourt [1835] 1977). The Romantics valued wild mountains for aesthetic reasons and because the 'wildness' led to sensory arousal through embodied experiences that was considered 'real' or authentic when set against the de-sensitising proclivity of urban life. The poets and guidebook writers who absorbed the values of Romanticism were 'ethnographers' in the way they became a part of the landscape they wrote about. They literally wrote about what they saw and sensed and felt about the wild places they visited: the wind in their faces, the details of a beetle scampering across a rock, the passage of clouds and the warmth of sunlight on the body. It is these kinds of sentiments that provide continuity through the different guide-books discussed below. Acquiring the 'taste' (Bourdieu 1986) for wild places was an embodied experience.

Changes in access to The Lakes, particularly through the arrival of the railway at Windermere in 1847, appear to have been important to the emergence of a very different place myth. Urry (1995) argues that a democratisation of travel possibilities changed our primary mode of consumption of place from second hand (via reading and listening) to first hand. People could now see for themselves, or 'gaze': "scientific knowledge of 'nature' (and civilisation) came to be structurally differentiated from travel which thus entailed a different discursive justification" (Urry 1995:195). This justification, he argues, became organised around connoisseurship of first arts and buildings, and then of landscapes which became objects of aesthetic evaluation. Landscapes became valued for their spiritual significance and places visited became a kind of curriculum vitae of taste and judgement. The evidence for this can be seen in my evaluation of the Baddeley and Wainwright guidebooks to the Lake District. As each new generation of mountaineers has appeared, the defining guidebooks for the lake District have further emphasised the values espoused and set down by Wordsworth in 1812. Thus, by the 1880s Baddeley, for example, discusses "fine distant views" and "real lake scenery" (1884: ix). His guide is an attempt to 'sell' the Lake District by comparing it favourably to more exotic locations as well as extolling the virtues of its natural attractions:

If we had never seen or heard of anything bigger than Scafell Pike, our English 'monarch of mountains' would realise our highest conceptions of natural grandeur. We can lift ourselves just as high as Nature has raised us, and no higher. Has any painter, working up to the acme of his own conceptions, ever surpassed the reality of nature? Has any poet ever described a scene transcending in beauty the experience which an observant tourist might gain in one or other of the favoured spots of the Earth during a month's travel? We think not (Baddeley 1884:xi).

The Wainwright guides, written between 1955 and 1966, have become the archetypal Lakeland walking guide. There has been a significant departure from the early

Bartholomew guides such as those written by Baddeley by this time. Two aspects of presentation of Wainwright's work stand out above the obvious practical consideration of being small enough to fit into a pocket. These are a visual presentation in the form of hand drawn pictures and a text that is printed as if it was hand written, and that overall is less prominent than the pictures. In this respect Wainwright anticipated the more recently conceived 'topo' guides[19] that have become common in rock climbing circles for example. His descriptions offer detail and are simultaneously pragmatic and prescriptive but he too has absorbed Romantic values. Consider the aesthetic assessment integral to this description:

> Loughrigg Fell...has no pretensions to mountain form, being a sprawling, ill shaped wedge of rough country...but no ascent is more repaying for the small labour involved in visiting its many cairns, for Loughrigg has delightful grassy paths, a series of pleasant surprises along the traverse of the summits, several charming vistas and magnificent views, fine contrasts of velvety turf, rich bracken and grey rock, a string of small tarns like pearls on a necklace, and a wealth of stately trees on the flanks (Wainwright 1958: no page numbers).

Here lakes become 'pearls', and the turf and the bracken offer all kinds of sensuous possibilities. The 'vistas' of the Fell are the reward for the effort involved in making the ascent. Even at the simplest descriptive level there is a language evident here that both reflects Romanticism and requires a common understanding to appreciate, for example 'rough country', 'cairns', 'traverse of the summits' and 'vistas'. So, whilst Romanticism might be the general construction, not everyone will be able to 'read', that is understand, what is written. For those that do, this becomes a point of distinction (Bourdieu 1986). This point is well illustrated by the way guidebooks featured on the climbing course in the Picos de Europa. Chris and Dave had bought the guidebook. Tom and Hugh had no idea about our proposed route to the top of Naranjo de Bulnes other than what was extracted from the FMA brochure where the mountain is described as, "the Matterhorn of Spain" and the climb itself as "an ascent of the stunning 300m. East face...one of the great rock climbs of the area" (FMA Brochure 1999:7). Tom cited this description to me and pointed out that

---

[19] Topo guides are a way of presenting information about the details of a climbing or mountaineering route that are essentially pictorial. Such guides use symbols to represent common features of an ascent such as 'crack', 'open corner' and 'belay stance' and numbers and letters to represent grades of technical difficulty. This circumvents the language problem for climbers operating beyond their own home mountains and, therefore, represents a 'universal' climbing language. Understanding such a 'language' is a constituent of cultural capital – see chapter seven.

when he saw the spectacular picture of the mountain next to the description: *"I just knew I had to climb it, and that is when I interested Hugh in the idea"*. When we arrived at the foot of the climb, Tim, the other guide with myself, positioned the four clients where they could view the climb and, holding the guidebook aloft, related the picture in the guidebook to the mountain as he said:

> It starts up these grooves, climbs out onto a big stance below a short unprotected wall, up this and trending left to that huge red corner, which can be a epic struggle...up the wall above and onto the crest behind that pinnacle...emerging onto the summit ridge beyond where we can see from here.

When Tom asked for clarification of the term 'groove' it was not Tim the guide that replied, it was Dave the client. I had observed that both Dave and Chris simply nodded in acknowledgement of Tim's description, and learnt later that they had already read (and understood) the description of the route we were about to climb. It was this incident, quite early on in the Picos de Europa course, that first alerted me to the differences between the two pairs of clients. Dave and Chris were climbers, and the description of the scenario above offers evidence that Dave and Chris could 'read' climbing guidebooks, a point of distinction for them when in the company of others who could not do so and who, therefore, needed 'guidance'. However, Tim's 'reading' of the climb had a practical purpose in alerting all the clients to the route of the proposed ascent. Hugh and Tom were being taught how to relate a guidebook description to the route of a climb and were, therefore, progressing towards being climbers. Chris and Dave, therefore, were able to position themselves as distinct from Tom and Hugh because they had the cultural capital of understanding guidebooks. From these observations I noted the manifest differences between these clients in terms of their existing and developing cultural capital. This direction of analysis helped illuminate the ideas of freedom and constraint. Freedom is an important value of Romanticism. Guidebooks, then, are an important medium for conveying the values of mountains and mountaineering. Guidebooks act to promote certain routes through which people can pursue their embodied experience(s).

There is a strong embodied component to the Romantic tradition that expresses itself through an active engagement with nature. The Lakes has become an important area for fell walking, but this achievement has needed a discursive justification. Just as the mountains themselves were originally seen as desolate places to be avoided, so walking was originally seen as a functional form of locomotion that people undertook because they could not afford to travel by any other means. Barron (1875) for example wrote: "pedestrianism is felt to be a little shabby. People do not generally dare to go on foot, for they fear the loss of social consideration" (Barron 1875:38). Barron was not writing of the Lake District specifically, where by this time in the nineteenth century recreational walking was well established, but expressing a more widely held view pre-dating Romanticism. The Romantic tradition re-invented walking and defined it, in cultural terms, as a form of recreation. This transformation has been clearly demonstrated by Wallace (1993). She discusses the literary connections between the emergence of a romantic tradition expressing itself in an affinity with nature and walking. She does this predominantly through reference to poets and novelists of nineteenth century England, Wordsworth, Eliot and Hardy for example.

Before the impact of the English Romantics on accepted perspectives on the peripatetic, walking was a necessity practised by those that could not afford to ride a horse or travel in a carriage. Wallace (1993) suggests that, in England in the early part of the nineteenth century, changes in transport combined with the enclosure movement to facilitate a change in the way walking was perceived, particularly by the educated classes who were most directly influenced by contemporary literature and poetry. She also suggests that changes in socio-economic conditions in nineteenth century England altered existing frames of reference in the way people saw the world and movement within it. These were "...material changes that caused or permitted changes in the material and ideological shape of walking" (1993:10). She goes on to suggest ways that the transport revolution impacted upon walking. First, fast and cheap travel became available to the labouring classes. Travel in general became more attractive and eventually this democratisation of travel removed the connotations of poverty and vagrancy hitherto associated with walking as suggested by Barron (1875). Second, as reaching distant destinations now became relatively easy, and choices became available as to how one should travel, there was a shift, Wallace (1993) argues, from destination to process. It was now possible to regard walking as a freely chosen mode of travel. Moreover, she continues, enclosures had a similar impact on walking. By the nineteenth century the enclosure movement was reaching its climax. By this time most agricultural land had been appropriated radically altering local landscapes. In this respect the physical landscape became subject to multiple frames of reference: "so that even those who lived in one place were subject to constantly shifting perceptions" (1993:10). Enclosure closed footpaths. This network of routes was fundamental to local communities because it connected villages to their markets, churches and homes. English law provides usage as the defining characteristic of a public footpath and, in this manner, walkers on a path through privately owned land were un-enclosing that path and re-appropriating it for common use. Walkers were preserving a portion of the old landscape against change (Wallace 1993:3-17), an early example of what was to become an important relationship between Romanticism and conservation[20], whereby certain types of landscape, and the features within landscapes, are retained and promoted at the expense of others. For example, in the Peak District farmers, who are generally happy to enclose their fields with barbed wire fences, are encouraged by the National Park Authority and conservation groups such as the Friends of the Peak District National Park to retain and maintain the dry-stone walls that have come to represent the farmed landscape here (www.peakdistrict.org.uk). Aitchison (2000) argues that the people who constitute such bodies are themselves inculcated with the values of Romanticism.

Wordsworth and those following this tradition invented the excursion (de Selincourt [1835] 1977, Urry 1995). This is essentially organised physical engagement. The excursion was a guided experience through nature, sensory, aesthetic and embodied. The point was to walk along set paths and tracks, through and over 'wild' nature, and to return. To undertake an 'excursion', particularly if this meant walking alone, was a point of 'distinction' (Bourdieu 1986). Not everybody could do this because it required, for example, an ability to map read and at least a rudimentary knowledge of mountaineering. The idea that capital acquisition in the form of excursions completed was / is linked to 'education' is an important one that will be explored more fully in chapter seven. Maps and guidebooks are not value free (Aitchison et al 2000, Harvey 1989), as content is selective and modes of expression promote particular sets of social relations. Commensurate with the more general argument of social construction, the 'excursion' as a pattern of engagement is very much alive today. Excursive routes, particularly in British mountains, have become 'the beaten track' in the sense of their physical presence. Some of these paths have now been engineered, for example the upper section of the 'tourist route' to the summit of the Old

---

[20] The terms preservation and conservation should not be thought of as interchangeable. The former implies a fixed and static entity such as might be found in a museum. The latter allows for some flexibility and a more dynamic interpretation of landscape, thus being more accommodating of ongoing changes to mountains.

Man of Coniston. Here, the National Park Authority has used slate and other 'natural' materials to construct a staircase that both guides and makes physically easier the ascent of this mountain by what has been called, the 'tourist route'. The tourist route is a term used by mountaineers to describe the easiest route up a mountain. In using such a term mountaineers are suggesting that to ascend the mountain by a route other than the tourist route is a point of distinction. This level of social differentiation implies that mountaineers not only have the skills and experience to operate independently of the 'masses' (by selecting and following a more challenging route of ascent) but that they also understand the principle of the excursion. In particular, the Romantics valued a mode of experience commensurate with the idea of 'solitudinous contemplation', that is, part of the purpose of excursive walks and climbs was to get away from the crowds. Lorimer (2000) makes this point when he suggests Bennet's (1985) guidebook to the Scottish Munros rarely shows people in the pictures of each Munro. When people do appear they are small, discrete, looking away from the camera and generally either in poses of active walking or poses of 'solitudinous contemplation' (see for example, the cover 1985, and pages 9, 10, 14, 15, 23, 58, 59). Thus, the Romantic values promoted through guidebooks frame the way people build an understanding of mountains.

Bennet's book (1985) clearly conveys the Romantic proclivity for solitude, and, such a position is not consistent with connotations of tourism. Some clients were very sensitive to any suggestion that identified them as tourists. When I met Paul from the Peak District course for the interview, before I had asked any questions he explained that the group I had joined for the week-end had felt aggrieved at the suggestion that they were 'tourists', even when the term was used with the prefix 'adventure'. This is the first thing he said to me:

> We were concerned about your use of the term adventure tourism: 'I travel, you tour, he trips'. We didn't like the connotations of tourism so we re-defined ourselves as mountaineers.

I had not even got as far as asking my usual opening question at this point, but as Paul had started I followed the direction by explaining that the word 'tourist' had emerged before in my fieldwork. I described a mountain walk I did with my group in the Lake District. We were ascending a mountain called Fairfield on a misty and damp morning when a solo walker came out of the mist behind us. The group had suggested he 'looked like a tourist'. When I asked why, they explained their use of this term in two ways. First he 'looked like a tourist', apparently because he had a small cheap rucksack, leather walking boots and nylon tracksuit trousers on.[21] Second, and perhaps more important for the discussion here, he appeared to be following us. When we stopped, for example to check our maps, he walked a little way past us and then stopped himself. He re-assumed progress more or less when we did. The group was sensitive to the 'tourist's' lack of independence. Their assessment of the situation was a point of distinction for themselves as they could read a map and were learning to position themselves, even in poor visibility. I presented a flavour of this observation to Paul as it offered a point of continuity in the discussion he had initiated. Paul was, thereby, able to further illuminate his point. This is what he went on to say:

> We are all tourists whether we want to admit it to ourselves or not. The true connotation of the word has taken on connotations [sic] of mass packing [sic] etc. So the more elitist would want to steer away from being associated with those things.

It is clear that Paul recognises a form of distinction is operating. He uses the word 'elitist'. Moreover, he associates such a position of distinction with non-alignment with tourism as in 'mass packing'. Further evidence that supports a non-tourist position for mountaineers, that is, a close alignment to the values of Romanticism, comes from Wally. Wally was a client on the Lake District course but he was not a part of the group I took onto Fairfield in the example I described above. His assessment of the 'tourism' issue is, therefore, independent of the group discussion described above. This is what Wally says about a proposed trip to Scotland:

> The problem with well known [mountains] is that they do become something of a tourist route. And I think this does detract from the experience to some extent. So I would be happy to go to a less well known mountain, not such a high one...and the less people I see the better....This year [the people I usually walk with] invited me to Ben Nevis and I politely declined. I thought if we are going to Scotland, why are we going to Ben Nevis?; what is so special about it?; why can't we go somewhere else? It seems to me it is a tick list and at the end of the day you can say to your family, I went to Ben Nevis.

---

[21] The relationship between clothing, fashion, and distinction is explored much more fully in chapter six.

So Wally rejects the idea of a tick list and articulates a resistance to the 'pull' of the biggest mountains. My interpretation of this is that Wally is using his knowledge and experience (cultural capital) to over-ride the symbolic capital that an ascent of Ben Nevis can provide and thereby position himself closer to the identity of mountaineer.

The 'guiding' component of the excursion is sustained by present day guidebooks which are a direct descendent of Wordsworth's 1812 *Guide to The Lakes*. Discursive strands of education, aesthetics and Romanticism emerge in patterns of behaviour characterised by walking 'excursions' and solitudinous contemplation of wild country. However, such analysis assumes an uncomplicated reading of such symbols and does not allow scope for human agency that may contest and re-define such discursive values. With such possibilities in mind the following section draws upon fieldwork data to examine more closely the multiple interpretations possible now adventure tourism has opened a gateway into mountaineering.

4.3 Building a Mountaineering Frame

I have argued that the terms mountain and wilderness are socially constructed. Here is a perspective on the Peak District offered by Tim, the FMA guide. I asked him whether the Peak District was either mountainous or wilderness. He replied:

> Size, nature of terrain and shape of the land determine mountains. The Peak District to me means rolling hillside with some valleys with gritstone outcrops for climbing on but not mountains with a summiting view or a climbing to the top view. A mountain is more about shape than height. Snowdon [the highest mountain in Wales] and the Glyders [Glyder Fach & Glyder Fawr are also mountains over 3000 feet] are definitely mountains; they have ridges, big drop-offs, deep valleys. This is not the shape we have in the Peak District. As for wilderness, to me it's untouched, uninhabited open area. So, to say we have wilderness in Britain is incorrect. We have some wild places and mountain spaces but it is not true wilderness in the sense of Siberia or parts of the Himalayas. The Alps is a superb mountain environment but I wouldn't use wilderness to describe the Alps. The Alps have telephriques and thousands of people moving everywhere at any time of the year. Wilderness is to do with the number of people who are living there and the ways of getting around. It also includes a consideration of how close rescue facilities are.

The guide describes a mountain aesthetic when he suggests mountains have 'summiting views', 'more about shape than height' and 'ridges and big drop offs'. Wilderness is understood to be about 'the number of people living there', that is, constitutive of Walter's (1982) 'earth-sans-man'. This interpretation is promoted through images and writing. When exploring client ideas of where an understanding of mountains and mountaineering comes from, my data supports the earlier suggestion that it is a combination of influences that includes books, maps, magazine articles and other people who may be mountain guides or simply friends (or both). Tom, an FMA client, summarised how his own perceptions are shaped as follows:

> Either reading about them or talking to people who have done them. I don't know, you seem to just hear about them and they grow in your mind, odd snippets and bits. I had read about the Cuillin Ridge. I've got one or two books on walking, 'Challenging Walks in the UK', 'Fifty Best Walks' and books like that. Probably, when I started reading about them, I would have thought that 'Oh, that looks interesting', but as I gained more experience and confidence and got into scrambling and you come across it again, you think 'Ah, now this is something I can do'. It just seems to gradually impinge on your consciousness and suddenly you find it becomes an ambition. The possibility of doing the Munros is growing a bit stronger, the more you do the more you tend to think I can do this. This friend of mine has finished the Munros and is now onto the Corbetts.[22]

'Experience and confidence' have opened up possibilities of exploration for Tom who also appears to be responding to the 'competition' provided by his friend. These are aspects of the identity of mountaineer. Tom has recognised that status is to be gained through accumulated experience and he has a developing 'ambition' to complete the Munros. There is a clear suggestion here that books, particularly guidebooks, establish frames of reference. But also that 'the more you do the more you tend to think I can do this', an articulation of the potential 'freedom' that mountaineering experience (cultural capital) can bring. Guidebooks promote certain places and types of landscape at the expense of others. This is well illustrated by the example of Skye. Skye has a history steeped in Romanticism (Marriott 1983, Swire 1961, MacDonald no date, Bull 1993). Of these sources Marriott is the most concise. He reduces the attractions of the island to the bare

---

[22] J. Rooke Corbett became the fourth Munroist in 1930 and, not to be outdone by Hugh Munro, constructed his own list of 2,500-foot mountains in Scotland. He subsequently climbed them all and today they are known as Corbetts. He defined a 'Corbett' as a hill 2,500 feet or over but having also a drop of 500 feet or more from any adjacent higher hill. This restriction ensured that there are fewer of them (221) than Munros (Dempster 1995:36).

bones and in doing so emphasises the culturally significant. So, Skye is described as, "the jewel of the Hebrides" (Marriott 1983:156) through its unique combinations of seascapes and mountain vistas. Facts and figures tell us that the jagged coastline is 900 miles long and that despite tourism, the island remains "unique and tranquil", steeped in Gaelic culture and dominated, from the mountaineering point of view, by the Cuillin Mountains, "the most dramatic in Britain" (1983:156). The mountains of the main Cuillin ridge are "gashed, pinnacled [sic] and sometimes knife-edged", Loch Coruisk is "remote and wild", and the summits, of which Sgurr Alasdair at 3309 feet is the highest, require much scrambling and climbing to reach: it was 1898 before the last peak was conquered (1983:156). The construction promoted here is of wild mountains not wilderness, but the alignment between 'jagged', 'gashed' and spectacular mountains is evident, as is the suggestion of remoteness (e.g. Loch Coruisk). The construction of mountains is no longer about 'killing dragons' (Fleming 2000) because, on Skye, the last peak has been 'conquered'. It is more about engaging with an environment that has been constructed as 'wild and remote', that is, the *idea* of killing dragons. Fleming (2000:1) suggests that one reason for a British dominance of the conquest of the European Alps was "an imperial confidence that had emerged from conquering much of Asia and Africa". Mountains became archetypal wild and inaccessible targets for conquest. The qualities of tenacity, endurance, determination and courage in adversity were considered distinctive, and, therefore, sought after by people who associated such distinction with being a mountaineer. Books, such as Fleming's, valorise such qualities, which become integral to mountaineering values. Tom, cited above, offers evidence that books have directed him towards mountaineering objectives. Books become an important medium through which the qualities required to be a mountaineer are re-produced.

Some clients do read books about the area(s) they visit. They are generally well informed of and sometimes experienced in the mountain areas of the holidays they choose. Anthony came on two FMA courses to Skye. I interviewed him following the first Skye course, when we failed somewhat dramatically in very poor weather to complete a traverse of the Cuillin Ridge. He said that he had had only the vaguest of notions about Skye, based mainly on family accounts:

My sister went to Skye and rented a cottage last summer and my uncle went there on a cycling trip. They reported back in general terms about the scenery. I hadn't seen it on television or read any articles so it was really word of mouth. I spoke to Tim about the Cuillin, and it was on his recommendation that I signed up for the trip.

Here he speaks of a guide (Tim) sustaining the symbolic importance attributed to Skye and the Cuillin Ridge in particular by 'recommendation'. At first I was surprised before the second Skye trip to find Anthony back again. His bedtime reading each night this time was Humble's (1986) classic account of mountaineering on Skye. Thus, Anthony readily absorbed passages such as this (1986:2):

All kinds of climbing are there for the cragsman's [sic] delight - faces, gullies, buttresses, cracks, chimneys - but the true glory of the Cuillin lies in ridge wandering, finding one's way along the narrow shattered ridges, sometimes among the clouds, with the weird towers and pinnacles looming up out of the mist and barring the way; sometimes on the very top of the world, with wondrous Hebrid panoramas all round. I can not think of the Cuillin as black. Light grey, steel blue, rose flushed in dawn, tipped blood red in the evening sun - all these I have seen and many others.

Here the aesthetics of a 'rose flushed dawn' and a 'blood red sun' are a reward for effort and patience. Anthony's understanding of terms like ridge, crag and mountain are learnt through social construction and re-enforced, and, therefore, re-produced, through his first hand experiences. This became apparent in the conversation we had as we sat on our rucksacks at An Dorus for our 'overnight' break when he and I were traversing the Cuillin Ridge. This conversation was not an interview, and I did not have the opportunity to write verbatim notes as I did not have the circumstance or the capacity to do so. Nevertheless, as the mountaineering was temporarily suspended while we rested, we had our longest conversation together since the interview that followed the previous Skye course when I had first met Anthony. Anthony used terms like 'ridge' and 'gully' to pick out 'lines' [that is, routes of possible ascent] on the mountains we could see. He was not self conscious about his language as he had been to a certain extent when I had first met him. Perhaps he knew me better now, and was, therefore, more relaxed in my company. However, it is my interpretation that this more confident Anthony felt himself becoming a mountaineer. He had read Humble's (1986) book and, having now spent more time with mountaineers, more fully appreciated the symbolic value that mountaineers place on completing a traverse of the Cuillin Ridge, even though his was a 'guided' crossing. The joy that he felt when, on the following morning, we stood on the summit of Sgurr nan Gillean, the northernmost point of the Ridge, was expressed in a huge grin that stayed with him for most of the descent to the Sligachan hotel, which he entered with his head held high. Here is support for my claim that clients have to be mountaineers to some extent in order to engage with the activities.

Elias and Dunning's work (1986) on civilising processes helps explain the ongoing dynamic between mountaineering and adventure tourism. Experienced mountaineers will resist the notion of buying a guide and rely upon their own carefully constructed accumulation of skill and experience to explore mountain wilderness whilst simultaneously avoiding the objective dangers inherent in such activity. This is why Dave and Chris, the climber-clients from the Picos de Europa course, set off several months later for an independent crossing of the Cuillin Ridge. They had recognised the symbolic capital associated with this specific mountaineering achievement, and they wanted the distinction that such an achievement conveys. In this example Dave and Chris are using their skill and experience as an expression of freedom because they are operating independently as mountaineers. However, they are constrained in their choice of objective by the symbolic value attributed to the Cuillin Ridge. To pursue such objectives is to aspire towards an identity of mountaineer. Adventure tourists, in contrast, are more likely to have the nature of their experience defined for them through a combination of a dependence upon guides, existing sources of information about mountains and a 'protection' afforded by constantly improving equipment and other resources such as mountain rescue possibilities. One of the problems, however, is that it is increasingly difficult to operate independently. Independent planning will still involve guidebooks, and, for overseas, chartered flights and liaison officers to facilitate arrangements. People will be guided by such systems. Such dependence becomes more acceptable because of the symbolic capital achieved by participation. However, cultural capital is more than the symbolic, it is about understanding that flying half way up a mountain and then climbing to the top is a lesser experience than a fully independent ascent. For example, Ross, a guide from Calgary operating in the Canadian Rocky Mountains said:

I fly clients to the 10,200 feet 'Dome' on Mount Robson and then climb to the summit. Have these clients climbed the mountain?

If they have not climbed the whole mountain, but because they have stood on the summit through their own physical efforts consider that they have, then the rule that delineates what is and is not a mountain ascent is being challenged. Ross expands on this as follows:

The capital exchange value of an ascent is not just about height and technical difficulty. It could be argued that height is the primary criteria [sic] for non-mountaineers to utilise but to those in the 'know', speed of ascent, solo ascents, un-roped climbs, alpine versus siege style and other investments all play a part.

Ross 'knows' mountaineering is about much more than achieving 'height'. However, to those who lack the cultural capital to 'know' this, height is broadly equated with symbolic capital. He does use the language of distinction when he separates mountaineers from 'non-mountaineers'. Moreover, he equates the distinction to 'knowing' that an ascent of Mount Robson in an independent style, that is without mechanical assistance, is a reflection of the distinctiveness of being a mountaineer as opposed to a client. Ross does use the language of the marketplace when he talks of 'investments', an intimation that, however one may ascend a mountain there is an expected return on that investment.

Western culture places a value on mountains of a certain height but also of a certain shape. Walter (1982) makes this point when he describes the Matterhorn as being the archetypal Alpine mountain. Ama Dablam, which has been described as the Matterhorn of the Himalayas, has been used as the symbol for an international insurance company, and appears on all its official stationary. Such shaped mountains have been given status, and, therefore, currency, through Western culture. Mont Blanc, although much higher than the Matterhorn, sits as the high point to a sprawling massif and as such is less 'dramatic' and has not emerged as a visual image in the same way but its importance is achieved because it is the highest mountain in Europe. It is not a coincidence that the pictures illustrating the brochures of FMA and JG are predominantly of the spectacular variety, examples include Naranjo de Bulnes and the Inaccessible Pinnacle on the Cuillin Ridge of Skye. Shape and form are important because people 'collect' images (Urry's terminology 1990, 1995) through photographs, postcards, calendars and other representations of mountains. Others, friends, family, and colleagues for example, will assess people's representations by broader cultural criteria. Mountains 'are', therefore, understood to be like the Matterhorn. The west coast of Scotland contains some of the most aesthetically appealing and therefore photogenic mountains in Britain. This is, as Hewitt (1996:44) argues, because the 'west coast mountain vistas can be enjoyed against a spectacular seascape and they look jagged, steep and formidable'. Closer, in fact, to a broad cultural understanding of 'mountain'. He continues:

> In the world of hills, lookism mainly centres on still photographs. Scotland has a series of megafamous views which recur endlessly on calendars and are hot-wired into the nation's brains...[examples include]...the northern Cuillin's fearful symmetry from the Slig. What all these have in common is spectacular westcoastness. Rare is the day - or, rather, month - when you see an eastern or central hill on a calendar: they simply don't present as well.

West coast Scottish mountains and spectacular peaks such as Naranjo de Bulnes represent considerably greater symbolic capital than mountains that 'simply don't present as well'. For interpreters then, value attached to different mountain spaces is set out by this established tradition and the target might become one of systematic accumulation. The example of Brendan, an FMA client and an avid collector of Munros, is discussed in chapter seven. Often, this is as quickly as possible, reflecting Harvey's (1989) 'virtues of instantaneity' and fuelled by the commodification process through which adventure tourist companies operate.

The rules of mountaineering form a reference point from which legislators formulate meaning about what they do. Far from being an eccentric and incomprehensible pastime that, to the non-participant, was characterised by risky endeavour and voluntary exposure to objective dangers such as avalanches, rock falls and extreme weather, mountaineering has emerged as predominantly rational. A modern framework of rationality is expressed in the rules defining what it means to be a mountaineer. As an experienced mountaineer and a guide myself I understand and act upon these. The rules are written down in climbing and mountaineering manuals (such as Fyffe & Peter 1990) and disseminated via clubs and organisations that are involved in climbing or hill walking. Such bodies include the Scout movement, the United Kingdom Mountain Training Board (UKMTB), the British Mountaineering Council (BMC), climbing clubs and adventure tourism companies. The motives of these bodies may be essentially recreational (e.g. climbing clubs) or educational (e.g. schools running the Duke of Edinburgh's Award Scheme) but the rules defining good and bad practice, and hence the way of 'doing' mountaineering remain the same. These rules involve knowing about planning, clothing, training and styles of ascent. Mountain expeditions of whatever scale (a day out on the local hills or the ascent of a Himalayan giant), are carefully planned with due reference to existing maps and information, weather patterns and the logistics of travel to and through mountains. In addition clothing and other specialist equipment is used to maximise comfort, training techniques are put into practice and ascents or journeys meticulously documented, not only with respect to height and distance but also to style. Rules set out by the legislators, I would contend, include the following. First, serve an apprenticeship, thereby, gaining experience of mountains and knowledge and skills from those already experienced. This will facilitate the development of fitness and mountaineering competence. Second, have the right equipment and know when and how to use it (if in doubt defer to a guide or undertake a training course). Third, attend to energy requirements particularly concerning diet and pacing through the mountains. Fourth, maximise appreciation of mountains by forming only small groups (or go alone). Fifth, always rely upon your own physical efforts and respect the environment.

The concept of a frame helps explain the extent to which these rules may be accepted, challenged or simply ignored. If people are unframed, Goffman (1959) suggests they will 'have a go' at a performance based on the nearest reference frame that they have. Thus, a novice mountaineer is more likely to contribute to 'frame mobility' across different settings. Frame mobility of this kind suggests people are likely to bring reference points to new settings and that inevitably these reference points are aligned to 'normative rituals' (Edensor 2000). Adventure tourism is, arguably, part of a democratisation of mountaineering. Expectations are different for clients like Hugh and Tom from the FMA Picos de Europa course, who have entered the field of mountaineering without following the apprenticeship that the 'rules' demand. For Hugh and Tom 'rules' can only be understood by a 'frame' that carries 'normative rituals' into an extraordinary setting. Only a person with a developed mountain frame can appreciate and, therefore, perform the script emerging from the rules. Understanding the rules is what leads to distinction in mountaineering.

There are observable differences between clients with different amounts of cultural capital. Position is determined by how well people understand the rules and how this cultural capital is communicated. So, for example, the popularity of mountains that convey significant symbolic capital, such as the highest peaks, may fail to convey the right distinctiveness precisely because of that popularity. The example of Wally discussed earlier has already been used as evidence to support this contention. The point about distinction is noted by contrasting Wally's statement to that of Tom, who has also noted the symbolic importance of Ben Nevis. Tom, using his previous mountaineering holiday in Peru as a reference point, had this to say:

> You see climbers poised on glaciers in pictures in books and suddenly you're there with your own ice axe and crampons. It's a thrill...I'd quite like to do Ben Nevis in the winter. Ticking is part of the way you choose what you want to do each year. It's part of the way you define your achievements.

Both clients recognise the symbolic importance of Ben Nevis but articulate different responses to the prospect of climbing it. Wally is drawing upon the constructions of solitude and exploration (as in 'the excursion') that are constituents of Romanticism. Tom is more focused upon the symbolic capital of 'ticking mountains'. Wally has taken a position of distinction based on his knowledge of the rules of mountaineering. Illustrated here is rule four in my list, go alone or in small groups and seek out solitude. Wally's cultural capital positions him as a mountaineer, but his desire to seek out places of solitude may take him to mountains that are relatively unknown outside the mountaineering field. His cultural capital has specific rather than general transferability. Tom understands the symbolic importance of climbing Ben Nevis and sees this as an objective that will give him the possibility of translating his symbolic capital into status or other benefits inside and outside the field of mountaineering. This is because Ben Nevis is the highest mountain in Scotland, and one that many people have heard about. Tom is bringing tourism to mountaineering because he wants to translate his capital gains into distinction outside mountaineering, that is, in urban society. For Tom, the values of Romanticism, such as seeking out solitude, are less important than the conquest of a mountain that is generally well known. For Wally, the values of Romanticism are prioritised above the symbolic capital of an ascent of a famous mountain. Wally is seeking distinction from the tourist alignment of Tom by rejecting the significance of Ben Nevis as a point of symbolic capital. This is different from the keenness of Dave and Chris to accumulate significant symbolic capital from an attempt on the Cuillin Ridge. Wally is exercising freedom. Such observations contest Harvey's (1989) suggestion that space is constructed around capital. According to the evidence I have set out above, the situation is more subtle and complex than Harvey suggests.

4.4 Summary

Ideas about mountains are embedded in our culture. Romanticism, which contains characteristics of aesthetic appreciation, exploration, solitude and sensory arousal has been espoused by mountaineering. Mountaineering legislators have mobilised a safety agenda that is consistent with civilising processes. This generates a set of rules that influence the 'freedom' generated by mountaineering. The rules are partly due to the entirely rational responses evidenced through the mountain safety agenda (everything from textbooks, and governing bodies to mountain exhibitions) required by a civilised society in response to the risks and dangers inherent in mountaineering. This presents legislators with a strong rationale for 'their' perspectives on 'mountain' and 'mountaineering'. Identity construction is related to the accumulation of cultural capital. Investments made by adventure tourist clientele involve an exchange of economic capital for the symbolic capital of ascents completed. Different mountains have different exchange values so that those with the greatest aesthetic alignment to a Romantic sensibility contain the greatest symbolic capital. The essential values of Romanticism are critical of all that is urban, the crowds, the noise, the pollution and the inauthenticity of life in the city. Many clients also reject such an artificial life in favour of 'firing up their boilers' in mountains. In this respect they espouse the values of Romanticism. However, 'freedom' is constructed around the cultural capital of mountaineering. There may be important differences between clients in the transferability of their cultural capital. This is turn reflects an alignment with the cultural (re)production of mountains whereby well known mountains have greater symbolic currency, although this may not operate as effectively within the mountaineering field. Translating symbolic capital into distinction has become complicated by the access afforded to clients through adventure tourism. Mountaineering legislators may perceive clients more as 'tourists' because they do not necessarily follow the rules of mountaineering. This is particularly noticeable in the rule that concerns serving a mountaineering apprenticeship. If 'tourists' can access mountains with considerable symbolic capital, this requires re-adjustments in the mountaineering field to retain social distinction. One such adjustment is the discursive creation of 'tourist routes' on popular mountains. Another is a reinforcement of the omnipresent safety agenda, which can only be operated by mountaineers who have considerable cultural capital. The next chapter explores the other main component of cultural capital, that of physical capital.

Chapter five: The Body and Physical Capital

5.1 Physical Capital

Shilling (1993:20) says bodies: "see, listen and think...feel (physically and emotionally), smell and act". Everyone is embodied, and how people control, shape and present their bodies would appear to be important in understanding the construction of identity through social distinction. Motility in mountaineering is 'inculcated' by techniques of physicality and disciplinary procedures "intended to communicate particular values and status positions" (Edensor 2000:98). Viewed from this perspective, mountaineering is about the acquisition of physical capital (Bourdieu 1986). To take an example from walking, "that dragon-slaying feeling of distance done" (Hillaby 1981:15). I will argue that the conventions governing appropriate performance of posture, gesture, stance, gait and deportment have come, in the first instance, from the mountaineering tradition.

Whitehead (1990:3) argues for the centrality of physical experience to our lives: "our bodily dimension is integrally involved in most aspects of our existence - not least in the establishment of a meaningful relationship with the world around us". When the 'world' is conceived as a field of political and cultural struggles, cultural capital becomes a currency for establishing position. Physical capital, a part of cultural capital, (Bourdieu 1986) places the body at the centre of a general theory of social reproduction. Physical capital concerns the construction of corporeality in a social form. Social production has symbolic value and includes ways that people carry themselves, walk, talk and dress as well as the modification of bodies through lifestyle management, dieting, training and other strategies. Bourdieu (1986) argues this distinguishes social position but that people are socialised into different types of physical capital by class and class affiliations. Three key concepts are social location, habitus and taste (Shilling 1993:58).

Social location refers to the degree of 'distance from necessity' that people have from financial and material want. Individuals thereby have unequal opportunities for acquiring the forms of physical capital most valued in society. Adventure tourism requires a significant financial investment for example, something that might exclude low earning sections of society. Bourdieu (1986) says that the way people treat their bodies, in the case of food consumption by way of example, reveals their habitus (Bourdieu 1986:190), that is, patterns of behaviour absorbed from the social environments in which people spend most of their lives. 'Taste' is the conscious manifestation of habitus, and refers to class choices that are actually rooted in material constraints. People may feel distanced from the circumstances in which they were raised but habits and preferences forged at this time remain inscribed (Shilling 1993:59). In particular, Bourdieu notes how a combination of social location, habitus and taste lead working class people to view their bodies as 'instrumental', that is, as a means to an end. By contrast, the dominant classes are removed from the immediate demands of material necessity and, therefore, have the freedom to treat the body as an end in itself. Bourdieu (1986:190) explains the relationship between taste in food and the body as follows:

> Tastes in food also depend on the idea each class has of the body and of the effects of food on the body, that is, on its strength, health and beauty; and on the categories it uses to evaluate these effects, some of which may be important for one class and ignored by another, and which the different classes may rank in very different ways. Thus, whereas the working classes are more attentive to the strength of the (male) body than its shape, and tend to go for products that are both cheap and nutritious, the professions prefer products that are tasty, health-giving, light and not fattening.

Thus, taste can lead to two different perspectives of the body. The first sees the body as an intrinsic function and expresses itself as a "macrobiotic cult of health" (Shilling 1993:60), the second sees the body as perceptible 'physique', that is the body as others see it. Moreover, there is a more finely differentiated orientation to the body within the dominant class. Bourdieu, for example, discusses the different forms of physical expression practised within the "aristocratic asceticism of the dominated fractions of the dominant class" (Bourdieu 1986:214). Executives, school teachers and young women are apparently disposed to "a sort of training for training's sake" (Bourdieu 1986:213) which rewards effort with satisfaction. This point is illustrated through the example of Hugh Symonds, a teacher from Sedbergh School in Yorkshire, and a record breaking fell runner who has said "I had come to learn that it was satisfying to repeat the movements of exercise" (cited Henderson 2001:15). His satisfaction comes from the efficiency of a healthy body propelling him over the fells. Walking also appears to express a health orientated function through the symbolic gratifications gained by practising a distinctive activity. According to Bourdieu, (1984:214) these practices can be: "performed in solitude, at times and in places beyond the reach of the many, off the beaten track". Such practice is encompassed by Wordsworth's "inward eye/Which is the bliss of solitude" (cited Henderson 2001:15).

Bourdieu's (1986) argument does have limitations. Some of these have been noted in critical appraisals of his work, (e.g. Shilling 1993, Chaney 1996), but I shall develop a more general discussion of the limitations of some of Bourdieu's ideas when the concept of physical capital is explored in mountaineering. Shilling (1993:60-61) points out that participation in body forming activities is not reducible to the convergence of social location, habitus and taste in the formative years. This is because finances, spare time and lifestyle have an ongoing influence on bodily orientation. Additionally, one's stock of economic and cultural capital can, and generally does, change over time. How much time and money clients have become important practical considerations in adventure tourism. Mike, a single, male client with JG, works as a freelance computer programmer on projects that demand short but concentrated bursts of work related activity, for which he is paid very well. This gives him both the money and the extended periods of non-work time to pursue his mountaineering ambitions. As a client with JG: he is, by his own definition:

> A kind of serial mountaineer operating through a company that I know I can trust to deliver what I want to do. I could not have afforded this when I was younger.

Shilling (1993) also points out that certain sports and activities become 'democratised' over time. Rock climbing is a good example. Among the activists who pioneered climbing in the Lake District, for example, Haskett-Smith and Botterill were clearly from Bourdieu's (1986) 'dominant classes'. They were leading acolytes in British climbing from the 1880s until well into the twentieth century. From the late 1930s onwards working class climbers like Jim Birkett and Bill Peascod emerged from their shadow and demonstrated that this sport was not necessarily the preserve of a moneyed and leisured elite (Birkett 1983). The distinctive qualities of a sport, Bourdieu argues, are lost through this process of democratisation. However, drawing upon Harvey's (1989) contention that commodification can lead to a legislative position, this means that the rules of mountaineering are strengthened in relation to adventure tourism.

It has been argued in chapter one that adventure tourism has made / is making a significant contribution to the democratisation of mountaineering. This, in turn, has set up established mountaineers as legislators and adventure tourists as interpreters. Legislators, it has been suggested in chapter four, draw upon the values of Romanticism to define 'their' sport and use a powerful discourse of 'safe practice' to maintain their positions in the field. Mountaineering can only be undertaken by physical endeavour; this requires a process of learning. As novices progress towards being mountaineers they will learn certain 'body techniques' (Williams & Bendelow 1998). Williams and Bendelow (1998) suggest these will be 'technical', in that they will take a specific form, 'traditional', in that they will have emerged from a mountaineering tradition and 'efficient', that is purposeful for mountaineering. There is an appropriate way of mountaineering, and when it has been learnt, that is the body has been socialised, it will lead, so Bourdieu suggests (1986, 1993) to an inscribed bodily hexis. Bodily hexis is a term Bourdieu uses to describe a durable manner of standing and speaking and, therefore, thinking and feeling. It is made up of body techniques and leads to habitus.

Mountaineers that have followed the rules and pursued an apprenticeship of systematic accumulation of experience will, hypothetically, have also acquired bodily hexis and, therefore, a mountaineering habitus. The body techniques of mountaineering are a set of practices operated by an understanding of the constituents of rational practice. The practices that define a mountaineering habitus are likely to be especially well inscribed in expert mountaineers, notably guides. Reflecting upon my own experience as a guide these practices include attention to training, diet and other aspects of preparation before going in to mountains as well as efficient movement through energy conservation once there. These would be expected to be least developed in novices, particularly clients who may have 'fast-tracked' the legislative principle of an apprenticeship by using the opportunities made possible through adventure tourism. Novices, it is assumed, have a great deal to learn about the body techniques of mountaineering. Because novices lack experience they will have a limited mountain frame of reference, and, it could be argued, that they are, therefore, more likely to bring different reference points or 'habituses' to mountains. As 'interpreters', novices thus have the potential to challenge the legislative position and thereby bring new interpretations to the identity of mountaineer. However, the 'flood' of adventure tourists into mountaineering is likely to have less impact on the field than might otherwise be the case for the following reasons.

First, the holiday format of adventure tourism makes the setting extraordinary. This, as Urry argues (1990), changes routines and raises habitual practices to the level of consciousness. It is common for people to behave differently from normal life when on holiday. Thus, over the period of time of the holiday, people may have different priorities that may raise the status of performing tasks from the habitual to the conscious. Second, as chapter four has shown, people already have encultured ideas of what a mountain is and how mountaineers behave. They may not understand all the technical jargon, but I have shown they have absorbed the symbolic significance of mountains. Moreover, ideas that mountains are dangerous places and that mountaineering involves taking risks are socially constructed (Furedi 1997). Finally, and a development of this point, people are likely to have absorbed a Romantic perspective through guidebooks, brochures and other media common to Western culture. They are likely to be familiar with mountain aesthetics, understand mountains to be escape locations where they can enjoy a 'natural' physical experience from which they can return enlightened and re-created having experienced freedom from urban crowds and a sense of embodied satisfaction from their 'excursions'. So, I am suggesting that, the extraordinary setting and an awareness of the risks in mountaineering place the novice in a malleable position. Each novice will have to learn the body techniques of mountaineering in order to be able to perform as a mountaineer. Guides and significant others thus have an opportunity, indeed a responsibility, to take the novice body and inscribe it with the physical capital of mountaineering. Moreover, such inscription will be closely aligned to the tenets of Romanticism.

Leanne, a female client with FMA who came on the first Skye course, illustrates this general argument. Leanne, as citations in earlier chapters have shown, positions herself as an experienced traveller but an inexperienced mountaineer. Here, Leanne brings together strands concerning the aesthetic, physicality, lifestyle-habit, comfort, the group experience and the experiential (and therefore the sensory) component of the mountain experience:

> I enjoyed the mountain spires; the scenery was very beautiful. I enjoyed pushing myself physically, even though I complained that day. I enjoy the feeling of physical exhaustion. I like to challenge myself, its something that I have done all my life and I probably

always will – it's a part of my personality. I didn't feel all that comfortable up there, even though the people and the scenery were fantastic. I know we are paying for someone to look after us but ultimately we all have to put one foot in front of the other and get ourselves up and down the mountain. No one can do that for you.

Mountains are described as 'spires' and the scenery is 'beautiful' and 'fantastic', a reference to the aesthetic, but mostly the dialogue concerns embodied action. The interruptions to ordinary experiences of comfort are noted through the bodily responses required by movement over the rock and up the mountain, in this case an ascent of the Pinnacle Ridge of Sgurr nan Gillean in the Cuillin mountains in wet and windy conditions. Leanne appears to relish the physicality of the experience because of the demands it makes, and there is pleasure to be gained from the 'feeling of physical exhaustion'. This supports Bourdieu's (1986) suggestion that there are rewards to be gained through physical effort. But such an ascent makes considerable demands upon skill and judgement, especially on wet rock in a wind and in exposed positions. Leanne was aware she was being 'looked after', an affective factor in her comfort zone, and that, despite having to put 'one foot in front of the other' her exploration of this experiential environment was limited by the directions afforded by the route and the guides leading her. Leanne understands that mountains are potentially dangerous places, qualitatively different from walking in the countryside because of rocky terrain and exposure. Leanne's embodied experience of this climb was highly directed and managed, a circumstance that undermined her potential for agency through personal exploration. On one section, for example, her feet were physically placed onto footholds she could not see because she was hugging the rock. The guides were exercising a control over the body techniques Leanne had to adopt in order to complete the ascent.

The legislative position sustained by experienced mountaineers is constructed around a discourse of safe practice. To not follow the rules and conventions of mountaineering is to place the body in physical jeopardy. Physical fitness, for example, becomes an unwritten 'convention' of mountaineering because mountains demand sustained physical endeavour. Only those who are physically fit can 'be' mountaineers, a point of distinction that excludes those who might not have the 'appropriate' physical conditioning. Thus, in recognition that she had struggled physically on our attempted traverse of the Cuillin ridge Leanne said:

If I had known I was going to have to carry that amount of weight I would have spent more time in the gym before coming on this trip.

Here, then, is a limitation of Bourdieu's (1986) argument, and it stems from his alignment of physical capital and class. For Bourdieu, the working class body is instrumental, that is, a means to an end. This is drawn from the likelihood of the working classes to work in manual jobs. Leanne is relating her physical performance on the Cuillin ridge to a lack of training. In particular she equates such 'training' to be general, that is 'in the gym' rather than specific. Lewis (2000) notes, that 'the best training for climbing remains climbing'. This suggests that 'training' for mountaineering is not an abstract phenomenon but, for mountaineers, it remains rooted in the activities themselves. The mountaineering body is 'trained' via the body techniques outlined earlier, and it becomes instrumental. Those people who have considerable mountaineering capital may well have a body physique that is attractive to others, that is a body trained through Bourdieu's (1986) 'macrobiotic cult of health'. However, the mountaineering body is trained to meet the rigours of mountaineering, part of the discourse of safety, and in this respect it is instrumental. The mountaineering body is not drawing upon the class specific habituses that Bourdieu suggests define distinction, but is moulded by a legislative position applying the 'rules' of mountaineering[23]. The rules of note here are, rule one (serve an apprenticeship), rule three (eat the right food, train and be physically fit) and rule five (rely on one's own physical efforts). To have an appropriately trained body becomes a point of distinction for those clients (and guides) who appeared to move more effortlessly in ascent and over rocky terrain. Anthony, another FMA client who has been cited in earlier chapters, and who was also on the Skye course, was clearly watching how others moved over the rocky terrain. Anthony was comparing his own motility in a conscious way to those of the more experienced people around him. Anthony himself was clearly 'feeling the strain' in the way his body was responding to the demands of the setting: this was a conscious response to an extraordinary set of demands. From my field notes I recorded that Anthony said to one of the guides:

You don't seem to be affected by the gradient and the heavy rucksack, why is that?

To which the guide, Tim, replied:

---
[23] The rules were set out in chapter four.

It's partly about pace but more about experience, I've done lots of this stuff and it always hurts but you learn not to show it in the same way.

Tim answers the question directly, 'it is about pace and experience', thereby taking a didactic role but he goes on to suggest that 'not showing' the pain is what mountaineers do. Thus, part of the performance of a mountaineer is to appear to move without pain, effortlessly, across and up rocky terrain. Tim suggests this is a conscious act because 'it always hurts', and therefore a point of social distinction. In this case at least, pain creates an awareness of body and breaks the mould of habitual behaviour. It affects both guide and client, but the guide has learnt to present a form of motility that is aligned to effortless movement. The safety agenda is apparent and broadly identified by this dialogue as 'experience brings inclusion, mountaineers are forged in mountains'. Part of the inclusion is to have a mountain-conditioned body that, when required to, can perform body techniques commensurate with a perceived safe and rational approach to mountaineering.

When Romanticism designated mountain spaces as environments for an articulation of its ideological position it also implicated a set of physical practices through which the values embedded in such a position could be transmitted. The way these practices have evolved has been influenced by an agenda of safety consistent with the idea of civilising processes and a rational society. A good example is the notion of the 'solitary excursion'. To walk alone is to maximise the sensuous possibilities of mountains, imbibing the tactile experience of moving amidst rocky terrain, 'smelling the grass of the fell-side hearing the crackle of lichen' (Winthrop-Young 1933). Vaughn, an FMA client from the second Skye course, said, "the rain trickling off my nose makes me feel alive". Mortlock (1984, 2001) goes further when he suggests the insights possible through outdoor experiences are heightened by the fact of being alone. However, walking manuals and instructive codes talk of 'minimum group size' and 'safety in numbers' (Langmuir 1995, Ashton 1987) the antibook of Wordsworth's solitary excursions. What exists today, therefore, is a code of physical motility and display defining the 'legislative' position of mountaineers that have emerged from the tenets of Romanticism but which have been moulded by an agenda of safe practice to sustain social distinction. The distinctiveness comes from a trained body fuelled by an appropriate diet that moves efficiently, probably with the appearance of effortlessness, through mountains and up climbs.

5.2 The Mountaineering Body

Edensor (2000:82) suggests walking can transmit identity and meaning through rhythm and gesture. In this respect the 'body-in-becoming' (Edensor 2000:84) of the walker is subject to "ongoing reflexive monitoring about the way in which it moves through, senses and apprehends nature". Experience of walking and climbing frees the body in a physical sense. Hart (1968), for example, says hills and mountains are "traditional symbols of the absolute" (1968:5). He suggests they represent 'religious and ethical postulates' and they are metaphorically inviolable. To Hart the hills represent continuity, stability and a "sanctuary to which men and women can escape from the pressure of the problems and tensions of modern life, and where these can be viewed, and perhaps solved, from a new and higher standpoint" (Hart 1968:5). Hart is, thereby, articulating a perspective that sees a less complex, more primal bodily engagement through escaping from a de-sensitising urban setting. Thus, he can argue that mountain recreation heightens body consciousness. The body techniques of mountaineering are constructed from Romanticism and yet, somewhat paradoxically, a legislative position has been developed that reflects the civilising processes. Hart (1968:8) explains how physical exertion brings out a 'heightened general consciousness':

All the senses become most alive when the fibres, the ligaments and muscles of the body are hardest at work. Strain and suffering, far from deadening the mind, increase the intensity of its vision, so that the colouring of skies and the forms of rocks stand out with preternatural vividness. One gains an awareness that this is not attributable to any single sense, but to a state of heightened general consciousness; one's body is transcended, and yet, paradoxically, one feels the movement of every muscle.

A key element of such a perspective is that physical effort frees the mind. There is, therefore, an implicit suggestion that mind and body are related yet separate entities. Thus, Hart (1968) projects the notion of 'opening oneself up' through physical engagement with a mountain environment. He connects mountains and up as 'good' and by contrast describes the "complicated trivialities of urban living" (Hart 1968:9), as superficial at best, suggesting a transcendence of 'bad' urban life through an educating mountain experience. However, to gain such insights one must perform as a mountaineer, and this means understanding the rules and acknowledging the conventions. Hart (1968:9) explains:

> The wise mountaineer climbs slowly, feasting his [sic] eyes on views whose incessant changes become, to his sharpened awareness, like a series of revelations. As he acquires disciplines and skills of his difficult craft, he learns that rhythm, rather than strenuous effort, is the secret to successful progress: the deliberate placing of feet and hands, the steady upward heave. Pitting himself against nature in her most savage and uncompromising form, he realises that the penalty of any lack of precision or clear-headedness, any momentary failure of concentration, may be disaster. Dependent upon and responsible for the other men and women on his rope, he gains the joyful fulfilment of community, the deep sense of fellowship that is born of shared endeavour and shared danger. Pressing himself to the limit, testing his capacities to the utmost, he gains a sense of personal release which opens up infinite possibilities. In discovering the heights he discovers his higher self.

This example illustrates how specific body techniques have emerged. Specific forms of movement (climbing, walking and scrambling) are learnt from a mountaineering tradition that provides a purposeful way of exploring mountains. There is a discourse of self discovery through engagement with the natural world. Hart (1968) suggests that mountains impact our lives in a number of ways. They provide a non-urban space to escape to (Romanticism); they represent continuity and stability (identity) in a changing modern world and they provide for a physical challenge that transcends everyday life by engendering a fundamental re-engagement with Nature. Moreover, they teach us (education) things about ourselves and symbolically unite us to others through the shared adventure of roped activities. To achieve a 'higher self', it is suggested, we need to approach mountains with respect and perform certain skills in ways commensurate with accepted mountaineering practice. This will then give us our 'personal release', freedom, presumably, from the shackles of everyday existence that deaden the senses and leads to ennui (Lewis 2000). So, discipline and rhythm are important for example, particularly if we are to maximise the revelations a mountain vista can provide: the prudent mountaineer 'climbs slowly'. Climbing slowly rationalises energy expenditure and exhibits a demeanour of control and 'a disciplined body' trained for the rigors of mountaineering. Hart's (1968) interpretation of mountain recreation emphasises a qualitative experience initiated by the physicality of ascending a mountain with rules to dictate the way we should walk and climb. Implicit in such determinants of behaviour is the idea that not to behave in this way is a demonstration of ignorance, meaning inexperience or stupidity. Experience, is demonstrated by the 'appropriate' forms of behaviour. Consider this description from the manual of the Mountain Leader Training Board. It clearly offers prescriptive advice on how to walk in the hills but in doing so it pre-supposes an accepted form of motility:

Rhythm is essential to good hill walking: jerky movements, springing and flexing the knees by taking too high a step tire the muscles and should be avoided. The leg should be allowed to swing forward like a pendulum; the natural swing of the body assists this movement. There should be no conscious use of the leg muscles. To assist rhythm and balance the hands should be kept free, particularly in descent. Spare clothes etc. should be carried in the rucksack or tied round the waist...The feet should be placed down flat with a deliberate step, resting the heels on any available projections such as stones or tufts of grass. Where the slope is very steep, zig-zagging will assist the walker. Good rhythm and setting the feet is the sign of the experienced hill walker...Running downhill, though good fun, can be tiring. An experienced walker uses downhill periods to rest his muscles (Langmuir 1995:72).

Of note here is the observation that 'setting the feet is the sign of the experienced hill walker'. Implicit in such advice is the suggestion that not to perform in this way is a sign of inexperience, evidence that one does not understand the rules and tantamount to placing oneself in danger by, for example, using up the reserve energy demanded by a rational approach to mountaineering. This point is well illustrated by the work of two guides I observed in their approach to leading a group of young adults onto a mountain scramble. Here is a summary of my field observations of this mountain day. Following a clear briefing to the group to move slowly for the first part of the day, the guides positioned themselves one at each end of the 'crocodile' which then set off from the hut. The pace was very slow; many of the group reacted to the slow plod, a perceived snails pace, by adopting a playful 'skipping and dancing' style. However, such frivolity had completely disappeared an hour or so later as the scale of the undertaking began to be acknowledged by the group; meanwhile, the pace set by the guides remained unchanged. The guides knew how important a 'steady pace' is and were particularly emphatic in the way they controlled the movements of this inexperienced group because these young people were the responsibility of the guides who were especially attentive to the safety agenda.

The rules, then, which determine the body techniques of 'mountaineer', might be thought of as a script. Knowledge of and adherence to the script becomes the mechanism through which a person can show distinction. In respect of physical capital, the script offers the following rules: avoid over exertion and move rhythmically; do not run; place one's feet carefully; show balance and poise as one moves over mountainous terrain, this is Hillaby's "ambulatory overdrive" (Hillaby 1981:14-15). Furthermore, absorb the atmosphere in poses of solitudinous contemplation and avoid crowds because they will undermine the quality of a mountain experience. Finally, be prepared to work hard, to be battered and bruised, and to feel exhausted at the end of the day. To follow such a script is to acquire the physical capital of a mountaineer. However, although to perform in this way is a social demonstration of one's status as a mountaineer, the 'rules' become a set of constraints. The rules limit freedom of behaviour and reinforce the mechanical aspects of the activities at the expense of an exploration of self that purports to be, so literature such as Hart (1968) suggests, at the centre of mountaineering. Performing physically in ways commensurate with accepted practice in mountain walking, as the example above shows, is to display knowledge and awareness in ways that project physical capital. Williams and Bendelow (1998:78) suggest this when they state, "the search for social distinction, in short, is a continual process of claims and counter claims". The claims can be reflexively monitored in relation to the discursive influences identified above. The following examples from FMA clients, Tom from the Naranjo course and Jim from the first Skye course, are explored in relation to these claims.

Tom clearly sees mountaineering as a kind of therapy. He suggested that:

> Part of the pleasure of doing trips like Naranjo is that you do something very physical, you get very tired, you eat a very big meal then you sleep a very long time. It's all relaxing and re-invigorating. That's one reason why it's good to do it fast, it's the contrast.

Here, the reward for Tom follows the physical effort. To walk and climb hard, as we did on Naranjo, is a complete contrast to Tom's more sedentary existence as a lawyer in Central London. The rewards include eating 'a very big meal' and sleeping for 'a very long time', two aspects of Tom's ordinary life that do not normally happen in such a manner. When I met him in London, we ate a meal together and he was very careful about what he ate. He also explained that he worked very long hours. The extraordinary experience of climbing Naranjo de Bulnes meant he could consciously abandon normal eating and sleeping habits. In this respect mountains, for Tom are 'relaxing and re-invigorating', a kind of therapy. Jim also suggests mountaineering has a therapeutic value through which he gets a 'buzz of health'. Jim said:

> The stress of work, dealing with customers etc. probably makes me enjoy my running and walking more. It is an escape and I do get immersed in it and I don't really think about work and problems. If I was just laying on a beach somewhere I think my mind wouldn't be actively engaged in the holiday and I would think about these problems. When you are walking your mind is totally taken over by what you are doing. You are either navigating or watching where you put your hands or your feet on the rock if you are climbing, or looking at the view. And I think it's a marvellous way of escaping from the pressures of everyday life if you like. It's regenerative, or whatever you want to call it... and we are out there doing it and I get a real buzz of health and a glow.

Jim clearly sees his mountaineering experiences as 'an escape', that is freedom from work, an alignment with a central value of Romanticism outlined in chapter four. This is also a perspective consistent with Hart's (1968) articulation of the 'benefits' of mountaineering. Moreover, the tactile engagement of hands and feet on rock appear 'regenerative'. Jim is a butcher, Tom is a lawyer. From the second Skye course, Brendan is an accountant, Lee is a motor mechanic. I have found little support for Bourdieu's (1986) contention that a propensity to pursue outdoor recreations is the preserve of the dominant classes. The 'distinction' operating among clients has more to do with an understanding of the mountaineering script. Thus, Jim does 'get immersed' in mountaineering and he enjoys 'looking at the view', and, most importantly, he does get a physical 'buzz' from mountains. Dave, another FMA client who came to Naranjo, said:

> London gets very heavy sometimes, for example the light at night means we can't see the stars from within the city. That's why I want to get away as often as I can afford to and that's why I came to FMA. When I can afford it I want to go on a really big trip with JG and be away for several weeks. Climbing mountains is important

because of the contrast to the city, although in the quiet moments from my office I can 'see' mountains in the high rise view of 'scrapers.

Drasdo (1997) discusses the visualisation of town-scapes as mountains, linking the intricacy of cathedrals with jagged mountain ranges, for example, offering some insight into how a mountaineers mind might function around the idea of escape. Dave is articulating ideas of freedom and escape and linking them to sensations of 'coming alive' outlined by Hart (1968). Jim takes his love of running into the mountains. The physical practice for Jim is about pushing himself to explore physical limits at the edge of his ordinary experiences. The notion of 'exploration' and self development remains but produces a form of walking which contests the accepted norms as Jim *"enjoyed the physical thing, heart pumping and everything going."* He goes on to say:

> I enjoy looking at the views, it gives me a lift. I think there is a physical side as well. The sense that you have achieved something. I like a pack on my back and really striding out. It gives me a great buzz. That's why I enjoyed it in the Cuillins because we had a fairly fit group and we were doing something hard. Most of my usual walking I feel I have to 'trim my sails' to keep up with people who can not walk at my pace, and who aren't as fit. A lot of people I know say you shouldn't move fast up a mountain, you should savour it and take your time. But if someone enjoys going up hard and fast then why not? Everybody to their own. Curved Ridge was great, just to go up and down so fast like that, although I have already done Buachaille Etive Mor. I like to blast up a mountain. There is a gain to be had from being able to do it and to do it well. A lot of the people I walk with will plod, then stop a lot more than we did.

Whilst not immune to the aesthetic elements of mountaineering, he 'enjoyed the views', Jim picks out his own practice to contrast with that of more conventional approaches that propose 'slow steady movement' in order to 'savour' the experience, he prefers to 'blast' up a mountain. A much more spontaneous physical response is suggested in contrast to a slow considered percolation of a mountain aesthetic via a steady 'plod'. But this can only happen when the body has 'fitness', that is, the appropriate form of physical conditioning. In this respect, by achieving an appropriate level of fitness the person has a greater freedom to move beyond the constraints of Hart's (op. cit.) plodding mentality. Jim clearly gains satisfaction from performing 'on the edge' of accepted practice because he likes to 'blast up a mountain'.

I have argued that the mountaineering body can be viewed as both a means to an end and an end in itself, that is, both as 'instrumental' and as 'physique'. This is contrary to Bourdieu's (1986) suggestion that class-habitus will inscribe a person's body as one or the other. The mountaineering body needs to be shaped and chiselled to inscribe the identity of mountaineer because mountaineers 'do' things, and the 'doing' relates to physical capital, which in turn can be translated into cultural capital and thus determine distinction. Additionally, there is an understanding that a physically fit body of the appropriate physique is a manifestation of that 'doing'. Climbers, for example, are particularly sensitive to 'power-to-weight' ratios as this becomes critical to body movements in the more technically demanding rock climbs (Bollen 1994). Guides and clients alike are sensitive to the requirements of body image commensurate with being a mountaineer, and have both suggested that they want to lose weight. A guide, Tim, sensitive to the passage of time he had spent in Sheffield, said:

> I'm too fat and I need to lose at least a stone, so I'm looking forward to some long hard days in the hills. My climbing is suffering, I need huge muscles because I'm carrying too much bulk.

Brendan, a portly client from the second Skye course, said:

> Doing the Munros is a great way to lose weight for me. Since I started last year I have lost over a stone, but I tend to put it back on again when I get home after trips like these.

Another client, Dave who came to Naranjo de Bulnes, in aspiring to climb harder routes said he wanted to train his body:

> Not because I want to look better but because I want to climb better. I want to be rippled. I must train harder.

Bourdieu (1986) has identified the distinctiveness of the body in his exploration of social identity and there is clear evidence to suggest the importance of body aesthetics amongst clients. Muscles, leanness and a weathered and tanned body all suggest a mountaineering body in making. However, there is evidence here to suggest the body as instrumental as well as the body as physique. Tim perceives himself to need 'huge muscles' as he is 'carrying too much bulk', here the end is predominantly instrumental. Brendan also has a target in mind for his mountaineering, that of 'collecting' Munros. However, Brendan, who is a large man, suggests the training of his body through mountaineering is to have some transfer to his ordinary, home society in that he regrets how easy it is to 'put it back on again' when he gets home. He did suggest that colleagues in his office commented that he looked slimmer after he returned from a previous mountain walking tour of Scotland. However, Brendan remains conscious that he does not look 'chiselled' and lithe as he understands the mountaineering archetype to be and, therefore, he expects to have problems in convincing people that he is a mountaineer. This is an example of physical capital in operation, except in Brendan's case, the currency of his physical capital may not be easily transferred. Dave clearly wants the instrumental benefits of a body that can 'climb better' although he is very aware that a 'rippled' body has the added advantage of presenting his physical capital as the aesthetic of a 'body for others'. For Dave, unlike for Brendan, the transfer is facilitated by the corporeal form he has, or hopes to achieve, through a rigorous training regime.

Training and conditioning the body becomes important both before and on the hill. Guidance is given in adventure tourist brochures of the fitness demands of different itineraries (see chapter seven). This is part of the control, and therefore loss of agency, generated by the malleable circumstance of the paying client as novice mountaineer. The impact of the physical demands of mountain days is still undiminished for many clients, Tom, said:

> The first time I did fourteen hour days in Peru I found the whole effort incredibly shocking.

However, having completed various Andean ascents with JG in Peru, Tom has acquired an experience of the demands of extended mountain days. When it came to the Naranjo course, as will be shown shortly, Tom was able to take a position of superiority over his brother Hugh, who did not have Tom's Peruvian experience as a frame of reference. Chris, an FMA client who took some pride in being a climber, said, initially about week-ends away generally and then about the Naranjo trip in particular:

> Monday morning I'm knackered, wrecked for the whole week. Spiritually you are re-energised but physically you are drained. It takes a week to recover, early nights and so on. I like going up a mountain but I prefer a degree of difficulty. I prefer scrambling to walking up a path. Walking never really appealed to me. I don't like long walk-ins. The Naranjo thing nearly bloody killed me. I would of almost preferred it if the climb started in the car park.

Attitudes to fitness, despite an accepted understanding on the physical demands of mountaineering varied. This is illustrated by the discussion about helicopters which emerged from dialogue between guides and clients on the Picos de Europa trip. On the walk-in to Naranjo de Bulnes one client, Hugh, had this to say in response to my question probing how he felt about the approach to that mountain:

> The walk up there almost finished me off but that was a fitness thing and the one factor that is most likely to stop people doing that. I do enjoy the technical side of climbing, it is the moves that I enjoy rather than the physical haul of trudging up with a pack in order to get to the more interesting part of an ascent.

Here Hugh is demonstrating his ignorance of the rules of mountaineering. In particular, he can not see the importance of rule one, serve an apprenticeship. Hugh wants to by-pass the least desirable aspects of a mountain ascent and get to 'the more interesting part of an ascent'. He does, however, recognise that the 'fitness thing' is a point of distinction in that it can 'stop people doing that', supporting the instrumental view of the mountaineering body. When I asked clients if they would have taken a helicopter to the foot of the mountain three replies were:

> Yes! Undisputably. If a helicopter had been offered I would have taken it. I liked the walk back down again, and I liked being up there. I'm happy to do a bit of walking up there. But, if I was being entirely honest, I found the walk up so uncomfortable that I would have happily taken the option. I know it's cheating, I know it's cheating, [his repetition] but I would have done it [chuckle] (Hugh).

If I had known what the walk-in was going to be like then I probably would of taken it. Hugh is probably thinking that anyone can walk up there, but not everyone can climb the mountain. So, I don't want to do what anybody can do, I want to do the hard bit. The walk-in is gruelling and there is nothing particularly challenging about it, it's just a bit of a drag (Tom).

I would not take the helicopter option because the walk-in is an essential part of the experience. It's a sweat and a grind and, therefore, not particularly pleasant, but the unfolding views are something special (Chris).

Hugh enjoys the 'climbing moves high on a mountain face' and would like to maximise his enjoyment of this aspect of the trip whilst minimising the 'physical endurance' required to get there in the first instance. Tom is more phlegmatic about the steep and long approach but recognises the successful completion of this conveys symbolic capital. He notes that 'not everyone can get here', meaning the hut under the mountain, and he remained:

Pleased that the training I did before coming has paid off, my body coped OK, and may even have developed some muscles.

Chris, the third example above, 'knows' what is appropriate to mountaineering and understands that pain and perhaps some unpleasantness are an integral part of the experience. Distinction is achieved by knowing the rules and being prepared to adhere to them. The three clients cited above represent a range of 'positions' in the field in relation to the extent to which they embrace, reject or simply side-step the rules. The last aspect of the mountaineering body to be considered relates to rule three, that is, the way food and an understanding of energy levels help construct the mountaineering body. Training and food intake have important links, not the least of which is the way that eating illustrates Bourdieu's (1986) concept of 'taste'.

Food sustains the physical. Food and drinks 'appropriate' to mountaineering are set out via the legislative agendas outlined above. Energy levels affect performance and are an important element of operating safely. The greatest legislative control is exerted on the mountain, and in the packing of rucksacks to carry the right foods and drinks. Because mountaineering makes huge demands upon levels of energy expenditure and at the same time geographically distances people from places like shops, restaurants and even home where food is readily available, eating, drinking and talking about food occupies a great deal of time. Ben, a guide said:

> One of the great pleasures of a hard day on the hills is thinking about all the food you can eat when you get back.

Several clients ate expensive high energy bars during the Naranjo climbs. They had been sold these by the staff of an equipment shop they visited just before the trip, and, when tasting them, disliked them intensely. They had purchased them in London, following advice from FMA pre-trip documentation about 'high energy mountain food', under 'expert' advice of the shop personnel. By acting in this way they were demonstrating an awareness of the need to feed themselves 'as mountaineers'. Another client, Hugh, following the same FMA guidance came to Naranjo with pork pies and mustard claiming:

> We were told to bring high energy foods we enjoyed eating – and I love pork pies.

Hugh did not have the level of understanding that Dave and Chris appeared to have about what mountaineers see as 'hill food', that is, snacks that sustain a mountaineer in the mountains. One of the requirements of 'hill food', for example, is that, ideally, it is light so that the energy required to carry it around does not undermine the energy to be gained from eating it! Adherence to the 'light and nutritional' characteristics of 'hill food' is evidenced by Dave and Chris, but has been interpreted differently by Hugh.[24] Tim's response as the guide who sent out the details of food and kit to bring on the course to all the clients was a rather neutral: "Well, it's not quite what I had in mind, but it will do the job".

Food remains important in the mountains for a number of reasons. It sustains physical engagement by providing energy in a high energy expenditure activity. It becomes a focus

---

[24] Several group members, including myself, said we were envious of the decadence shown by Hugh, particularly as he had mustard! Food becomes a bit of an obsession in the mountains.

of fantasy because mountain food, certainly that provided by mountain huts, is, by virtue of the difficulties of getting it into the mountains and then preparing it when there, tends to be "simple fare", an expression used by Hugh. Aspiring to eat favourite food(s) becomes an obsession at times because the satisfaction of this particular need is seen as a reward for effort expended. Beyond this however, eating food becomes a shared pleasure and incorporates an important social dimension. In the hut under Naranjo and in the bothy on Skye preparing and eating food became both relaxing and purposeful. In contrast to the physicality of walking, scrambling or climbing, sometimes in unpleasant weather conditions and always at the expense of energy expenditure, the hut or bothy is a haven. Moreover, it is a place to share individual achievements and identify with similar achievements of others. Eating is a ritual of the familiar, it is habitual and provides a sense of continuity with normal life. The stresses of the day are displaced by engagement with a familiar activity albeit in an unfamiliar location. This is why Tom and Hugh 'got dressed' for dinner, it is something they always do. The rest of us, Tim and myself as guides and Chris and Dave as climber-clients stayed in our climbing clothes. Because we were in the mountains it did not occur to me, and probably to the others too (although I have no record of a conversation about this), to get changed for dinner. The habitus operating here for Hugh and Tom was from their ordinary lives. The habitus operating for the rest of us on this course was a learnt response to an extraordinary setting that, in effect, normalised behaviour for that setting. In other words, experience leads to a set of practices that operate at a habitual level and which come out of the mountaineering tradition: mountain clothing forms the protocol for mountain huts, and Tom and Hugh were not fully conversant with this social constraint. However, no one chided them for this because the hut is not as serious a place as on the mountain, where dress codes do matter for safety reasons. Tom and Hugh were self conscious in the clean clothes, and took a while to relax into the group atmosphere of celebration. The awareness of their dress sense had been raised to the level of consciousness so that they were, it could be argued, 'learning' from the codes on display in that social setting. Huts might be described as 'supporting stages' in performing as mountaineers. The dangers that are characteristic of active mountaineering, and which demand a conscious engagement, are temporarily suspended and thus, through the process of relaxation, more sub-consciously constructed behaviours emerge.

Lewis (2000) argues that climbing leads to a 'coming alive', something that transcends habitual behaviour. If habitus is involved, when it matters i.e. in the nitty-gritty of mountaineering, a mountaineering habitus may emerge but, just as class issues do not appear to be important in mountain based adventure tourism, neither are habitual forms of behaviour. Lewis (2000) suggests that urban bodies, (although Lewis uses the term 'metropolitan' bodies), are "highly regulated, defensive, passive, sensually deprived, performatively inert and, therefore, not conducive to reflective practices". In contrast to this inorganic 'metropolitan' body, Lewis argues that the 'climbing' body is "organic, self-determined, tactile and of the ground" (2000:59). He argues that "the train, the car, the aeroplane and the package holiday merely bring us up to date with our sedentary nomadism" (2000:64). Furthermore, he suggests that life in the city has become comfortable because we no longer have to make decisions and "our modernity of ever-increasing choice and possibilities may be nothing more than a masquerade of enslavement to commodity capitalism" (2000:67). Packages and not making decisions are characteristic of adventure tourism, the whole thrust of which ironically is adventure and challenge close to the edge. Walter (1984:74) says, "danger does indeed exist, but awareness of it comes only in those passive situations which are the very antithesis of the essentially active sport of climbing". Lewis argues that climbers are 'alive' because of their proximity to death, that is, part of the climbing experience involves operating at 'the edge'. Modernity, Lewis argues, has 'anaesthetised death'. By taking a position that argues for climbing as 'coming alive', Lewis (2000) is contrasting a habitual and quotidian regime of ordinary urban life with the life awakening possibilities of an extraordinary climbing experience.

Lewis (2000:67) goes on to suggest that adventure climbing offers a counter experience to the "shifting cerebral and ocular tendencies of the civilising process". Climbing, he argues, presents an opportunity for an unmediated tactile experience of sensual possibilities within the natural world. He is particularly concerned with the hands, which, for climbers in particular, act directly upon that environment to bring the body alive through kinaesthetic awareness. The climbing clients from the Naranjo trip saw the intricacies of the vertical roped climbing as a defining element in their experience on the mountain. Hugh, the least experienced of the four clients on this course, said this to support Lewis's (2000) contention about coming alive through climbing:

I loved the movements on steep rock and the technical bits, you know fingers tingling, knees scraping. I was completely absorbed, even on the stances while waiting for Tim to lead the next pitch. Apart from my toes hurting because of those rock boots we were given it was fantastic – one of the highlights of my year.

Here, Hugh mentions how pain, 'toes hurting because of those rock boots', is part of the experience. Pain is an embodied response to stress. When climbing steep rock the hands are constantly active and involved in body movements. Hands are less obviously required for walking and therefore become an interesting component of deportment. Observation of experienced mountaineers suggests a number of positions are adopted. Thus, for those for whom Hillaby's (1981) 'ambulatory overdrive' is the norm, hands are not required until the terrain demands 'hands-on' activity, and even then, the point at which one uses one's hands becomes a matter of distinction and a display of skill. By way of demonstrating one's position, experience and knowledge of such things, guides and the more experienced clients commonly walk with hands in pockets, a description of my own preferred practice. Field observations of client performance when walking noted a variety of practices, some reflexive and others, apparently more habitual. I use the term apparently because, as Tim has suggested in the earlier example, such mannerisms and bodily movements may be consciously acted to convey an effortlessness, or flow. These included hands clasped behind the back appearing to support the rucksack (Bruce); firmly grasped trekking poles used as 'exploratory feelers' of the terrain in front and to the side of the walker (Vaughn) and hands hitched under rucksack shoulder straps (Wally). Such practices were enacted by clients (and guides) who were generally more experienced in mountain walking and appeared to be unreflexive in that the positioning of the hands was a 'natural' part of the body 'flowing' over the ground. Inexperienced clients moved less fluidly and appeared, at times, to be unsure of what to do with their hands. It was possible to observe reflexive experimentation in action amongst such clients. One, for example, Peter from the Lake District course, walked with his arms folded across his body but also tried many variations on a theme, notably the positioning adopted by the guides and others. Another swung his arms for balance, (Lee from the second Skye course) particularly when moving over broken terrain. There is clearly some awareness of what others in the group are doing in a physical sense but also a reflective self monitoring evidenced in that practices that did not 'feel' right, or failed to facilitate a more fluid form of movement were characteristically discarded. One client, from the second Skye course, said this about trekking poles:

I used them once but didn't get on with them. But although I felt they just got in the way, I felt out of place because the others all had them.

This explanation suggests the bodily configuration using poles did not feel right, and they were discarded but, inexperience leaves doubt as to how appropriate they might be in terms of identity. Having something in one's hands does alleviate the problem of what to do with them. When the 'something' is trekking poles or a map, for example, then such features become props in the performance being undertaken (Goffman 1959). This is not to say, however, that such motility and deportment is consistently replicated but appropriate embodiment is a manifestation of physical capital.

A key element of Lewis's (2000) work is that the 'doing' via tactile experiential engagement supersedes other means of 'knowing' such as guidebook descriptions or videos. He also explores the idea that climbing 'inscribes' the body, for example through scars and injuries, and by the predominance of muscle over fat. The body has to be prepared for the proposed activities (training) and then used in a controlled way (discipline) during the activities.

Lewis (2000:70) says, "metropolitan life suggests reservation, spectatorship and a spiritual life remote from the personality" Life in the city is civilised and rational. Such efficiency and emotional de-sensitisation appears to generate unreflexive forms of behaviour heavily dependent upon a person's habitus. Adventure climbing, in contrast, offers a counter perspective. Heywood claims (1994:185) that "there is about the notion of adventure climbing something fundamentally at odds with the outlook and values belonging to the process of rationalisation as it has been understood and described by writers from Weber onwards". So, the prospect of adventure has the potential to become emotionally arousing. However, there is much evidence to illustrate the emergence of rational and 'civilising' practices amongst clients in adventure tourism. This includes the packaged format, deferment of decision making to guides and the determination to pursue specific mountaineering objectives that have been given a cultural 'value' through the symbolic capital they represent. The more determined clients become to accumulate physical, and therefore symbolic capital through achieving the completion of certain climbs or standing on certain summits then the less freedom they have.

In the field (Bourdieu 1986) of mountaineering however, the equation is not as simple as 'I have climbed the mountains x, y and z and therefore I have a quantifiable amount of cultural capital to establish social position. There is, for example, the route of the ascent: was it by the 'tourist' route, that is, the most accessible line of ascent, or was the choice one of remoteness and technical difficulty, a climb rather than a walk for example. Furthermore, was the style of the ascent guided or unguided, solo or in a group, summer or winter? Such matters appear to be important to distinction in mountaineering. This argument is supported by evidence from the Picos de Europa course. At various times, either out in the mountains, in the hut or at the post-course interview, each of the four clients made direct reference to their climbing achievements. In discussing their mountaineering aspirations they each implied they understood the relationship between different climbs and modes of ascent and the identity of mountaineer. Using the evidence presented hitherto in this chapter, and that yet to be set out below, I have developed the notion of a client continuum. This continuum has 'tourist' at the left end and 'aspirant mountaineer' at the right end. The continuum is introduced with these four clients in mind, but the principle will continue to inform the remaining chapters and, therefore, all clients can be located on the continuum. Each client's position is based upon their cultural capital, and this includes their physical capital. A position is not fixed, and clients will generally move from left to right as their experience, and therefore their cultural capital, grows. I have set out the evidence below and suggest that Hugh is closest to being a tourist, with Tom close to him on the continuum. Dave is the most experienced aspirant-mountaineer, and, therefore, at the right of the continuum, with Chris close to him. Hugh said:

> I don't think I will ever be as much of a climber as anyone else there was, because I would need to stop doing some of the other things that I do and I can't see that happening at the moment, especially when you live in London. To be able to climb from here means a hell of a lot of time travelling. So what I think I'll do is, do some more climbing (I'd happily climb with anyone else who was on that trip), and, as I said to Tim before and after the Naranjo trip that I should imagine that he and I would see each other once a year. It's that sort of arrangement, where it will be a

> big highlight in my calendar. In all the things I do, it is the mountaineering trips that I really look forward to more than anything else. The climbing thing is once a year, different, abroad, challenging, looks exciting. For all these reasons it means I know I'll do it again. I will never buy a rope [chuckle].

I feel this is a clear articulation of Hugh as an adventure tourist. He acknowledges the symbolic value of the rope, for example, but will never buy one. Tom, Hugh's slightly more ambitious brother, had this to say:

> I'm not that fired up by doing more and more difficult rock-climbing. I am relatively inexperienced but curious about leading, conceptually, because it is clearly very different from seconding. I would like to gain leading experience but I have no desire to do difficult rock-climbing. [I then asked: 'what type of climbing does appeal to you? Tom continued] Well, I was quite taken by Tim's [FMA mountain guide] description of the Cuillin. It was mainly walking and scrambling but with some abseiling and climbing. That I found interesting, and was attracted but in the context of gaining experience of looking after yourself in the mountains. Overall I am more interested in doing things in the mountains rather than rock climbing.

Tom acknowledges an interest in lead climbing, that is, taking the rope up a climb at the 'sharp' end when a fall has greater potential for injury. This would extend his experience beyond 'seconding', that is, following a leader on the 'blunt' of the rope when the consequences of physical harm from a fall are far less serious. In doing so, he is articulating an ambition, albeit carefully stated, of operating more independently in mountains. He is, however, directed towards the Cuillin Ridge as an objective by Tim. Chris is considerably more ambitious than Tom. Here is Chris talking about his climbing over the week-end before we met. It contains a language of climbing and statements of different modes of climbing illustrating his position of distinction:

> Met Dave and Nat [Dave's girlfriend] in Lanberis, Snowdonia. The mission was to go and do Centotaph Corner [a climb graded extremely severe that appears in Ken Wilson's book 'Hard Rock' and has become a 'test-piece' for the aspirant 'hard-man']. It was far too wet so we ended up by soloing Flying Buttress on Dinas Cromlech in the rain [a climb on the same cliff in the Llanberis Pass, but graded as technically easy, that is 'difficult'. The climb appears in Ken Wilson's book 'Classic Rock', indicating that it also has considerable symbolic value for climbers, but at a lower level of difficulty]. Both me and Dave had done the route as one of our very first leads, six pitches and we felt 'oooh' [sic] very exposed. Dave said it had come

full circle for him because when he was leading it, thinking he was doing well, this guy had just soloed past him. It was satisfying because you got to do a lot of quality climbing in not much time. It took us 15 minutes, whereas to do it the proper way takes two hours. We, in turn, passed a couple of guys who were roped up on it. After coming back down we picked up Nat and went round to Little Tryfan [an outcrop set back at an easy angle for climbing, located below Tryfan, a 3000 feet mountain in Snowdonia]. We messed around on the slab and tried to persuade Nat to do some leading, but she didn't, she just freezes. She's a good climber though, and climbs at least 5b[25] On the Sunday we went to Tremadoc [a climbing location on the coastal fringes of Snowdonia, popular with climbers when the weather is bad in the mountains themselves] and looked at Vector [another extreme climb in Hard Rock] but didn't climb it. We did Striptease instead, and The Fang, VS and HVS respectively [very severe and hard-very severe, one grade below extremely severe]. It had dried a bit by the time we did The Fang, it was a little bit wet with puddles in some of the holds but OK. It was really good.

A great deal of detailed analysis is possible here but I will restrict myself to emphasising the distinctiveness of the position Chris is projecting here. He measures his progress by an un-roped ascent of a climb he had once led, aware that he is extending the challenge to himself but also demonstrating a higher level of judgement and skill to the team on Flying Buttress that they soloed past. Chris is also keen to climb routes promoted in books as being high in symbolic capital for climbers. He uses the language confidently and, because he was talking to me, assumes that I will know the places and routes he describes as I will have had a similar set of experiences in serving my own apprenticeship. In other words, he 'knows' how to convey his mountaineering identity. Dave, who is mentioned as Chris's partner for the week-end of climbing described above, adopts a similar position at the right hand end of the continuum. Here Dave articulates something of the freedom that his skill and experience in climbing have given him:

If I don't do something I feel, not guilty but, uhm [sic] I like to challenge myself physically and mentally. That's why climbing is so good, its not just the physical side it's the mental side as well, getting your head around the fact that you're a long way off the ground. It's a rope harness and working with this gear on the rock. I just find it fascinating, the whole part of it, even if you're on an easy route you are somewhere that not many people can get to. I was climbing Leviathon at the Dewerstone [a granite crag in south Dartmoor] at the week-end. We arrived in the afternoon so daylight was likely to be a problem. There was this one bloke there so we dashed up to him and asked about the good routes. He said, 'what grade?', we

---
[25] See chapter seven for an explanation of climbing grades.

said 'VS to HVS', or something like that, and he said 'well try this one' and we had like an hour left. We geared up and went for it. I felt like we'd reached a level where I was so much more comfortable on the rock than I have ever been. It all came together. I felt really strong, like I could hold on; I knew what I was doing, I felt like the gear that I was placing [on leading the pitch] was like bomb-proof. It was fantastic.

Dave has to ask for recommendations from a local 'expert' about climbs as this was his first visit to the crag but he uses his 'gear' to maximum efficiency and applied his skill and strength to the successful ascent which left him elated. Following the Picos de Europa course, Dave said he *"wanted to come back here to do some leading"*. Dave clearly positions himself as a mountaineer-climber and is keen to move into the freedom of independent mountain exploration, away from guided ascents.

Thus, when Urry (1995) talks of 'a curriculum vitae of taste and judgement', this appears to apply as equally to mountaineering as it does to other areas of social distinction in tourism. However, such taste is interwoven with the discursive strands of Romanticism which combine to shape constructions of mountain. So, for example, one guide Mike, recalled an experience when he had *"cramponed directly up good neve [compacted snow] solo, directly to the summit of Ben Lawers"* one winter. For Mike, *"it felt fantastic to be alone under a blue sky on the top before the crowds arrived via the ordinary route"*. In this respect, cultural capital gained within the framework of a Romantic perspective, again emphasising solitude as a value, appears to convey greater authority because of the line and style of ascent. A traditional legislative perspective, therefore, can articulate what a 'real' mountain looks like and can position lines and modes of ascent in a hierarchy. Such social exclusivity is based on an understanding of the aesthetic subtleties of line and the educational values implicit in undertaking challenging ascents. In this respect knowledge and experience do equate to power. This becomes a defensive strategy used by legislators for limiting the incursions into the field of mountaineering made possible through adventure tourism.

5.3 Summary

The chapter began by recognising that the body is the medium through which people experience the world. People have different backgrounds and social influences through which, over time, an individual habitus emerges. Bourdieu (1986) argues habitus, and its evaluative dimension taste, are the determinants of a class-based social distinction. This leads to a view of the body that, from the working classes is predominantly instrumental, and from the dominant classes is the aesthetic 'body for others'. I have argued that the class alignments proposed by Bourdieu (1986) do not fit adventure tourists. More specifically, a mountaineering body requires shaping and training in ways that may create 'the body for others' but which is also instrumental in adhering to the rules of mountaineering. Novice mountaineers are socially malleable because they have yet to learn the rules of mountaineering, some of which, such as follow an apprenticeship, adhere to training regimes and energy control systems and pursue an efficient body shape, are directly relevant to the acquisition of physical capital. Physical capital has been discussed in relation to therapy, fitness and training, body image and food. The discussion has shown how clients have various degrees of understanding of these aspects of physical capital. Bourdieu argues that bodily hexis, that is the way that people carry themselves, is learnt unconsciously from immersion in a social environment. I have argued the limitations of the bodily hexis-habitus dimension of learnt body techniques as a way of theorising how physical capital is accumulated in the mountaineering body. The work of Lewis (2000) has been used to illustrate how the adventure setting may transcend ordinary habitual practices. However, it has also been noted that as novices move forward in the accumulation of cultural capital, that is they gain more experience in and of mountains, a type of mountaineering habitus is likely to evolve incorporating its own bodily hexis. The mountaineering body requires a conscious response to learning body techniques because of the extraordinary demands of the setting. In particular, the physical capital of mountaineering requires an understanding of the rules of the sport which, in turn, are a manifestation of a discourse of safe and rational practice – the essence of the legislative position. Interpretation of these rules by clients, particularly those that are novice mountaineers, is limited to the social spaces away from the action of the main mountaineering stage. There are real objective dangers in mountaineering and these provide operational constraints for clients who are not adventure climbers but adventure tourists. Embodied practices of 'interpretation' do exist, but the place(s) and times at which they are permitted to operate remain in the 'non-serious' parts of the mountain day when more habitual practices from people's ordinary lives may emerge. Legislative control remains in the body techniques of mountaineering.

Chapter six: Clothing, Equipment and the Fashion of Mountaineering

6.1 Fashion Systems

In chapter two it was suggested that mountaineering is not immune from the impact of 'civilising processes' (Elias & Dunning 1986) understood as a rationalisation of adventure, particularly through using equipment and systems of organisation. There are a number of ways that mountaineering is influenced by this broader context in ways that inform the central issue of social distinction, however, it is the interplay of technology (functional) and fashion (symbolic) that is discussed here where the theme is clothing and equipment. Clothing and equipment have a functional purpose in mountaineering as they facilitate the activities. Clothing provides, for example, some protection from an elemental environment and equipment contributes to a safety context by offering support technologies ranging from instant weather forecasts and navigation aids, through specialist footwear to ergonomic rucksacks and kernmantle[26] climbing ropes. Much clothing and equipment is also fashionable. Craik (1994:4) suggests, "codes of dress are technical devices which articulate the relationship between a particular body and its lived milieu, the space occupied by bodies and constituted by bodily actions". Craik suggests clothes construct a personal habitus, however, I will suggest that fashion statements in mountaineering are much more consciously constructed around an agenda of legitimacy based on safe practice.

Bourdieu's (1986) analysis of the place of fashion emphasises the role it plays in class distinction. For example, he equates working class paucity of cultural capital to a limited supply of economic capital so that 'prudent choice' dominates working class 'fashion' (1986:378). He suggests working class people have a propensity to collect and display 'trinkets and knick-knacks' for maximum effect for minimum outlay (1986:379-380) utilising:

---

[26] Modern climbing ropes have an outer sheath protecting an inner core of parallel nylon strands. The rope is designed to stretch when loaded (as in a climbing fall) making it stronger than the hawser laid and hemp ropes it has replaced. Modern rock climbers are therefore less likely to abide by the adage that Tom Price (2000) advocates 'in my day the principle was the leader must not fall'.

A formula which for bourgeois taste is the very definition of vulgarity (one of the intentions of distinction being to suggest with the fewest 'effects' possible the greatest expenditure of time, money and ingenuity).

Mountaineering clothing, and to a lesser extent equipment, has a functional purpose in the way that it contributes to the rational approach to mountaineering promoted through the legislative agenda. Earlier chapters have shown how a mountaineering discourse has emerged that is reinforced by exhibitions, guidebooks and the institutions of mountaineering. This discourse brings together ideas of safe practice with clothing and equipment. This is not a function of class, except in so much as clothing and equipment are expensive, a fact that favours those people who have significant disposable income, but a function of comfort in what can often be adverse weather conditions. Mountains can be dangerous and life threatening environments. In mountaineering the selection and use of clothing and equipment reduces (but does not eliminate) the risks, so that having the right footwear, for example, becomes crucial to safe practice. The uncertainty integral to the setting requires functional clothing and equipment. However, the mountaineering culture also builds symbolic expectations. It was Billy Connolly who said: "there is no such thing as bad weather, only the wrong kind of clothes!" Connolly is using humour to make the important point that 'comfort' is socially constructed. Similarly, when Bourdieu (1986) suggests taste, that is, the evaluation of habitus, emerges from everyday life, the application of this to mountaineering is also problematic. The argument set out and evidenced in the previous chapter can be developed here. Experienced mountaineers understand the rules and have developed a mountaineering habitus grounded in an extended period of socialisation among people (mountaineers) and places (mountains and other places such as equipment shops and climbing walls). This is not necessarily the case for novice mountaineers who generally have a relative dearth of experience and, therefore, may bring other fashion frames to mountain places. However, the discourse of safe practice is powerful, and it provides a strong rationale for the legislative position. The indignation voiced by Hugh, an FMA client from the Naranjo de Bulnes course at the way Tim, a guide, modified the weight of Hugh's rucksack before the demanding walk to the foot of our intended mountain illustrates this well. Hugh said:

> I could not believe what Tim threw out of my rucksack, my leather shoes for example, perfectly good footwear!

Clients have to perform as 'mountaineers' because the setting requires this. There are two components of this performance, that which is physical and functional and that which is symbolic. According to Cannon (1998) people will gauge the effectiveness of a performance through comparisons that will draw heavily upon the 'props' provided by clothing and equipment. Cannon (1998) suggests fashion has a relevance to all small scale societies, and in particular he notes (1998:25), "virtually any situation that creates social uncertainty can lead to the elaboration, diversification and emulation of distinctive forms of expression". Cannon, therefore, emphasises the symbolic role that 'props' have in performance, that is, people use clothing and equipment codes for social evaluation. In this respect he is drawing upon the idea of social distinction, without which there would be no demand for fashion. Fashion, he suggests, is a universal process. I would argue that clothing and equipment in mountaineering are a manifestation of the civilising processes (Elias & Dunning 1986) in that they make a contribution to the legislative agenda of safe practice. However, this functional component sits alongside the symbolic dimension, and it is this that appears to be important to social distinction. The following evidence from my field notes and interview data can be used to explore ways that clients may interpret the symbolic value of mountaineering clothing and equipment.

Pam, from the Lake District course, confided in her guide before the first significant mountain day:

> I don't feel qualified to be doing this. [When asked why not, she replied:] Well, I don't have the right gear for a start.

When asked about why she thought this, her explanation was based almost entirely upon her observations of what other clients were wearing or carrying. She perceived her rucksack to be *"old and too small"*, her boots to be *"too heavy"* and her cagoule to be *"rather basic, hardly breathable and far from waterproof"*. In fact, the course leader Mike, a guide, had checked her clothing and equipment and 'passed it' as functional for the walking and scrambling activities to be undertaken on the course. Safety per se was not an issue. It may well be that Pam was concerned for her own physical comfort, but my interpretation of this exchange is that Pam was comparing her 'fashion' to others and drawing conclusions about herself in that social group. As a novice mountaineer she was constructing a frame of reference from what others were wearing. She was equating a perceived lack of appropriate clothing and equipment with a self assessment through which she found herself 'lacking confidence' in relation to the identity projected by others. Such a position was based on what she looked like in the eyes of others and was, therefore, a social construction. Implicit in her appraisal is the suggestion that she did not meet the fashion standards demanded by mountaineering codes, which in turn presupposed acknowledgement that such a code (or rules) exist, and that she knew what they were.

Jayne, part of the HK Peak District course, wore Buffalo clothing, which is the trade name for an innovative layering system of fleece and Pertex, a breathable shell material. She felt comfortable in this clothing in a physical sense but took an opportunity to explain herself to one of the guides as follows:

> When the talk came round to clothing I did not say very much because I thought you might all think that Buffalo gear is 'naff'. So I'm quite relieved to learn that it's OK for me to wear what I want to.

Here another social comparison is being made. As with Pam, Jayne is making a fashion assessment given some immediacy by her arrival as a member of a small group of clients who have never met each other before. Buffalo clothing is what Smith (2001:21) would call a 'Soft-Shell System' which means it is breathable, supple, light, wind resistant and warm. Smith argues such garments are 'cutting edge' in terms of function and are the future of mountaineering clothing. Jayne's concern, articulated through the comparisons she was making with others in the group, was to belong. Despite being extremely functional, as a style or fashion her choice of clothing might identify her as 'different' – perhaps socially inferior – at a time when she clearly wanted alignment with the group identity being forged. Here, choice of clothing is consciously made based on a layering system[27] that Jayne feels comfortable in, but the symbolic value of such a set of clothing needed social approval. The fact that she was reassured by the guides, who endorsed her choice, validated her decision. As a relative novice she needed re-assurance of the legitimacy of the fashion choice she had selected from an increasingly diverse range of possibilities. It may not,

---

[27] The principle of having layers of clothing to trap and heat air for body insulation remains. This is explained more fully in section 6.3.

therefore, be enough to be functionally equipped. For Jayne, there was a psychological comfort to be gained through 'belonging', which suggests an aspect of safety beyond the physical.

Vaughn, an FMA client on the second Skye course, produced a different slant as he made comparisons, not between clients, but rather between mountain and urban settings. He said:

> I am amazed by the things you can get for leisure today that aren't worn as they are meant. I see young Afro-Caribbeans[28] wandering around Birmingham with full Berghaus fleeces on and they will never go near the mountains.

Vaughn is assuming what these people will not do and taking a position of social distinction here. His knowledge of mountain codes symbolically represented by clothing leads him to align specialist clothing (Berghaus use a tightly woven fleece material called Polar-Tec which is superior in its insulating properties to many other fleece materials) to 'being a mountaineer'. This garment, for Vaughn, is a symbolic statement of mountaineering achievement and Vaughn's observation is the articulation of a position that contests the 'right' to wear such garments as fashion. In the discussion above, Pam is the least experienced and has the greatest concerns of these three clients for her appearance. As a completely novice mountaineer[29], she can only construct a frame of reference from what she sees around her. Jayne has more experience[30] than Pam, and, therefore, despite an apparent initial lack of confidence about the social acceptability of her mountaineering clothing, has a more established frame to draw upon. Vaughn is the oldest and most experienced of these three clients. Vaughn has been trekking in the Himalayas, and he had certainly been on Skye before his arrival on the course during which we met. He felt socially comfortable in his choice of mountaineering clothing (poly-cotton trousers,

---

[28] A parallel line of analysis, not undertaken here for reasons of space and focus, concerns the racial theme implied by Vaughn's observation. The countryside has been viewed as dominated by a white and middle class hegemony (Harrison 1991), a position endorsed by Bourdieu (1986).
[29] Through the week of the course I talked to Pam on several occasions and learnt that her walking and scrambling experience was limited to the Lake District and an ascent of Scafell Pike was something of a pinnacle of her achievements.
[30] Following several conversations with Jayne I learnt that her experience was not limited to the UK but that she had Alpine experience, and, in particular, had made an ascent of Mont Blanc.

fleece and pertex jacket), but, because he saw this as symbolic of 'being a mountaineer' he has taken a stance of distinction. This discussion, therefore, illustrates the connection between experience and 'fashion' confidence. Clients who are relatively inexperienced, such as Pam, may be more inclined to be sensitive to the fashion on display around them. Craik (1994:x) suggests identity today is more likely to be constructed from the "kaleidoscopic bits and pieces of cultural debris". I take this to mean that fashion has become increasingly eclectic in its construction by drawing upon different cultural influences. When clothing is predominantly symbolic this is less problematic than when symbolic and functional dimensions come together, as in mountaineering. The evidence cited above shows that there remains a strong legislative agenda of safety operated by guides who 'check' rucksacks and who endorse the functional capacity of clothing and equipment for reasons of safe practice. For more experienced clients, the body and how it is clad has been 'trained' through "sanctioned codes of conduct in the practices of self-formation and self-presentation" (Craik 1994:5). Mountaineer legislators have set out the 'sanctioned code' that constructs identity, and it is the symbolic importance of wearing and knowing about clothing and equipment that contributes to the cultural capital necessary to create position in the field of mountaineering.

Michael (2000:117) draws upon the notion of fashion when he discusses walking boots as: "objects of semiotic consumption". He suggests that certain boots (Caterpillar for example) signify urban walking and are, therefore, for non-serious walkers. Karrimor, Saloman and Berghaus on the other hand produce state of the art walking boots offering style with performance for serious walkers. Michael goes on to suggest (2000:118) that although serious walkers purport to choose their boots using practical criteria such as cushioning, ventilation, durability and sole construction, in fact they have a "tacit discourse of needs". This discourse signifies that a 'serious walker'[31] should not be concerned with the trivialities of aesthetics and style, but the evidence suggests they are. Mountaineers are very much concerned with style. Clothing and equipment facilitates performance in a functional sense and addresses the 'needs' for comfort and safety but simultaneously constructs identity around a mountaineering fashion system based on rules and codes. These points are well illustrated through the following dialogue with Chris, an FMA client from the Naranjo de Bulnes climbing course:

---

[31] My understanding of this term is someone who has accumulated substantial cultural capital through walking activities predominantly operating independently of the institutionalised setting of adventure tourism.

P: The kit seems important for you at a functional level, but is that all that it means to you?

C: No. Not entirely I must confess. When I'm buying some gear I don't want to look a pillock. I jokingly say to people 'the first rule of climbing is that you've got to look good', [Chuckles], yeah, safety is about four or five! [More chuckles]. There is a lot of fashion in climbing. I don't think I'm a complete and utter fashion victim. You have also got to be good enough to wear certain things. It's a strange kind of climbing wall thing. You can't possibly take your shirt off unless you can climb French 6b[32]

P: And this is your local climbing wall?

C: Well, this is how it is in Bristol[33] No one talks about it, it's like an unwritten rule. You go down there and you're a rookie. You've got all your gear on and you're wearing your jumper and you wouldn't dream of taking your shirt off or wearing tight fitting clothes or anything that makes you look good, or look like a good climber, because you're not. It's like having a souped-up car with a tiny engine; it's got flames down the side, big wheels but a tiny engine. It's ridiculous. It's a strange climbing wall culture that you don't take your clothes off until you're good enough.

Craik (1994) suggests that the civilising processes have problematised bodily display so that fashion today is a subtle mixture of revealing and concealing the body. Atavistic activities such as climbing are premised upon body-action and part of the 'freedom' is to do with being able to display the performing body. However, the civilising processes are evidenced in the codes, articulated by Chris, that constrain such agency. Chris, like Pam, is sensitive to what fashion systems are saying about one's ability to perform. The codes articulated by Chris appear particularly clearly defined in this indoor setting. The codes here are operating to restrict climber freedom, or at least position climbers socially in a location that is demonstrably more social than the ascent of a mountain in a remote area. The climbing wall setting puts climbers in the social spotlight to a greater extent than outdoors precisely because of its independence of weather and time of day and its city centre location. Having entered into such an area of discussion, it seemed opportune to explore this further. Our dialogue continued:

---

[32] An example of the grading system commonly used on climbing walls to distinguish indoor climbing, with its almost complete lack of objective danger, from climbing on crags and mountains. Grading is explored in chapter seven.
[33] Undercover Rock is an indoor climbing complex built inside the de-consecrated church of St. Werburgh's in Bristol. Imaginative use has been made of archways and the original pews still feature in the changing areas.

P:- Is that restricted to climbing walls do you think?

C: No, it's very much a crag thing as well. There is a lot of fashion and a lot of money to be made in climbing gear, you only have to go into any climbing shop. Now fleeces are hitting the mainstream market. I see my Rab down duvet jacket as a very functional piece of equipment, it's brilliant and I love it. I see people walking down the high street wearing them, they've got no right! It's like taking your kids to school in a big four wheel drive. Outdoor equipment has hit high street fashion shops now and you can buy fleece and quilty things from Gap. I look on them with complete scorn and contempt. They are not the real thing, not the genuine article.

Here Chris is articulating real indignation based on the perceived dilution of his cultural capital through the appropriation of 'his' fashion system by people who are not climbers. I would suggest, drawing upon my professional judgement as a guide, that Gap gear and other fashion garments are not functional in mountains and may compromise safety standards if people thought that they were. Chris is aware of this functional dimension but is here voicing indignation at the symbolic dimension of clothing. Taken in conjunction with his sensitivity to codes of display at climbing locations he clearly feels that the right to such identity has to be earned through mountaineering endeavour. This is an expression of social positioning based upon his own stock of cultural capital. The concluding section of this example shows Chris's awareness of how fashion systems construct distinction between sub groups in the social field of mountaineering.

P: Are these people buying in to an image?

C: I suppose they could be but I don't think they know what that image is. Because they are outsiders they don't go to Llanberis[34], they don't go to these places and hang out in the places climbers go. I think it's just somehow become fashion. In a gear shop there is some stuff that I would buy and some that I wouldn't.

P: What wouldn't you buy?

C: I wouldn't buy a ramblers outfit!

P: What's a ramblers outfit?

C: Um..it has got to have a bobble hat in there somewhere. This may sound pathetic but I wouldn't wear thick woolly socks with my rock shoes, and I don't like Ron Hill Tracksters much. I quite like climbing in jeans. I wouldn't go up a mountain in jeans, but for messing around on a crag....

---

[34] The Llanberis Pass is a well known climbing area in Snowdonia with appeal to both adventure climbers (on the mountain crags) and sports climbers (climbing with bolted protection) in the more recent developments in the disused Dinorwic slate quarries.

P: Like Seb Grieve?[35]

C - Exactly. If Seb Grieve can climb in bloody jeans then I can too! I was down at the local climbing wall the other evening and there were these typical twenty year old lads down there and they asked me to show them this move that virtually involves doing the splits. I was wearing jeans and this lad said... 'he's wearing jeans as well!'. And then he suggested that it was a kind of 70s thing. I said, or thought, 'cheeky bastard', haven't you seen Seb Grieve climbing?

This section of our dialogue shows a number of elements of the construction of identity. Chris is aware climbers and walkers may use clothing in different symbolic ways. He is, therefore, cognisant of projecting the right image. It also shows Chris is aware of safety factors in climbing as he rejects wearing denim for mountaineering thereby showing his understanding of the limitations of such material when wet. Additionally he is aware of what he does want to wear driven by the 'style' set by significant others. Clothing for climbing and walking activities has, then, moved out of the functional environment of the mountains and into towns and cities. The fluidity works both ways, however, as what one wears in the mountains has to be fashionable as well as functional. Moreover, as Chris's dialogue suggests, what one wears, how one wears it and when and where one wears it appears to be symbolically representing a social hierarchy. The crossover of the urban-mountain frames is well represented by the emergence of indoor climbing walls, which replicate the outdoor rock-climbing arena of the mountains in our towns and cities. These walls are very popular (BMC 1999) and are themselves the result of an emerging technology that can simulate a 'natural' rock climbing setting. Walls today are a common starting point for someone interested in climbing. It may well be where people first hear about climbing and walking courses when they read notice-boards, absorb advertisements and interact with lots of other people. The climbing wall setting is very different from the 'solitudinous contemplation' that informs a Romantic construction of mountaineering as there are lots of people around all the time. This creates an extensive stage upon which people can perform. There appear to be 'unwritten rules' operating which create social distinctiveness in a climbing setting. Moreover, on a broader level, there is a suggestion that a social hierarchy operates in mountaineering that places climbers above walkers and both groups above those people who only possess symbolic attachments to mountains via clothing.

---

[35] Seb Grieve is a 'cutting edge' adventure climber, a contributor to High magazine and featured prominently in a recent extreme rock climbing video called Hard Grit.

6.2 Technology, Equipment and Comfort

Mountaineering clothing and equipment relates to being 'comfortable' in a physical sense and in a social sense. Mountaineering clothing now comes in 'systems' that are highly instrumental in sustaining personal homeostasis and are a scientific development of 'civilising processes' (Elias & Dunning 1986). Understanding how the systems work thus becomes a part of the cultural capital of mountaineering. Chris Smith (2001:20) explains how modern clothing systems for mountaineering use layers to sustain a micro-climate that facilitates comfort:

> The complex activity that exists on the surface of the skin, and also between each layer within a clothing system, is sometimes referred to as a 'micro-climate' where varying amounts of perspiration (moisture and moisture vapour), accumulate and diffuse, depending upon levels of activity and the 'temperature differential' between the layers. The primary aim of any layering system is to manage these individual micro-climates, and to quickly move or transfer perspiration through the system.

Summit Magazine, from which this extract is taken, is, together with the other popular magazines such as High, On The Edge and Climber, an important source of the knowledge that constitutes this cultural capital. So, at one level there is bodily homeostasis, this is physiological comfort and is objective and functional. At another level there is social comfort that is subjective and symbolic. Clients are very aware of this latter aspect. This is well illustrated by Dave, a client from the FMA course to the Picos de Europa:

> The gear is a status thing: you are an outdoor person, you are almost showing another side of your personality. So you are fairly conscious when you wear the stuff that you've got outdoor gear on. You are definitely making a statement about what you do and where your aspirations lie.

Making a fashion 'statement' is, for Dave, a *conscious* act of identity construction. Analysis of my field notes and scrutiny of my interview transcripts provides many instances of clients 'making fashion statements' commensurate with identity issues surrounding 'mountaineer'. Here are some examples.

Bruce came to Skye with FMA because he wanted to get on to parts of the Cuillin Ridge he had hitherto been unable to visit, such as the Inaccessible Pinnacle. Bruce walked smoothly and talked freely of his mountain walking and scrambling experience all over the UK. His boots and rucksack were well worn, a point of pride to him, as was his patched 'shell layer' (meaning an anorak or cagoule[36] or, or more commonly today a 'mountain jacket') which was a Buffalo jacket. He wore his clothes as a 'statement' of his experience, and stood out in sharp contrast to other clients from this group and others (such as Paul and Michael from the Lake District course) who wore new and colourful mountain jackets. Bruce felt comfortable in his choices, he made it appear that he was a part of his clothing. Bruce conveyed this feeling of social comfort in a number of ways. He had, for example, a relaxed demeanour both in and off the mountains, he smiled a lot and did not appear stressed when the terrain became more demanding. He unzipped the side ventilation slots on his buffalo jacket when going up hill and zipped them up again in the windier situations experienced on ridges and on the summits. He was confident in his foot placements and appeared to be comfortable in his boots: he never complained of blisters and he wore his boots to the pub at the end of the day. Bruce's performance exuded effortlessness and he appeared *comfortable* in and off the mountains in a manner that recalls Tim's (the guide) performance noted by Anthony and discussed in the previous chapter. Bruce's clothing was a part of him, creating what Craik (1994) calls a fashion system, bringing person and clothing together in a way that conveys a distinctive position. Bruce's fashion system showed a mountaineering habitus whereby it *appeared* that his movements and demeanour were 'natural' rather than a reflection of the fashion of others around him. However, although he was clearly comfortable, part of the 'comfort' has come from knowing his clothing and boots are what is legislated for, he is wearing the 'right' things. It is possible that Bruce is acting out a role and that, like Dave, his fashion choices are consciously taken.

---

[36] Cagoule is a term emerging from my apprenticeship years to describe a water and wind proof outer garment. Original designs were basic. The more sophisticated (and significantly more expensive) 'mountain jackets' sold today are technically superior in the level of comfort they afford. This contrast is made in the comparison between Peter, who had a cagoule, and Vaughn, who had a mountain jacket.

Peter, in contrast to Bruce, was not at ease with his choices. Peter is a younger client, and I met him on the Lake District course. Peter often appeared to be self-conscious both on and off the mountains. My field notes record that he changed the clothing he was wearing more often than anyone else. Through observing him closely I noticed he was constantly looking at what other people were wearing; his eyes were rarely 'at ease'. He was curious about Wally's ventile mountain jacket, for example, and asked Wally about how the fabric worked as he lightly ran his fingers over it. I have interpreted this observed behaviour as Peter consciously 'picking up' on the clothing of others around him. For example, on the first morning in the Lake District he was not sure about wearing gaiters as very few others were, so he left them off one day yet wore them on another. He made similar apparently conscious decisions about over-trousers which were left off even though it was raining because the guide was not wearing them, yet on another occasion were finally put on when the rest of the group had chosen to do so. This taking off and putting on of clothing was partly functional, to reflect the changing weather conditions of different aspects, heights and times of the day. However, Peter had to take his cagoule off when he got too warm ascending whereas Bruce had simply surreptitiously unzipped the sides of his jacket. Where Bruce was smooth and understated, Peter was discordant and overt. Where Bruce appeared to be oblivious of the fashion statements all around him, Peter was reflectively experimental. The conclusion that I would draw from this analysis is that Peter's stock of cultural capital, evidenced by what he wore and his understanding of clothing systems appropriate to mountaineering, was relatively low when compared to the same with Bruce. Bruce, therefore, through his understanding of 'being a mountaineer' used the social settings provided by the adventure holiday to position himself in the field.

The two examples above concern fashion systems operating in the actual mountains where safety is a strong determinant. At other times however, and in other more peripheral places, the codes defining mountaineering clothing are relaxed. On Skye, for example, most evenings were spent in the pub and this provided an opportunity for variations in dress codes. Derek, for example, wore his kilt on more than one occasion and Lee wore his Alan Shearer England football shirt. There may well be an element of national identity being projected here but the main point is that any pretensions to sustaining a mountaineering identity in this non-mountain setting were ignored by the fashion systems chosen by these two clients. Almost all the others (including Bruce) continued to wear at least some mountaineering clothing – fleeces and boots were common. Clothing can therefore make people comfortable in a functional sense and in a social sense depending on a person's understanding of the rules and codes operating in different settings and the choices that each location may offer. It is possible, for example, that Derek and Lee, who were both novice mountaineers, felt more comfortable in the alternative identities of 'Scotsman' and 'footballer'. Wearing a kilt and a nylon shirt were legislated against by the codes of sensible clothing for mountaineering, but the rationale of safety underpinning such rules do not operate in a pub. Clothing, then, is part of the construction of identity. Moreover, knowledge of what to wear and when to wear it constitutes cultural capital. Issues of identity and distinction, can be 'managed' depending upon how that cultural capital is deployed. Having and using equipment serves a similar purpose except that, to a greater extent than with clothing, equipment becomes a facilitator in that it can ease an average mountaineer into territory hitherto occupied by the more elite performers. An example of this is Dave's guided ascent of the west face of Naranjo de Bulnes. This route[37], Merciana, has several hard pitches that have been climbed 'free' by very good climbers, that is, without recourse to using pitons or slings as holds, that is without 'aid'. However, by using such aid, climbers of more modest ability, such as Dave, can make the ascent. A consideration of equipment needs, therefore, extends the concept of a fashion system, which is highly suggestive of clothing and style, to include the 'actor-networks' advocated by Urry (2000). The inter-dependence of equipment and person is suggestive of the concept of 'actants'. Urry and Macnaghten (2000:8) suggest:

> Actor networks consist of sets of humans, objects, technologies and scripts that contingently produce durability and stability, a social order of particular leisure landscapes involving various hybrids that roam the countryside and deploy the kinesthetic sense of movement (as when walking, sailing, climbing, driving on the open road and so on).

Urry (2000:78) suggests, "objects thus appear to be crucially part of how humans effect agency". From this perspective Urry (2000) suggests agency is an accomplishment achieved by objects and humans coming together to form inter-dependent networks. He uses the term 'actant' to describe a machine-technology and human hybrid. Thus, he argues, the human is decentred and no longer to be viewed as separate from the non-human. Rather, the human is redefined as a mediator or translator of empirical experience.

---

[37] Route is climbing jargon for a line of ascent. When of considerable length the ascent is broken down into pitches, that is sections.

The history of mountaineering clearly demonstrates how higher and more difficult objectives have been achieved as more efficient and effective forms of equipment have evolved (Frison-Roche 1993; Bernstein 1989a.) However, it is suggested (Urry 2000, Michael 2000) that the relationship between human and equipment is not straight forward and evolves over space and time. The following examples illustrate this point.

In May 1999, George Mallory's body was discovered on Everest – he had died in 1924 and it is still open to debate whether he reached the summit or not, nearly thirty years before Hillary and Tenzing in 1953. Mallory's clothing system consisted of tattered woollen sweaters and a cotton wind jacket. "By today's standards, a climber wearing Mallory's clothing system, even on a 3000 ft. mountain in the UK, would be ridiculed, never mind on the highest mountain in the world" (Smith 2001:20). Nevertheless, such attire was 'state of the art' for its time. Smith's point is to compare 'then' to 'now', but it also implies the 'ridicule', that is the social evaluation or taste (Bourdieu 1986), likely for transgressing the mountaineering code that has evolved around the twin ideas of greater safety and greater comfort today. As the following example from Tom a client with FMA, shows, plastic boots and 'second generation outdoor clothing systems' (Smith 2001), which offer performance and comfort in a single layer, are now common.

I bought a rucksack, boots, North Face top and bottoms, a balaclava, some good skiing gloves. I bought all this stuff for Peru, including a ludicrously expensive pair of mountain boots that will take crampons. I don't know if I will use them again but they are incredibly comfortable. They're a kind of flexi-plastic. I had no blisters. I thought I might buy some crampons this year especially if I was to do the HK Scottish winter mountaineering course this winter.

Clothing and equipment has become more sophisticated, more functional, lighter, stronger and thus more comfortable. It has contributed to safer mountain experiences for most people. Following Urry (2000), clothing and equipment mediates the mountaineering experience in ways that create networks of inter-dependency between mountaineer, equipment and environment. Thus, Michael (2000) uses his discussion of the walking boot to suggest that the mediation of the constituent parts of the boot (vibram, leather, gore-tex for example) makes the 'walker' an example of such a hybrid. He goes on to describe the concept of 'affordances', which are (2000:111) the interface of environment as a set of surfaces and potential human behaviour in that place. Affordances are both objective and subjective and derive from our kinesthetic activities. A path through the mountains is an affordance[38]. Affordances are "intrinsically social insofar as for humans, activity is always culturally invested" (Michael 2000:111). Not to use a path is to exercise freedom but not to wear walking boots would set oneself up for ridicule. Freedoms thus afforded operate in fashion systems that reflect the prevailing culture.

Boots and paths facilitate a relatively safe and comfortable experience. However, as actor-technology-networks continue to expand and become more complex so legislation becomes harder to achieve. Network expansion increases the likelihood of cross-fertilisation of technologies from other sports and activities. It is not unreasonable to speculate that people interested in mountaineering may have developed their curiosity of this environment through skiing for example. When activities no longer stand as mutually exclusive there is likely to be a destabilisation of the relevant fashion systems so that a re-alignment is required to incorporate the new technology. The example of trekking poles illustrates the case. The technology seems to have been hybridised from skiing. There is no doubt that trekking poles have emerged as 'essential' to the trekking-walking experience. An analysis from walking magazines will demonstrate how trekking poles have become an important part of a walker-mountaineer's presentation (Trail 1998a:7, 12, 15, 83, 108; 1998b:19, 62-65, 87, 109; The Great Outdoors 1995: cover). Part of the attraction of trekking poles appears to be the scientific rationale that is commonly found supporting their use. Fundamental to this rationale is the idea that poles operate as an 'affordance' that reduces pain by protecting the body and facilitates movement over rugged terrain. Consider this from the newsletter of a mountaineering clothing and equipment shop (Outdoor Shop newsletter 1998:1):

Take a typical walker, kitted [sic] with clothing and boots but no backpack, weighing in at say 140lbs. He or she walks a distance of 15.5 miles over undulating terrain over a period of 5 hours - not unreasonable. The calculated total weight loading on the lower joints in that period is 2375 tons! or 237.5 tons per hour on each leg. No wonder they are tired and aching. Walking poles are all about weight transfer. It is calculated that an average person can transfer between 5 and 9 kgs. per stride onto the upper body and

---

[38] At a recent meeting with the Head Ranger for Edale, one of the most popular areas of the Peak District national park, he implicitly evoked the concept of affordances when he explained the management idea of 'desire lines'. These are routes between certain specific wild places used by walkers to construct their journeys through the hills. Foremost amongst such routes are footpaths, a manifestation of human construction of a wilderness setting.

limbs with the use of poles. In this way the loading on the lower limbs can be reduced by between 37 and 67 tons per hour - a considerable saving on those joints. Modern poles are lightweight, telescopic for ease of carrying and adjustment of walking length. Most have easy grip ski pole type handles and integral wrist strap. Some have internal springing for additional shock absorption. They can be bought and used as single poles or in pairs.

Here the mechanics of walking have been laid bare and reduced to a set of figures. The purpose of trekking poles appears to be to facilitate bodily locomotion in ways that reduce the stress on vulnerable joints. Walking becomes 'safer', because the body is operating away from the point of physical overload – at which point it could break down. Additionally, the experience becomes more comfortable because there is a feeling that the body is less stressed. Trekking poles have become part of a fashion system in that they combine mechanical object and bodily motility. Thus, trekking poles have a function as an affordance in mountaineering, but they also have a symbolic value in the image of 'mountaineer'. This is a relatively new development and, therefore, an example of how fashion symbols can change.

Trekking poles clearly have a practical function but they also provide an example of a way of accepting or rejecting a key visual symbol of social positioning. The wariness outlined in the examples cited below is a result of the 'newness' of this mountaineering symbol. For those clients who have a frame that has been developed without trekking poles, this new symbol is a challenge. To accept or reject such a symbol are options, but, as the examples show there is some prevarication pending 'guidance' from others in the group, especially the guides. This is about conscious choices not habitual usage. A deeper analysis reveals that the symbolic value of trekking poles has not been lost as an opportunity to claim symbolic capital. Paul, for example, has created some distinctive individuality out of using poles by opting for one only. So, views from the clients were mixed. For example, in the HK group from the Peak District, several of the clients admitted to using poles. As a relatively new innovation, it was noted that clients were careful about how they displayed, used or talked about trekking poles. Mike for example, said that he found them very useful on expeditions such as his trip to Aconcagua in the Andes and Denali in Alaska, but did not have them with him for the Peak District activities. Mike is, therefore, aligning poles technology with 'serious mountaineering', something that Paul also implies when he mentions the Himalayas. Paul, also from the HK group, had developed his own system and admitted to using one pole. Paul said:

> It operates as a third leg when doing river crossings in the Himalayas and is very useful, if not essential in that setting.

Paul had his pole with him and did get it out to use on one of our walks in the Peak District, but only after carefully reviewing the group, and even then he was initially very self conscious. Chris and Richard the two HK guides from that trip both said they used them, a statement that appeared to ease uncertainty about the extent to which one should, or should not endorse trekking poles. Tom is very keen on trekking poles. He explains why:

> I did use trekking poles in Peru, and very good they were too. I saw some people in Wales on Saturday using them. I think they are good things. It's the saving of energy gained by a better sense of balance on difficult terrain. They really are good.

Tom appreciates the functional qualities of trekking poles. Tom is a relatively inexperienced client still learning about how to move over rough terrain. Experienced mountaineers will 'flow' over rough terrain, their bodies making minor sub-conscious adjustments to balance constantly. This observation is explored further in chapter eight, however, the point for the present argument is the facilitation to balance provided by trekking poles. For Tom the poles are both functional and symbolic. Poles enable Tom to reach a level of 'flow' comparable to that of more experienced mountaineers, he has a 'better sense of balance on difficult terrain'. He also feels included in a collective symbolic element of identity as he notices those around him using poles. Tom does not have a reference point of mountaineering experience without poles. In contrast, Wally, who has a lot more experience of mountain walking than Tom, has a more ambivalent view. When I asked Wally, an older client from the Lake District course, if he used poles he said:

> No. The only time I have used a stick was when I was in Indonesia and I was carrying a huge pack. It provided an extra support on rough ground and river crossings. I understand the principles of taking some of the weight off your knees and your hips, which may be admirable but I can't bring myself to get them or use

them...they get in the way crossing obstacles and anyway I've usually got a map in my hand when hill walking.

Wally has an extended experience of mountain walking without poles. He also makes a moot point concerning the context in which poles are now being used. People with extensive mountaineering cultural capital may have a more fully realised sense of 'freedom' through operating the skills and knowledge they have acquired. The ability to read a map and use the information it provides to make route choices that might take in terrain 'off the beaten track' is an exercise in freedom. Using poles suggests a 'following' mentality with paths and / or guides providing the lead. The main point is, however, that Wally does not use trekking poles. Part of the explanation for this is that he has developed a sense of balance through immersion in mountains without using them. The emergence of trekking poles in mountaineering is an example of how technology has made it easier for novices to achieve mountain ascents and journeys whilst simultaneously providing a symbol of 'being a mountaineer'. Having the 'right' clothing and equipment is part of the rules of mountaineering. With trekking poles, rule one (serve an apprenticeship) is being 'interpreted' to encompass the possibilities 'afforded' by the equipment. Rule two (use the right clothing and equipment) is enforced in an adventure holiday setting by guides legislating for a safe and rational approach to mountaineering. This, together with the other rules concerning food, training, effort and environmental awareness, reduces the 'freedom' of the mountains.

Greenway (1995:191) argues that trips into mountains are encapsulated by both physical and psychological insulation. He says: "Most people, leaders or participants, play out their cultural ideas of wilderness, so the trip enhances their power as defined by the culture or their ability to integrate into the culture." Greenway is suggesting that clothing and equipment insulates us from the outdoor environment, and by implication this alters the experience. In Greenway's example mountaineer and equipment form an 'actor-network'. The affordances operating here are both objective (hard ground, wind and rain for example) and subjective (such as levels of comfort from 'ordinary' home transferred to 'extraordinary' mountains). The mountaineer-client becomes hybridised through the reciprocity of person and environment. Thus, a tension emerges revolving around comfort as people's experiences of mountains are mediated by the clothing and equipment used.

The clients observed in my fieldwork illustrated this tension. Some, such as Wally, actively sought to apply high levels of comfort in the mountains. He said:

> The expedition was good for me. It was my little tent, that I had carried, that I found quite pleasing. I was by myself in this little tent feeling very self contained and self satisfied.

For Wally, feeling comfortable is an important part of the attraction of mountaineering. The elemental conditions offer an ongoing challenge to such a circumstance so that satisfaction comes from demonstrating that one can be comfortable through one's own efforts in what might be adverse weather conditions. Wally went on to explain as follows:

> I don't mind being temporarily cold and wet and fighting on through it but I wouldn't want to be particularly uncomfortable. And there is some satisfaction from making yourself comfortable in extreme conditions. I have just bought myself a new Paramo jacket and I really love having that thing on. It is such a wonderful piece of kit and I really enjoy wearing it. It has zips to ventilate all the right bits and the hood is extremely comfortable.

Wally's new jacket is an actant: it makes him feel comfortable, (warm and dry from the effects of wind, rain and bodily exertion). This has moved beyond style, although he clearly does 'love having that thing on'. Dave takes a contrasting view when he describes his personal ambition for camping, particularly when he leaves London for a weekend of mountaineering. He wants to emphasise the difference between the ordinary and the extraordinary as much as possible:

> I don't want to be comfortable all the time because that destroys the point of it all. You're not there to feel warm and cosy, you want to feel a bit cold, it's a balance. Sometimes we won't put our tent up because we'd rather sit outside under the stars and be a bit colder. You may get a bit wet but it's worth it because you get more out of the fact that you're not in the tent, it's a great place to be. In the city you can't see the sky. You can't see the stars because of the reflections from all the lights, the city blanks it out. The sky at Naranjo was incredible; all the Milky Way was there and shooting stars: it was wicked.

Here, then, is evidence of a degree of resistance to the momentum of civilising processes, yet, what also emerges from both examples is a different sensory awareness afforded by a combination of person and environment. Wally delights in embracing the feel and performance characteristics of his jacket while Dave actively resists such comforts. This raises an interesting point of discussion. There are many different manufacturers producing unprecedented quantities of mountaineering clothing and equipment. This is a function of consumer society (Chaney 1996). People can buy mountaineering clothing and equipment and, thereby, almost instantly project the image of a mountaineer. Using only visual hints and cues it becomes more difficult to identify 'mountaineers', especially in the areas of social activity at the outskirts of mountains (pubs, hostels, bothies and climbing walls for example). Wearing trekking shoes or fleeces to the pub is no longer as distinctive as it has been, although rarely today is the 'sling and carabiner' seen as it has been in the past (Gray 1979, Whillans 1971). This means that the strategies adopted to display distinction are changing. One enduring image of the mountaineer is of 'hardness', that is, of the capacity to absorb and even delight in adversity. Clothing and equipment operates to change the 'hardness' of mountaineering so that it may need to be created artificially. To what extent should one be seen to be comfortable in mountains? In the above example is Dave's position a 'superior' display to Wally's practice? The relationship between clothing and equipment and social distinction, in other words how cultural capital is deployed, is explored in the next section.

6.3 Cultural Capital and Distinction

Mountaineering has rules, and, as has been shown in earlier chapters, activities in this social sphere are concerned with symbolic and physical capital. The interaction of mountaineering and tourism has facilitated access to this capital. There is an agenda of social positioning implicit in such a perspective that in turn suggests that hierarchies exist created by the deployment of capital. Such hierarchies are constructed and sustained by all elements of the actor-networks operating in the mountaineering-client world. Thus, the idea that walkers are of a 'lower order' than climbers comes through strongly in the evidence presented here. Anthony, an FMA client who came on both Skye courses, assesses his social position in relation to his perceived ability to perform as a climber. He clearly has an idea of the codes that legislate for 'being a climber' and they include knowledge and understanding of, as well as practice in using, ropes and harnesses:

> I see myself as a hill-walker and a scrambler. I'd like to be a climber. But my definition of a climber is someone who can use a harness and can lead: to look at something and lead it. I've never led a climb so I am not quite a climber...It's not just about putting on a pair of boots, it's about planning a route, getting equipment ready and knowing how to use it.

Anthony's reading of his own social position brings person and equipment into the arena of social identity, and illuminates the notion of hierarchies in particular. Thus, a climber is, in Anthony's understanding of the term, 'someone who can use a harness and can lead'[39]. Moreover, it is more than having this equipment, it's about 'knowing how to use it'. Certain descriptive terms do raise references to social stereotypes, which in turn appear to draw upon perceptions of status. In the example above, Anthony associated being a climber with expertise in using specialist equipment. Wally suggests 'walkers' might be just that or they might be 'serious walkers', the term used by Michael (2000:118). According to Wally, serious walkers are defined by how often they go walking. Although he stops short of positioning himself as a 'walker' or a 'serious walker' he is articulating an awareness that, just as a hierarchy exists amongst climbers, a similar hierarchy exists within walkers. Wally describes his own walking as follows:

> I walk three times a week. Mostly low level walks and then whenever I can get away, within reason, at week-ends.

When the issue of a 'serious walker' was explored to draw him out over the idea of hierarchy, and by implication distinction, this is how Wally explained himself. Wally's explanation drew upon the 'place' of both clothing and equipment:

> I buy it because it is the most practical and functional. But, and it is very easy to get swept into this, you buy what other people tell you is the thing to buy. I am always pleased to see people walking in things other than the latest fashions. But I think that some of these people are probably doing a lot more than me. I also think there are gear

---

[39] That is to take the rope up the route rather than follow the leader or guide with the rope acting as direct security.

freaks out there who buy all the right stuff and never actually do anything. They find it difficult to read a map and they go out with their GPS and their mobile 'phones and probably end up having to be rescued.

Here Wally is using his cultural capital (Bourdieu 1986) to position himself. He compares himself to people 'doing a lot more than me', a suggestion that the 'doing' is quantifiable. He then inverts the idea of fashion systems by suggesting that not having the latest gear, and / or having gear that is worn and well used is a sign of experience. Here, it is the 'gear freaks' that are driven by fashion and do not have the requisite skills and knowledge to operate independently of the safety net of rescue teams. A capacity to interpret such evidence is important and is itself an indicator of status through experience. To more fully understand the legislative position (Bauman 1987) and the interpretation of this, the following section draws upon my own understanding of mountaineering to explore ways people might be influenced by the images promoted in mountaineering magazines. This section is a development of the discussion of hierarchies outlined above and returns to the clients of my study at appropriate junctures to more fully illuminate the relationship between clothing, equipment and distinction.

A glance through any of the mountain activity magazines will consolidate for the reader an image of the contemporary mountain scene. This literature is full of spectacular images of mountains and those that use them for sport and recreation. The pictures and text are amply complemented by advertisements from retailers and manufacturers and almost every one of these magazines has a gear review section. It could be argued there are two ways that these magazines influence behaviour in their readers. The first is through the concept of the role model. Climbers and walkers at the cutting edge of mountaineering developments, who take on the most demanding and challenging aspects of their activities and who are often referred to as 'hard', offer a level of performance to which others can aspire. These significant individuals, whether consciously, unconsciously or by more subtle means such as editorial expediency, set the trends. Recent front cover photographs from the magazines show British climbers in exciting positions wearing shorts and athletic type vests (High 1999a: cover; Summit 1999: cover) climbing in 'sticky' rubber rock boots but without helmets. This has become popular attire for many climbers. A further example is the spectacular shot of a climber 'deep water soloing' (High 1999b: cover). This aspect of rock climbing, when the climber wears nothing but a swimming costume and rock boots and climbs un-roped up and around cliffs that drop directly into the sea, is becoming more popular. Alongside articles in the press (High 1999b:14-17) there is a new video of this activity (High 2000:89; Summit 1999:33). This is not the preserve of pioneering 'experts' as the following observation from Dave, the FMA client, suggests. Dave thinks this form of climbing is becoming fashionable:

> More and more climbers, particularly like me from London, are heading for the south coast. It's cool, and there are some wicked routes!

A further example of the power that these significant others have to influence behaviour and display amongst mountaineer-clients is that few of them climb in helmets. The magazines show that aspirant 'hard' climbers rarely wear helmets (High 1999a:12-15; 1999b:26-29; Summit 1999:9; High 2000b: cover). In contrast, off road cycling has an image that clearly connects helmet and rider (Trail 1998b:112-113, 116-117; 1999:136-137 for example).

A second way that magazines might influence presentation and behaviour is through the ubiquitous 'gear' section. Here, experienced outdoor practitioners wear specific garments or use certain pieces of equipment for a period of time and then write a report on it. These reports are organised thematically, edited and presented via the magazines. In the final assessment certain criteria are established, commonly objectively definable ones such as cost, size, weight, capacity, waterproofing and some more subjective ones like feel and comfort, and direct comparisons made, usually with a star system. It is clear from discussions with clients that the gear section is popular with readers. For example, one client, Paul from the Lake District course, had bought his waterproofs on the recommendations of the gear reviewer in Trail magazine. Indeed, Paul has taken out a subscription to Trail magazine as he explains:

> ...not just because it is packed full of useful information but also because their introductory offer included a free K.I.S.U. [a lightweight emergency shelter] which has got to be worth sixty quid by itself!

The presence of experts (Bauman 1991:200, Giddens 1990) supersedes the need for individuals to make choices for themselves, although sometimes, when those choices have already been made, it is an endorsement of choice that an individual seeks. Mike has an impressive list of guided mountain ascents from around the world, mostly undertaken with Himalayan Kingdoms (HK), now Jagged Globe (JG). He has accumulated considerable mountaineering experience. He had, however, brought four pairs of boots the week-end course. He explained: *"I still need to sort out my crampon situation"*. Mike still defers to expert experience. There is also a suggestion here that what was previously a simply choice between what is considered safe and equipment that met that standard is now more complicated because of the diversity of choices that exist. The fact that Mike brought four pairs of boots to the Peak District course is evidence of how confusing fashion has become as the dimensions of function and symbolic merge.

Knowledge of clothing and equipment is extremely important to cultural capital (Bourdieu 1986) in mountaineering. The difference between Hugh and Tom (novices) and Dave and Chris ('aspirant' mountaineers) on the Picos de Europa course illustrates this point well. Chris and Dave, had approach shoes, light poly-cotton clothing and fleeces, harnesses, helmets and their own rock boots. When it came to roping up at the start of the climb, Dave and Chris put on their own harnesses, tied themselves in and needed little guidance on what to carry onto the route and how to attach it to their harnesses. The brothers Tom and particularly Hugh, had very little idea about what to bring, how to carry it and had no specialist climbing equipment of their own. Hugh had brought smart leisure wear for the trip in a suitcase. At the start of the climb, Tom and Hugh had to be shown how to put their harnesses on and how to adjust their helmets, then they had to be tied into the rope and the rope management systems explained to them. Dave and Chris have since gone on to an independent traverse attempt on the Cuillin Ridge, an objective, they had 'learnt' from their time with Tim and other FMA guides, that carries considerable symbolic capital in the field. Tom and Hugh meanwhile look forward to their next adventure holiday with FMA or JG.

6.4 Summary

The tension identified in previous chapters between the more traditional values of mountaineering and the challenge of greater accessibility is sustained, at least partly, by the way that clothing both facilitates mountaineering activities in the mountains and symbolically represents the identity of 'mountaineer' in urban areas. Clothing in particular becomes a symbol of inclusion. However, to perform the identity of mountaineer means endorsement from others who understand the script. Part of the performance involves conveying a flavour to the audience for how established one's frame of experience is. In this respect frames become self-reference points and external identity indicators. It is not surprising, therefore, that social exchanges hinting at and detailing walking and climbing experiences dominate conversations when groups of people meet to go mountaineering. What one wears becomes a very important part of the image one projects in such a setting. Equally, knowledge of and experience in the use of specialist equipment, and even whether one owns it or hires it, become important benchmarks against which an individual is judged. So, an experienced walker who does not know how to put on a climbing harness is included in the collective of 'mountaineers' but excluded from the more selective group of 'climbers'. Such subtle distinctions require evidence to support a person's positional claims. Evidence has a wider impact if lots of people have heard of a specific mountain or a particular rock-climb. This may be one reason why people gravitate towards objectives that are highlighted by role models, guidebooks and other more general cultural media. It also goes some way to explaining why people go to great lengths to measure and record mountaineering activities. Measurement is the focus of the next chapter.

Chapter seven: Measurement and Grading Systems

7.1 Mountaineering, Modernity & Measurement

Anthony, an FMA client, explained that he was keen to do an Alpine training course with Jagged Globe (JG) so that he could climb Mont Blanc. When asked why, and, after he had given a humorous response of 'because it's there'[40], he had this to say about Mont Blanc:

It's a recognised symbol, a mountain that people have heard of. It's a way that I can tell non-climbers what I have done and they would understand.

Mont Blanc is 'known' as the highest mountain in the European Alps. It is its stature rather than its shape that makes it well known and Anthony, it appears, wants to use an ascent to establish some symbolic capital that he can translate into social status outside the mountaineering field. The 'people' who have 'heard' of Mont Blanc are not restricted to mountaineers: the symbolic value of this mountain is high. However, although there is the potential for the transfer of cultural capital outside the field, it is for distinction within the field that knowledge of measurement and grading systems is most relevant in the first instance. I will endeavour to show how such knowledge is an important constituent of cultural capital (Bourdieu 1986). Cultural capital in mountaineering becomes an important part of the legislative position (Bauman 1987) because knowledge of the systems and experience gained through the systems conveys distinction. Additionally legislators can direct novice mountaineers towards a structured apprenticeship through which they can learn the rules of mountaineering outlined in chapter four. Measuring and grading systems are a framework through which power can flow, an example of Rojek's (1995) 'carceral networks'.

"Everything started with Mont Blanc" (Frison-Roche 1996:44), first climbed by Paccard and Balmat in 1786. It was Paccard's great rival Saussure who initiated: "the era of true mountaineering, which...would long be identified with the scientific study of mountains" (Frison-Roche 1996:44). The two men represented different approaches to climbing,

---

[40] In using George Mallory's famous off beat remark about why he intended to climb Everest, Anthony is displaying his knowledge, an expression of cultural capital.

Saussure the scientist and Paccard the: "true sporting amateur, the first person to climb without a guide" (Frison-Roche 1996:49). However, the emergence of guides was a sign of the merging of the two thrusts of mountaineering that Frison-Roche (1996) suggests were separated into 'science' and 'adventure'. Guides became professional mountaineers, and Mont Blanc, as a 'known' mountain became a focus for Alpine mountaineering as others sought to acquire the status that Balmat and Paccard (and in 1787 Saussure too) had generated for themselves by reaching the summit. Such people, wealthy, healthy and leisured, were the first mountain adventure tourists. Their guided ascents were facilitated by an increasingly detailed local knowledge, and innovations in understanding crevasses, avalanches and qualities of snow. Moreover, ice axes and crampons were invented and ropes used, as well as dark glasses to prevent snow blindness (Frison-Roche 1996:44). The most immediate result of the conquest of Mont Blanc was that climbing the mountain represented: "a somewhat exalted feat" (Frison-Roche 1996:49-50). Moreover: "climbers delighted in returning to the valley as conquering heroes, welcomed by the sound of cannon fired in their honour and escorted to the hotel by a swarm of admiring young women" (Frison-Roche 1996:50). Mont Blanc became, and remains, a powerful magnet of symbolic capital. Climbing this mountain conveyed a certain status and provided a social location consistent with the emerging identity of mountaineer.

The principle of 'firing cannons' remains today and operates through media of newspapers, magazines and the internet so that a successful 'cutting edge' mountaineer can achieve an enhanced social profile. The sophistication of such media provides a forum for claims and counter claims to be debated at the press of a button. High Mountain Sports (www.highmountainmag.com), for example, has a section called 'Mountain Info' that documents significant new mountain ascents from around the world. A more specific example of how the internet and magazines combine to promote 'exalted feats' (Frison-Roche 1996 op.cit.) is found with On The Edge, (www.ontheedgemag.com). In issue 113 of On The Edge, (January 2002:6), there are a series of corrections to a profile previously published about Ian Vickers a young, talented climber who is prominent on the climbing competition scene. The points of correction set out that Ian did have a "traditional apprenticeship" and therefore, "did not, as is often implied, come from a sport climbing or wall orientated background". I have selected this example to illustrate my point about the principle of 'firing cannons', but it also illuminates a mechanism through which cultural capital may flow. In this example the point of indignation comes from an intimation that, to come from a 'sport climbing or wall orientated background' is to diminish one's distinctive position as a climber. In other words, those people that practice climbing indoors are not 'real' climbers.

Real climbers, I have suggested in earlier chapters, operate outdoors and in all weathers, fully cognisant of the risks that are present in mountains. However, the 'playing field' of known mountains is much greater and status can only be attributed if the relative symbolic capital of mountains is established and (internationally) known. Thus, when Saussure stood on the summit of Mont Blanc in 1787 with his barometer and declared its height as '2,450 French fathoms or 15,626 feet' (Frison-Roche 1996:43), he began a process of quantification and measurement that became an essential part of the mountaineering experience. Mont Blanc remains an important 'tick' for mountaineers because it is the highest mountain in the European Alps (4807m.), just as the more modest Ben Nevis (1344m.) is for British mountains. Height is important to distinction, as in the definition of Munros[41] in British mountains (Bennet 1985), and tends to operate as a focus for mountaineering activities.

Chaney suggests (1996:43-44) that we invest certain aspects of everyday life with symbolic value as a way of 'playing with identity'. Chaney's (1996) intimation that identity and symbolic capital are connected is a useful theoretical starting point as he demonstrates (1996:48-50) that 'badges' (as in artefacts and clothing) are used in "networks of symbolic exchange" to confirm identity. However, this raises questions about how symbolic capital that is measured is valued. Walter (1982) suggests that goods can be divided into 'positional' and 'material'. Material goods are available to everyone and, to use an example from Walter (1982), include gazing upon the Matterhorn. Positional goods are, by definition, restricted to certain groups or sections of society. Standing on the summit of the Matterhorn is an example. Implicit in such a model is the notion of distinction (Bourdieu 1986). The ability (or even the desire) to climb the Matterhorn is not an option for everyone as it requires, for example, fitness, technical knowledge of climbing

---

[41] A Munro, named after Sir Hugh Munro who published his first Tables of Scottish mountains in 1891, is a mountain over 3000 feet. Munro died in 1919 and, as Bennet (1985:1-3) suggests, the impact of the tables upon hill-walkers has been immense, not the least of which concerns debate about what exactly a Munro is. Bennet (1985:1) suggests: "no definitive criterion exists, and such distinction as does exist is based on the drop in height and the distance between adjacent summits, their character and the character of the intervening ground and the time that might be taken to go from one to the other".

equipment and a level of skill generated through training regimes, that is, the rules of mountaineering in operation. This equates to the cultural capital commensurate with being a mountaineer. Moreover, even within the group of people who have such mountaineering experience, not everyone will be able to climb the Matterhorn as some of these mountaineers will see their activities restricted to walking or scrambling and an ascent of the Matterhorn is definitely a climb. So, once again it can be seen that the notion of social distinction is inevitably linked to a hierarchy of possibilities in mountaineering. Measurement, therefore, becomes an important element of understanding social dynamics in the field of mountaineering. Broadly speaking it is suggested that 'technical difficulty' is an important factor in determining position in the hierarchy. 'Technical difficulty' may be interpreted in a variety of ways, but it is undoubtedly closely aligned to the application of technical knowledge and competence, itself a product of the scientific foundations of modernity and representative of the cultural capital of mountaineering. This has already been illustrated in the previous chapter when clothing and equipment were discussed. The following section begins the discussion by examining grading systems. Grading systems demonstrate the systemisation of technical difficulty and they are very much part of civilising processes (Elias & Dunning 1986).

7.2 Grading Systems, Capital & Mountaineering Careers

Because mountaineering purports to be about freedom this raises the possibility of resistance to 'structures'. As the following discussion will show, there is some resistance to the principle of being guided by adventure clients who aspire towards greater independence. However, the mode of ascent, or style, becomes a factor in measuring the symbolic capital involved. So it might be reasonable to assume that some clients are aspiring towards the additional capital 'available' for an independent (that is non-guided) ascent that requires, by definition, a greater accumulation of skill, judgement and competence. As early as the 1960s Lito Tejada-Flores presented the climbing world with a model typology of climbing styles ([1967] 1978). In his essay 'Games Climbers Play' he identifies seven climbing 'games'. These are bouldering; crag climbing; continuous rock climbing; big wall climbing; Alpine climbing; super-Alpine climbing and the expedition game. The term game is used because "although the player's actions have real and lasting consequences, the decision to start playing is just as gratuitous and unnecessary as the decision to start a game of chess" (1978:19). He goes on to explain that a handicap system has "evolved to equalise the inherent challenge" (1978:20). Although he does not articulate how this has evolved (which is the intriguing question), he does explain that the most complex game is bouldering. Bouldering is climbing in its most basic form. It is climber against rock, the challenge being to solve the 'problem' of moving up or across the boulder. Performance is governed by rules which exclude any of the aids such as ropes, pitons, harnesses, belay partners[42] and even ladders, all of which are 'allowed' in the expedition game at the other end of the model which operates with the least rules. The application of such a model to the argument of this book concerns climbing 'style' and its relationship to capital. Tejada-Flores suggests that this model has a dynamic component so that the rules of a lower order game can be applied to the activities of a higher order game. This increases or sustains the element of challenge (or 'adventure') integral to the 'game'. The 'referees' in these games are climbers, usually more experienced climbers, who validate styles of ascent and in doing so thereby 'allocate' symbolic capital to success. For example, if a climber applies the rules of the bouldering game (no ropes, belays or climbing partner) to an ascent of a 'big wall' like the west face of Naranjo de Bulnes that climber's stock of symbolic capital is significantly enhanced. Such rare moments in mountaineering achievement are noted and recorded (in journals, club archives, guidebooks and other mountaineering literature). It then becomes generally known that a climber has made the first (or second or third) solo ascent of a climb that might have been first ascended using the rules of big wall climbing. Person, date, time, style will be written down and become available for any mountaineering archivist or guidebook writer to uncover. The following discussion draws upon this framework to illuminate the relationship between rules, style and 'measuring' mountaineering.

Originally, gaining and returning from the summit defined the rules of mountaineering. As the 'known' world of mountains expanded so diversification emerged. For example, rock climbing became distinguishable from mountaineering because completing a rock climb did not necessarily mean reaching a mountain summit. W. P. Haskett-Smith 'invented' the sport of rock climbing in the English Lake District in the 1880s (Birkett 1983:12). When Haskett-Smith, 'the Father of Rock Climbing' (Birkett 1983:37), distinguished climbing

---

[42] Belaying has two elements. To belay means to anchor oneself to the rock but the term 'to belay' refers to rope management systems. A belay partner is someone who feeds out the rope as the 'leader' ascends. Bouldering does not use ropes and can not, therefore, involve a belay partner.

within mountaineering a different system was required to inform climbers of the relative difficulty of individual routes. In 1894, Haskett-Smith published 'Climbing in the British Isles, Volume one, England', which: "was of course the very first rock-climbing guide to England" (Birkett 1983:36). However, the book was not a commercial success. The most influential of the early guide books was written by O.G. Jones and published in 1897. In his 'Rock Climbing in the English Lake District' (1897) Jones provided the foundational grading system for rock climbs:

A rough classification is here appended of some sixty of the well known courses judged under good conditions. They are divided into four sets. The first are easy and adapted for beginners, the second set are moderately stiff, those of the third set rank as the difficult climbs of the district, and the last are of exceptional severity. Some attempt has been made to arrange them in their order of difficulty, the hardest ones coming last; but the variations of condition of each due to wind, temperature, rain, snow or ice are so extensive that no particular value should be attached to the sequence. But even if only approximately correct, the list may help men [sic] in deciding for themselves where to draw the line that shall limit their unaided performances. As for the items in the fourth class, they are best left alone. Mark the well-known words of an expert (Mr. C. Pilkington): 'The novice must on no account attempt them. He may console himself with the reflection that most of these fancy lists of rock-work are not mountaineering proper, and by remembering that those who first explored these routes, or rather created them, were not only brilliant rock gymnasts but experienced cragsmen' (O.G. Jones cited in Birkett 1983:57).

A number of points of analysis emerge. Rock climbing was seen as a male preserve, moreover, even this early in its history hierarchies based on cultural capital are evident, here between 'novice' and 'expert'. That 'the novice must on no account attempt them [hard climbs]' is the language of prescriptive legislation (Bauman 1987). Experience, it is suggested, is the key to safe and competent performance and the mechanism to achieve this is to spend time becoming an 'experienced cragsman'. I will return to the issue of an 'apprenticeship' shortly. Meanwhile, a crucial observation is that Jones was setting out a framework for grading rock climbs. This 'structured' rock climbing from the beginning and has continued to do so. As Birkett notes (1983:57): "His grades were Easy, Moderate, Difficult and Exceptionally Severe. Many of these routes are still graded as Jones first graded them". Today, there are more sophisticated grading criteria used in climbing but systems remain close in principle to Jones's framework.

The principle of grading has transferred in more recent years from climbing to other aspects of mountaineering. Scrambling, walking and trekking have all now been subjected to grading by a variety of criteria, usually distance, height, terrain, technical difficulty and remoteness, or combinations of these depending upon the activity. An example can be seen in the coffee table book series conceived and published by Ken Wilson of Diadem books, now Baton-Wicks. The series began in 1974 with the publication of Hard Rock (Wilson 1974) which established the format. Significant others from British climbing were invited to write an essay based on a selection of 'important' climbs in the harder grades from the most popular climbing areas in Britain. The grade range covered 'very severe' to 'extremely severe'. The areas included a geographical spread from 'The South-West' to Scotland taking in the Peak District, the Lake District and Snowdonia. Each essay was the individual's expression of his or her experience(s) of the climb and included an overall grade, technical pitch grades, a visual route description and lots of pictures of climbers on the route. The book was so popular with climbers it quickly went into second and then third editions with the only obvious changes being an upgrading of some of the photographs. In 1978 Classic Rock (Wilson 1978b) was published. It utilised the same format but described easier climbs, broadly the category from 'difficult' up to 'hard severe'. This book was even more popular and the format was quickly transferred to walking. Although detailed grading systems for walking had not evolved in the same way, it could be argued that the publication of two books in this series made a major contribution to a general perception that walks could be categorised into quantifiable levels of walking. These two books were The Big Walks (Wilson & Gilbert 1980) and Classic Walks (Wilson & Gilbert 1984). The walking series was completed with Wild Walks (Wilson & Gilbert 1988). The books constructed a series of climbing and walking challenges that have been selected by experts from the world of mountaineering. These experts have defined what is hard / big and 'classic'. Moreover, the fascination with grades has been moved from one part of mountaineering (climbing) to another (walking) and the classification trend is still evident today.

The biggest single point of classification is 'difficulty', and, although variations on a theme clearly exist, in climbing, a progressive scale from easy to strenuous bears a close resemblance to Jones' framework published at the end of the nineteenth century. The trend to grade treks and expeditions is demonstrated by all the major adventure tourist companies that specialise in mountaineering. This structuring tendency has evolved quickly in recent years. In 1991, for example, White Peak Adventure published its first brochure and did not include any form of grading system. This company, at this time, offered packages as diverse as trekking in the Karakoram mountains (Pakistan) and Lapland (Northern Sweden), ascents in the Atlas mountains (Morocco) as well as British based climbing and walking. The authors of this brochure had made an assumption that the market targeted by such holidays consisted of people who had mountaineering experience and could, therefore, make informed choices about the demands of such undertakings for themselves. By the end of the 1990s, such assumptions have been exposed as naive when comparisons are made to other companies and their annually produced brochures. For example, Terra Firma, a Himalayan trekking company, had, by 1997, not only introduced a grading scale for their treks that ranged from 'easy' through 'varied' to 'serious' but represented this diagrammatically like a car speedometer with every trek description (Terra Firma Brochure 1997). This is an example of careful niche marketing.

The purpose of the grading system purports to be an essential guide to choosing the mountaineering challenge that most closely corresponds to a client's existing experience. Thus, an agenda of client awareness from the companies and, therefore, a caring and nurturing approach becomes evident. In a competitive market, none of the major adventure tourist companies can afford to ignore such an important trust generating position. It is not therefore surprising that, by the 2000 round of brochure publications the categorisation of treks and climbs has become well developed, even sophisticated. Each company uses a broadly similar approach to walking and trekking whereby itineraries are published highlighting hard days and rest days with an overall grade ranging from easy, through moderate and demanding to strenuous (Exodus Walking & Trekking Brochure 2000:6-7; Classic Nepal Brochure 2000:4; High Places Brochure 2000:2; Worldwide Journeys & Expeditions Brochure 2000:110). It has already been noted that the caring and trust generating climate that this approach promotes amongst clientele may lead many people to re-apply for subsequent holidays with the same company. In the case of HK trekking, 60% of the people on any one trip will have already completed a holiday with HK[43].

Both Himalayan Kingdoms (HK) and Foundry Mountain Activities (FMA) operate grading systems to help clients to choose suitable objectives. HK originally operated as two companies in one, Himalayan Kingdoms Trekking (HKT) and Himalayan Kingdoms Expeditions (HKE). In 1993 HKE were the first company in the UK to guide clients to the summit of Everest. This arm of HK has now become a separate company called Jagged Globe (JG) which retains its focus on organising climbing expeditions. HKT continues to organise trekking itineraries with a geographical locus of the Greater Himalaya. HKT's trekking grading system is based on hours spent walking and remoteness (HKT Brochure 2000:6). This company offers six grades ranging from Mild or Moderate, through Vigorous or Strenuous up to Expedition Grade 1. A further category of Reconnaissance tops the list and encompasses trips that: "should appeal to the really adventurous and the trekking itineraries may be less predictable than most" (HKT Brochure 2000:6). Clients from HKT and JG are very familiar with these grading systems. In the latter case the climbing expedition grading system is set out in the latest JG brochure. The system is based on a combination of technical difficulty (1 to 5, low angle to very steep respectively) and fitness requirements (A to D with A described as 'good basic fitness' and D as 'exceptionally strenuous'), (JG Brochure 2000:2). FMA utilise a simpler grading system. This has been made explicit in the 2000 brochure and, as with White Peak Adventure, this appears to be a conscious move to bring the company into line with competitors. The brochure explains the system thus:

This simple grading system will help you to match your personal aptitude against the trips at a glance. By their very nature all of the trips need a degree of endurance, but it is our aim that most will be within the attainment of a person of average fitness (FMA Brochure 2000:5).

The numerical grades range from 1 ("fine for the absolute novice") through 2 ("Long days, we may ask for some previous experience") to 3 ("All of the above plus altitude and / or several hard days in succession"), (FMA Brochure 2000:5). The brochures operate as a

---

[43] The source of this data is a newsletter from Steve Berry, the director of Himalayan Kingdoms, dated January 1999.

regulating mechanism. Purporting to be driven by health and safety issues (which are, quite rightly, an important consideration for any commercial mountaineering company), brochures encourage clients to reflect upon their existing experience and perceived competence and, thereby, position themselves in the hierarchy implicit in their constructions of mountaineering. The hierarchy has been set out through the marketing undertaken by companies and is, in turn, consistent with other more established forms of grading operating in the world of mountaineering. The client has clear reference points and even the more experienced ones recognise that the 'ladder' exists. Thus Mike, a regular with HKE/JG has worked his way up from Aconcagua (1B) via Denali (3C) and now, Mike says:

> I am really keen to try Gasherbrum II in the Himalayas (8035m.), not just because it is an eight thousand metre peak and JG go there, but because it is in the 4 category and I haven't done one of those yet. I am a bit concerned that its a 4D, and, after my experiences on Denali when a storm delayed our departure from the mountain by 10 days, I know it will be tough. But I've definitely set my heart on it, it looks stunning in the brochure.

This is a very structured and rational approach to mountaineering. Mike is the client who 'still had not sorted his crampon situation' and yet is climbing some of the highest mountains in the world. Mike's symbolic capital is substantial but, unlike Dave and Chris, the FMA clients who attempted an independent crossing of the Cuillin Ridge on Skye, Mike does not use this to establish cultural capital in the field of mountaineering. Paul suggests some clients get too "worked up about grades". Paul demonstrated his own understanding of, and experience in, mountaineering by distancing himself from issues of grading. Paul responded to my question that grades might be used to establish a 'pecking order' in the following way:

> Or, they think - whatever happens I can do this because it's a grade 2, and I can do grade 2. And this, to some extent, blinds them to conditions in the mountains around them. So, something that is graded C for average conditions might be a grade D in good conditions or a grade B in bad conditions. But that seems to have been missed somehow. To others on my last trip they kept going on about this being a grade C trip. Whereas I had chosen it because of where it went, when it was scheduled and, to a certain extent, how much it cost. I had looked at the description of what was involved and thought, 'yep, that's within my experience, no problem'. I hadn't gone with the idea that this would be a great C to do, but it seems that others had. Today, there has been a

vast increase in commercial trips into the hills compared to the past when the only access was by joining a club, or being invited along by friends, by being the 'boy' or the 'lad' or whatever. Now the access is different.

So, symbolic capital leading to cultural capital is to be gained from accomplishments that are graded. Additionally, however, Paul appears to use a more subtle strategy for his own distinction (Bourdieu 1986). This is most notable when he says "I hadn't gone with the idea that this would be a great C to do, but it seems that others had". Here he is distinguishing himself from those who appear to be driven by the 'grade'. Finally, his point about access is apposite, and perhaps explains the need he has articulated to be apart from the masses, 'included in the social but differentiated as an individual' (Jenkins 1996, Chaney 1996). Paul and Mike's comments seem aligned to Sharpley's (1994) notion of a tourist career, here best conceptualised as a 'mountaineering career' and predicated on the idea of an 'apprenticeship'. The idea of an apprenticeship is that there are codes to learn and rules to follow which can be seen as part of a mountaineering 'legislative' process (Bauman 1987). In effect, as chapter four has argued, mountaineering might be seen as having developed its own discourse which embraces the idea of controlled development and learning not dissimilar to other discourses surrounding Romanticism. Measurement and grading have a role to play in this mountaineering discourse because they are mechanisms to position a person in this learning process at any one time. Drawing upon the example of Paul is illustrative of this point.

Paul sent me a detailed spreadsheet of all his mountaineering activities around the world. This dates back to 1986 and clearly shows a balance between individually organised and commercial holidays, with an emphasis on the latter as his disposable income has grown. Whilst this is clearly Paul's way of showing that he is more than an 'adventure tourist', it quantifies his mountain experience. It also shows his individual progression through walking and scrambling in the UK to European destinations and finally the Greater Ranges with an ascent of Mt. Kenya a recent achievement of note. This 'diary' may lack some details but it clearly shows an 'acceptable' progression through an apprenticeship of modest activities and locations to those on a more international stage. It also shows a tension not evident with the example of Mike above between mountaineering independently and dependently, that is, through buying mountaineering holidays. When this information about his background is absorbed it becomes easy to see why he might choose to deploy this cultural capital in a way that distinguishes him from 'fast-track' adventure tourists. The analogy of a 'career' seems appropriate because it raises comparisons with working (as in physical engagement with mountains) but it also suggests a structure to the accumulation of capital. As in a working career, people can make choices about directions to follow, but each direction offers its own set of constraints because the criteria by which a person's career is evaluated are 'created' by a combination of factors beyond any one person's control. The suggestion emerging from the evidence presented here is that by pursuing a 'career' one must accumulate capital in ways commensurate with established understandings of what it means to be a mountaineer. The less experience clients have the more closely they are guided by the marketing of brochures and those that write them.

Paul clearly feels proactive in the choices he makes for his mountaineering holidays, others are much more reactive. On a smaller mountain scale from Mike's and Paul's experiences, Leanne, having successfully completed a British Three Peaks holiday with FMA, a '1' on the FMA scale, was keen to further her experience and try a '2' which is one reason why she signed up for the Cuillin Traverse course. However, Leanne was not an experienced mountaineer and, therefore, relied upon others to guide her in these choices. Leanne said:

> I'd never even heard of the Cuillin ridge before I got involved with FMA. It was during the Three Peaks trip that I learnt more, particularly through listening to people like Tim. He convinced me that I could do something that was graded harder, and he made Skye sound like a magical place.

Clients who already had experience, that is had accumulated the cultural capital of mountaineering to include knowledge, understanding and practice, were better positioned to discuss measurement. As the climbing grading systems are more extensively developed, and more detailed, than those for walking and scrambling, discussion of measurement was particularly prominent on the Picos de Europa course. Dave and Chris engaged me in discussion of climbing histories almost from the moment we first met. As I was to be guiding them on Naranjo, I was keen to learn about their existing experience just as they wanted to know about mine. Our conversations were therefore dominated by details of climbs completed, climbing locations visited and the grades of climb normally 'led' (literally leading the rope up a climb) and 'seconded' (literally following the leader once this person is secure). Numbers, heights and criteria of difficulty featured prominently. This is an example of what I mean when I differentiate between positions on the continuum I first set out in chapter five. The continuum locates experienced climbers at the right hand end and inexperienced or novice climbers at the left end. I have produced evidence to suggest the 'novice', which is a term clearly used in the FMA brochure (FMA Brochure 2000:5), is more likely to accept the label of 'adventure tourist'. Chris had limited leading experience up to Hard Very Severe (HVS), Dave had led some Extremely Severe ('E' grades) climbs. They had both completed a basic course of training and had climbed in mostly south British locations, usually on adventure climbs (placing their own running belays) but more recently on bolted limestone routes. There was a common language being spoken, for example, the difference between a 'crag' and a 'big face' route did not need to be explained. Thus, Chris said:

> I am really looking forward to climbing HVS on a big face. I have no real experience of climbing with the level of exposure that the mountain [Naranjo] clearly offers, or at least appears to from the photos in the brochure. I'd like to come back and do some leading here.

However, the limitations of cultural capital transfer are illustrated by the use of specialist language. Learning to operate the technical language is a social skill that evolves over time as it requires constant (re)adjustment in different social contexts. When two other British climbers arrived at the Naranjo hut on our rest day, they were keen to find out about the climbs on Naranjo. Their concerns were with height, completion times, technical difficulty of crux pitches and so on. This information was offered and received like a common currency: for those who knew the language of measurement this becomes a point of social inclusion. In contrast to Dave and Chris, Tom was relatively inexperienced and his knowledge of this language was more embryonic. Tom had this to say following our ascent of Naranjo de Bulnes:

> I would really like to do some leading, but at a lower grade than we climbed today. I want to look at the new FMA and HKE brochures. There are three things that I want to do, a Himalayan peak, the Cuillin ridge and some lead climbing on rock. I want to do

two of these things next year. There is no looking back, only forward to the next chance to do something like this.

Despite his inexperience, reading brochures and other literature and going on previous adventure holidays has given Tom an understanding of how his 'career' ought to unfold. He clearly understands that to become a mountaineer requires a move into exploration that is independent of being guided, although the term must be used carefully. Dave and Chris were able to specify their future projects in terms of certain graded climbs. The grade of these climbs was as least as important as where they were located. To be able to say one has led, or at least climbed, E2 5b for example, conveys a *gravitas* irrespective of what route of this grade has been climbed. Tom, lacking a broad experience from which to draw, sets his ambitions more generally, as in 'a Himalayan peak'. Mike, more experienced than Tom in mountaineering, is quite specific about his Himalayan ambitions in 'Gasherbrum II'. Ben, a climber and an aspirant guide who joined the first Cuillin course identified his own social position by using grades. Ben said:

> I consider myself a boulderer [un-roped climbing on small outcrops] and a mountaineer. I have bouldered 6c, but rarely lead above 5b.

Such self analysis reflects the measured approach to mountain training adopted by the Mountain Leader Training Board (MLTB) and other such bodies such as the Association of Mountaineering Instructors (AMI). Here, instructors and guides have to meet clearly defined parameters of experience before submitting themselves for training and assessment at the different award levels (High 2000b:14-15). Gary, also an aspirant mountaineering instructor, who joined FMA for the second Cuillin course, gives a flavour of the measuring system when he explained his personal aspirations:

> Just to get on to the MIA [Mountain Instructors Award] course you have to have completed summer MLA [Mountain Leader Award] and have 30 multi-pitched VSs under your belt, or better grades, of course. They do have some flexibility though if you have done things like the Cuillin ridge, which is right up there in the scheme of things.

It would appear, therefore, that for all clients, quantification of the mountain experience is important. For the less experienced clients, completing certain grades gives a reference point and locates them in relation to other adventure tourists. The more experienced clients, who may have ambitions to operate independently of commercial companies or may aspire towards becoming guides themselves, are likely to build a detailed mountaineering 'curriculum vitae' of their career. In the example of Paul, he had even documented this on a spread sheet and sent me a copy. This example includes lists of graded routes completed and opens up comparisons with other mountaineers who may have established their own credentials over a long period of time. In other words, mountain adventure tourism is organised as a measurable experience which appears to be attractive to all clients, and which can aid social location within adventure tourism groups, between groups from different companies and between adventure tourists and 'real' mountaineers. This is to assume that a distinction between adventure tourists and 'real' mountaineers exists. In the next section this point is explored in more detail with reference to Scottish mountains.

7.3 Munros and Bagging Munros

Hugh Munro, the man who first listed the Scottish mountains now named after him, might, because of his scientific approach to quantifying mountains, be considered a linear descendent of Saussure. Lorimer (2000:1) introduces his paper on the commodification of Scottish mountains by explaining the origins of Munro's Tables:

Dated September 1891, the sixth issue of The Scottish Mountaineering Club Journal includes an inventory of Scotland's mountains rising to 3000 feet and above. Divided into seventeen separate geographical sections, the 283 mountains are numbered, recorded by name, height and by grid reference numbers corresponding to the recently drawn, if extremely patchy, maps of the Ordnance Survey.

Lorimer (2000) suggests orographic[44] knowledge has been controlled by political interests in Scottish mountains of which the Scottish Mountaineering Club (SMC) in general and

---
[44] Orographic means 'of mountains'.

Bennet's (1985) book on the Munros in particular, have been primary influences. Lorimer's analysis suggests contemporary behaviour in Scotland's mountains has been formulated by a discourse that can be traced back to the point at which Munro bequeathed 'his' tables to the SMC. There has been an 'explosion' of interest in Munro 'bagging' from the 1980s onwards (Lorimer 2000:5); Dempster (1995:9) puts the figure at "40,000 in Scotland and at least 100,000 at present", although he doesn't specify the source of this data. Lorimer (2000) argues this democratisation of interest in the Munros has contributed to internal conflicts between different groups of mountain users. The reaction from the SMC has been to publish literature and use other, more subtle actions, such as promoting scientific evidence to support threats to bio-diversity, soil erosion and other elements of the delicate mountain environment. For example, Walker (1989:208-9) puts the case for the conservation of the Picos de Europa. Such a strategy, Lorimer argues, supports the 'protection' of the Scottish wilderness experience in line with the Romantic vision of 'solitudinous contemplation'. The significance of Lorimer's argument lies in his identification of the influence of legislators (Bauman 1987), that is, experienced mountaineers who have the cultural capital to sustain positions of power in the field of mountaineering. Lorimer (2000) identifies the legislators in this example as the Scottish Mountaineering Club (SMC) and Bennet's (1985) book as an important medium of 'legislation'. Bennet's book (1985) has been, in mountaineering terms, a best seller. This book: "institutes a complex of enacted pathways, steering readers towards conditions of recreational regulation and bodily constraint" (Lorimer 2000:6). These include the following; information presented to suggest car dependent, 'in-and-then-out' routes, prescriptive instructions to follow certain paths, an admonitory tone concerning safety issues and the need for experience. Moreover, pictures in the book suggest drab dress codes amidst snow plastered wilderness and a locale inhabited by respectful male walkers: "not an overflowing car-park, florescent Goretex, Global Positioning System (GPS) or winding snake of summit-bound teenagers in sight!" (Lorimer 2000:6).

Such analysis bears evidence of resistance to 'new' interest groups in the mountains; in this case a small, yet disproportionately powerful mountaineering body, is using its veracity as controller of official information concerning the Munros to protect its own vision. It is using an agenda of safe practice to do so, an argument first introduced in chapter four and developed in subsequent chapters. Nevertheless, Munro 'bagging', that is, the planned and systematic accumulation of ascents of the 284 Munro mountains, remains a strong motivation for many people. The groups I worked with on Skye generally support this propensity to accumulate ascents of these mountains as symbolic capital. Brendan, an accountant from Hampshire was driven by his desire to collect Munros. When the group gathered for the first evening of the course Brendan said:

> One of the great attractions of Skye is the concentration of Munros. I'd heard about them, and read about them, of course, and that's why I came up a day early for this course. I've done Bla Bheinn today, not too technical and, therefore, one I could do by myself, although I got a bit worried in the mist near the top because its pretty flat up there. With any luck I will have done the rest by the end of the week.

Brendan took great delight in reaching a new summit. As the group arrived at the top of Bruache na Frith at the heart of the Cuillin ridge, Brendan stepped forward, touched the summit cairn and said: *"that's thirty-eight"*. Others in the group were less outwardly demonstrative when reaching a summit, but equally pleased. Derek was also very keen to tick the summits. In particular he said:

> I signed up for this course because, although I have done plenty of the Munros now, I know the ones on Skye are much harder than many of the ones I have done. There is no way I am going to do the In Pin [Inaccessible Pinnacle] without some guide hauling me up on a very tight rope.

Jim from the first Skye course was very keen to 'bag' Munros. He used the term without any prompting from myself:

> Recently I've got interested in Scotland and Munro bagging. I feel a sense of achievement if we can go away, climb mountains and then be able to say, look I've done this and that. There seems little point in just meandering about.

Munro bagging, then, appears to offer a structure to mountaineering in Scotland. Companies such as FMA have been quick to exploit the phenomenon. The first Cuillin trip I worked on was advertised as a Cuillin Ridge Traverse, a major mountaineering undertaking with considerable logistical complexities and the need for settled weather and a small fit group to succeed. In the 1999 brochure such a course had become 'The Cuillin Summits' (FMA Brochure 1999:6), which breaks the holiday, and the ridge, down into sections with specific Munros as the focus for each day. This becomes a more manageable situation with a higher chance of success and a return to a comfortable valley base at the end of each day. In this respect the 'demands' of the clients, in this case to maximise the number of Munros 'bagged', have influenced the form of mountaineering undertaken.

Not all the clients were driven by the need to conquer Munros. Leanne said:

> I didn't know what a Munro was until I came on this course. I'm actually interested in having fun. If we make it to the top of something then that is a bonus.

Robert and his brother Lee from the second Skye course were similarly ambivalent about making it to the summits of certain mountains. Lee said:

> I am amazed that I've made it to the foot of this last bit of the Inaccessible Pinnacle. I never thought I would get this far in a million years. He [Robert] has been winding me up about this mountain ever since we arrived.

Robert himself did not climb the last bit of the Inaccessible Pinnacle either. He said afterwards:

> About 25% of me wanted to do that last bit, and I could see all the others going up and down and knew it would be safe, but 75% of me didn't want to do it. Like Lee, in the end, I was just pleased to have got this far.

Brendan, on the other hand, drew blood from his knuckles as he kicked and spluttered his way to the top of the Pinnacle on a very tight rope. As the guide said later: *"Brendan's determination was significantly greater than his climbing technique. It's just as well I had my first aid kit with me!"*

In contrast to the clients on the Skye courses, who were generally walkers and scramblers, Dave and Chris, from the Naranjo trip, set out to undertake the Cuillin ridge by themselves, with mixed results. Their experience as climbers led them to attempt an 'unguided' crossing of the ridge, an attempt to take their mountaineering careers forward by adding the Cuillin Ridge traverse to their curriculum-vitae. They followed the 'normal' approach from the Sligachan hotel because: "the Loch Coruisk side of the Ridge, though magnificent, is remote and forbidding" (Bennet 1985:222). Bennet is, thereby, suggesting such an approach to be the preserve of experienced mountaineers. Dave told me after this independent trip:

> We had a bit of an epic on Am Basteir in rain and high winds. We got the rope stuck on the abseil and had to retreat to the Slig. The rope's still there and we didn't get very far across the Ridge.

Dave and Chris viewed their Cuillin trip as an independent enterprise, but they were 'guided' by books, magazine articles, maps and the knowledge of other mountaineers. The following section explores in more detail how maps, books and magazines in particular provide structures that guide mountaineering activity into where to go, what to wear and how to behave when there.

7.4 Maps, Guidebooks & Magazines

In chapter two it was suggested that the ability to read a map is a point of distinction by being a skill integral to the cultural capital of mountaineering. Cartographically, in Britain, the hegemonic position of the Ordnance Survey (OS) has been challenged by private businesses like Bartholomews and Harveys. Harveys' maps in particular are making a major contribution to a reinforcement of mountaineering mores. Harveys has taken what might be considered to be the requirements of walkers and climbers from OS maps (for example clear presentation of footpaths, appropriate contouring to show shape and nature of terrain and an innovative use of scale) and 'improved' the functionality of British mountain maps through this attention to detail - subtle nuances of shade and colour for example. However, the ready availability of Harveys maps alongside OS maps in our shops operates to sustain the expectations of walkers by deliberately emphasising those elements which have a direct bearing on mountain recreation. For example, Harveys maps are geographically selective, they are competing in the niche market of mountain recreation not attempting the comprehensive British mainland and islands coverage of the OS: so one can only buy Harveys maps for mountain areas, although the company also specialise in orienteering maps. Furthermore, the actual geographical coverage of these maps as in The Snowdon Massif or The Central Lakeland Hills was determined via a consultation process with mountain users.[45] Thus, the 'requirements' of the mountain walker are catered for through these more specialist maps. Of particular note is the fact that the Harveys map of Skye has the Cuillin Ridge as its focus and, not only is the detail displayed at two different scales, but all the 'Munros' are highlighted. Following minor adjustments to Munro's original Tables there are, currently, 284 Munros in Scotland. Eleven of these summits are located on the Cuillin ridge, including the most difficult Munro of all, the Inaccessible Pinnacle, so called because it requires rock climbing to reach its summit. By highlighting the position and heights of the Munros, and thereby distinguishing them from other potential mountaineering objectives, Harveys maps are sustaining the pursuit of Munros as a defining trait of the culture of mountaineering in Britain. An example illustrates this. Waymark Holidays have constructed a package for hill walkers called the Irish Munro Tour (Lay 1999). This company have an itinerary lasting one week that takes in the ten Irish mountains over 3000 feet. This is a package that includes accommodation and travel between mountain ranges. The ten summits are located in the Wicklow mountains close to Dublin, the Galty mountains south of Tipperary and Macgillycuddy's Reeks in the far south west. So, not only has the idea of a Munro moved out of Scotland, but a mountain 'round' has been established that is achievable in a week. This will be an attractive undertaking for many adventure tourists combining achievement with geographical diversity; it could easily enter mountaineering folklore. Based on the previous example, I suspect that a 'record' already exists for this round, although I have, as yet, no evidence to support this suspicion.

Guidebooks, as Lorimer (2000) shows, have an influential role to play in patterning our behaviour. Guidebooks reinforce the Romantic visual aesthetic by including photographs which are dominated by craggy faces and snow covered peaks and notable for the scarcity

---

[45] As a member of the Association of Mountaineering Instructors I was a part of the consultation process.

of humans present or evidence of human activity (ski lifts for example) in general. All the visual symbols point to a pristine wilderness in which occasional humans respectfully recreate. Guidebooks also describe the 'best' routes and their veracity is assured because they are written by 'experts' steeped in the values and traditions of mountaineering; these are, after Bauman (1987) the legislators.

Part of the legislation process relates to measurement. This in turn is part of a larger picture of 'scripted performance' that is explored more fully in the next chapter. If mountaineering experiences do equate to the accumulation of symbolic capital then it seems logical that people will be interested in certain criteria such as how far, how high and how difficult a walking route or a climb may be. In order to make such an assessment there is a need for objective criteria to categorise activities. The British rock-climbing grading system has evolved from the framework set out by Jones (Birkett 1983). This currently combines overall seriousness (moderate, difficult, severe, very severe and extremely severe) with a numerical representation of the hardest moves on any one pitch (for example the range 4a, 4b & 4c generally covers the severe to very severe categories). It is therefore possible for a climber to know the grade of climb being undertaken: to be a climber means being able to 'speak' this language, that is, to know the system. The grade of a new climb is established by the team completing the first ascent and then 'moderated' by those making subsequent ascents. Over time the route is written up in a guide book and revisited, and the grade adjusted as necessary every time the guide book is updated. Guides and other experienced or expert climbers control this process. Climbing guide books, which may have additional features like a star system to distinguish the best climbs, therefore, direct people towards certain crags and mountains at the expense of others. For any climber, including the paying client, the system outlined above simultaneously creates feedback about the level of any specific achievement and a 'ladder' of possibilities for the future. It is a reflection of the competitive element of climbing that when conversations between climbers explore 'the grade one can climb at', this seems to carry more significance (at least in initial dialogue) than the breadth of a person's climbing experience in different areas. So, climbing in lots of different places but always at a modest grade of difficulty, appears to have less symbolic significance than how 'good' a climber one might be. Here the 'goodness' is measured by objective grading criteria recognised as a universal language. It follows that technical expertise is valued in a way that contributes to distinction.

Since the emergence of adventure tourism in the last third of this century such measuring criteria have been applied to both walking and, more recently, scrambling routes. From certain perspectives such developments can be seen to reflect broader modern concerns. This process of grading and rationalisation is not exclusive to paying clientele in the adventure tourist industry but part of a broader process of civilising driven by the rational propensity to reduce risk (Dunning 1996, Furedi 1997). The case of scrambling is a particularly interesting example of how the 'moral consensus' operates to make this aspect of mountaineering more rational through the construction of grading criteria to direct choices. There has been a spate of scrambling guide-books published over the last ten years focusing on popular mountain regions such as Snowdonia and the Lake District (e.g. Ashton 1995). Most British mountains can be ascended via a walking route; some have climbing routes on their steeper faces. Scrambling offers a hybrid activity somewhere between these two extremes. Scrambling routes offer 'interesting' ways up mountains that are off the beaten track but not as serious as climbs. Nevertheless, sound judgement concerning route selection and movement over potentially loose rock is paramount and it is no coincidence that adventure tourist companies are amongst the experts competing for clients interested in this activity. FMA offer a 'Scrambles in Snowdonia' course (FMA Brochure 2000). It is part of this logic that, once such an activity has become established as part of the British mountain scene, a grading system will emerge whereby people can quantify achievement. For example, Bull's scrambling guide to the Cuillins on Skye was first published in 1980; he takes several pages to explain the reasons for and the operation of his grading system (Bull 1993:10-12). The criteria, and to some extent the geographical context, are legislated for by experts. Experts operate a discourse of safety through publications such as scrambling guidebooks, examples include 'Scrambles in Snowdonia' by Steve Ashton (1995). In the first sections of his book, Ashton sets out 'how to do it safely' with details about equipment, access and retreat, planning, weather forecasts and a three tier grading system. Thus, despite purporting to increase mountaineering options and thereby enhance 'freedom' the proliferation of guidebooks continues to direct mountaineering endeavour towards specific objectives and modes of ascent. This is also part of the script utilised by 'guides as choreographers', which is more fully discussed in the next chapter.

Finally, the popular mountain walking and climbing magazines have a role to play in supporting the patterns established by maps and guide books. For example, Trail magazine, which in December 1998 had a special feature on the Cuillin Ridge, has a section called 'The Guide'. This is specifically aimed at training and dietary regimes to get readers fit for the hills. This is followed by 'This Week-end', which contains suggested walks from around the country. Highland and lowland walks are catered for, the Somerset Levels to Scottish Munros. Full details are given via a gradient profile, distances, outline maps, highlights and viewpoints, places to pick up food and water, maps, guides, accommodation and transport options. Although predominantly walking routes there are references to climbing options, mostly of the lower grades rather than the more serious routes that dominate the climbing magazines. Mountain biking is also included. Whilst a detailed analysis is not possible at this juncture, such a colourful and varied presentation from a relatively recently published magazine is clearly intended to present a less staid approach to mountaineering recreation than the SMC Journal for example. Trail magazine is relatively 'new' and could be said to be more representative of the breadth of contemporary interest in British mountains than On The Edge, for example, which has a specific rock climbing readership targeted. There may not be pictures of 'crocodiles of school children' (Lorimer 2000) in Trail, but there are certainly plenty of bright mountain jackets and trekking poles on display whilst the 'human' element is much more prominent in the photographs than is the case in Bennet's (1985) book. Trail magazine is designed to appeal to a broad section of people interested in different mountain recreations. It represents many of the changes, such as an emerging adventure tourism scene, that the traditional school of mountaineering continues to resist. However, despite some tension between the two groups, being able to position oneself socially is dependent upon having accumulated mountaineering cultural capital. Such accumulation requires systems of measurement.

7.5 Summary

A number of points can be drawn from the discussion outlined in this chapter. First, the Romantic idea that mountaineering is about freedom to engage with wild nature through a qualitative engagement is increasingly reduced to a set of measurable indices such as height, length and technical difficulty. Such a reduction establishes a hierarchy of social positioning that reflects an individual's cultural capital and determines its potential deployment in the field. Second, despite challenges to established ways of reading and performing in a mountain landscape, the media through which such a reduction is operated (guide books in particular) both inform and constrain at the same time. This reinforces the pre-eminence of some locations and certain forms of behaviour. Third, mountaineering offers an ambivalent response to civilising processes that project a discourse of risk reduction. Increasing risk raises the potential for greater cultural capital. Thus, Dave and Chris, having been paying clientele with FMA, attempted an independent crossing of the Cuillin ridge. Fourth, clients appear to be strongly influenced by the quantifiable indices of measurement discussed in this chapter, however, there is some evidence of alternative ways of 'measuring' one's mountaineering experience. Weight loss emerged as an objective for some clients, as did 'having fun' at the expense of gaining a summit.

Mountaineering is broken down into manageable sections, compartmentalised, ordered and graded by objective criteria. In the same way that 'travelling' has become virtually indistinguishable from tourism (Boorstin 1963), so it becomes increasingly difficult to operate as an independent mountaineer. Maps, guidebooks and magazines help us maximise the productivity of our mountaineering activities by allocating symbolic capital to different walks, climbs and scrambles. As an adventure tourist, or as a 'real' mountaineer, or as both, distinction both within and outside the mountaineering field is partly dependent upon such accumulated mountain experience. Such symbolic capital conveys mountaineering *gravitas* and contributes towards social position. In a Goffmanesque sense (Goffman 1959) projection of indicators of this capital are hints, cues and gestures that one understands the language of grading and measuring mountaineering achievement. These might include nodding or smiling when certain mountains are mentioned, using abbreviations such as HVS or the E numbers and sending postcards saying 'climbed this one'. Having learnt these social nuances, it becomes possible to display an identity of 'mountaineer'. What appears to be happening is that a person's stock of symbolic capital is more readily added to by the achievement than the style through which that the objective is achieved. The rules of the game(s) set out by Tejada-Flores (1978) reflect a legislative position that has relevance for those who are at or aspire towards such a position. To achieve distinction means to understand measuring systems and rules about the different levels of performance. Once 'mountaineering society' is diluted through the inclusion of people whose careers do not coincide with the codes set out by the legislators then the emphasis switches from the subtle 'inside-knowledge' detailed grading systems to cruder indices such as height. This point is illustrated through the ambition offered by Anthony at the start of the chapter that he has to climb Mont Blanc, *"a mountain people have heard of"*. In this respect the accumulation of capital becomes a distinguishing element in mountaineering and, therefore, more important, for some people, than the 'quality of the experience', escape, catharsis and re-creation which are the values informing the Romantic view of mountains. Adventure tourism embraces the accumulation of symbolic capital by projecting a clear articulation of graded walks and climbs. Mountain guides, who are the people sitting astride the two worlds of mountaineering legislators and interpreters, hold an interesting position. In order to obtain their qualifications they have had to serve an apprenticeship, with all this entails, for example logged experience of climbs completed and their grades. In this respect they are steeped in mountaineering tradition. Yet guides also conduct adventure tourists in mountains and, as the next chapter will show, they can have a strong influence on the patterns of behaviour that adventure tourists absorb. The final analytical chapter considers more closely the role of guides in directing performances in mountains.

Chapter eight: Performing in the Mountains

8.1 Introduction to Performing in Mountains

The previous chapter examined the contribution measuring makes to the construction of social distinction. It has been suggested that not everyone can read a map or understand the language used in guidebooks. Such a capacity represents cultural capital and becomes the currency of distinction (Bourdieu 1986). A person's level of understanding, technical competence, that is, stock of mountaineering cultural capital, creates and sustains hierarchies. Hierarchies are a reflection of status amongst people in the field. In Rojek's (2000:3) terms, all leisure activities are status statements in which performance is "understood as the social cement which binds life with others". He argues (Rojek 2000), all performances are mediated by scripts which others must see and understand. Moreover, as leisure is a performance in which we act a role and follow a script, activities such as mountaineering can not be simply escape routes through which people find freedom. This argument for social construction draws heavily upon the framework set out by Goffman (1959) and is echoed by Cloke and Perkins (1998b:214) in their discussion of adventure tourism:

> In our view the notion of tourist performance more adequately captures the experience of adventure tourism because it connates both a sense of seeing and association with the active body, heightened sensory experience, risk, vulnerability, passion, pleasure, mastery and / or failure.

Measuring, precision and standardisation reflect rational (scientific) control within the social world. This, in turn, Rojek (2000) argues, has led to a performative pluralistic culture. People are constantly under pressure to behave in predictable and standardised ways and "the quality of the performance is the main criterion for establishing validity in the power and authority relations between actors" (Rojek 2000:9).

The aim of this chapter is to examine the performance of 'being a mountaineer'. It is particularly concerned with the extent to which clients may or may not be socialised by their interactions with experienced mountaineers. It will do this by discussion of the construction of mountaineering scripts, a focus that requires a closer examination of the role of the mountain guide. Here the notion of a continuum of 'dependence' becomes an important conceptual tool to operate alongside that of 'hierarchy'. Clients on adventure holidays have opted for a 'dependent' mountaineering experience whereby the power and capacity of guides to both formulate and control behaviour is paramount. The amount of experience that clients have is likely to make them more or less dependent upon the directions of their guide. This has been evidenced from chapter four onwards. The idea of a 'client continuum', first introduced in chapter five, thus suggests itself whereby the most dependent clients are closer to a role broadly identified as 'tourist' and the least dependent, that is, those with the greatest existing cultural capital, might be thought of as 'aspirant mountaineers'. Mountaineering guides have a level of responsibility that is of a different order to that of a conventional tour guide (Edensor 1998), because of the omnipresent objective dangers of wild places. Mountain guides have a responsibility for the safety of their clients in inhospitable terrain: clients' lives may literally depend upon the guide's expertise.

8.2 Theorising Performance

Chapter four has introduced a framework for exploring the metaphor of space as a 'stage' for performance. Edensor (1998) suggests that performance in enclavic space is about reinforcement of identity stereotypes, and tourist modes of performance are most likely to be disciplined rituals. This is the kind of setting utilised by package holidays, and perhaps the packaged nature of adventure holidays will construct mountain spaces in a more predictable way. Enclavic space is what mountaineers want to get away from because, by definition, such spaces are constructed around normative rituals. Heterogeneous space however, is more likely to be occupied by backpackers and demand improvised or unbounded performances (Edensor 2000). This is a useful framework to apply to mountain spaces for several reasons. First, there are parallels between backpackers and mountaineers concerning the accumulation of cultural capital through going to places that have recognised symbolic value and by utilising and developing 'life skills' which facilitate safe passage through 'spaces of adventure'. For backpackers:

Status and distinction is acquired and transmitted concerning how far off the beaten track they have gone, the quality of their encounters with 'locals', the bargains obtained through skilful haggling [and] their commitment to back-packing (Edensor 2000a:9).

Locations visited, the number and difficulty of ascents made, the development of skill and the engagement with adventure are all part of mountaineering. Second, the identification of constructed space as enclavic or heterogeneous provides a framework for discussing mountains, particularly as it has been noted that enclavic characteristics emerge from packaged formats and appear to invade heterogeneous space over time. Lastly, this framework places fluidity at the forefront of its central book. Not only is it possible for space to change and evolve (as in the arrival of enclavic characteristics in heterogeneous space referred to earlier as the urbanisation of wild places) but tourist responses evidenced through their performances do not remain constant. A tourist may enact: "a medley of roles during a single tour or holiday" (Edensor 2000:341).

Edensor (2001) suggests the roles that a tourist performs will be more or less determined by 'habitual enactments'. He advances the work of Goffman (1959), who places the emphasis upon reflexive behaviour on 'stages', by emphasising that any performance may also contain habitual and unreflexive enactions so that "tourists carry quotidian habits and responses with them, they are part of their baggage" (Edensor 2001:61). He goes on to argue that the fragmentation of tourism into 'niche markets' and specialist areas (such as adventure tourism, itself a broadly defined area) has led to a "proliferation of stages, activities and identities" (2001:61). By arguing that common-sense habitual performances link culture and identity Edensor is drawing upon Bourdieu's notion of habitus. However, although tourist practice is "never entirely separate from the habits of everyday life, since they are unreflexively embodied in the tourist" (Edensor 2001:61), I have argued in previous chapters that the extraordinary setting of mountains is likely to raise 'client' performance, for people at the left end of my continuum in particular, to levels of consciousness. Tourism, as Urry argues (1990:10-11) takes place in socially 'liminal zones' which may suspend quotidian forms of behaviour and facilitate an enhanced level of social and sensory awareness operating in the conscious domain. I have argued in earlier chapters that conscious behaviour needs a frame of reference. In mountaineering, because of the dangers that are part of the activities, previous experience of the activity provides that frame. Where such experience is limited, or even non-existent, as is the case with people at the 'tourist' end of my continuum, clients become unframed. Without a frame clients may select a frame that is a 'close fit' to the demands of the setting but the seriousness of mountains determine that unframed clients have to respond consciously. Edensor's (2001) 'quotidian behaviour', I have argued in previous chapters, will be limited to the non-serious spaces of mountaineering. The result is that dependent clients become 'socially malleable', that is, they have everything to learn about the rules of mountaineering, which, in turn, constructs the script. Performing the script in a convincing manner is the essence of 'being a mountaineer'.

The most convincing performances will come from experienced mountaineers because these people have the greatest stock of cultural capital. This cultural capital will manifest itself in body techniques that represent the inscription of physical capital and in a personalised curriculum-vitae of measured and graded ascents and journeys that represent symbolic capital. This has been evidenced in previous chapters. Pursuing such a line of analysis, experience is likely to bring performances that operate through a mountaineering habitus. A client may indeed 'enact a medley of roles' within a holiday as Edensor (2001) suggests, but 'dependent' clients are likely to be socialised by more experienced mountaineers, clients or guides into restricting 'interpretative' (Bauman 1987) performance to the side-lines of the main stage. 'Independent' mountaineers continue to be constrained by a more broadly defined cultural interpretation of mountains and mountaineering that promotes certain places and certain forms of behaviour at the expense of others. Guides, therefore, have an important role to play in the process of 'client-socialisation' but are only teaching what they themselves have learnt.

So, mountaineering as a performance, therefore, casts clients as actors and guides as both producers and directors. The scene is set by a Romantic reading of mountains in which jagged peaks, blue lakes, and spectacular vantage points that simultaneously reflect an atavistic position of prospect and refuge (Appleton 1996, Jerome 1979) become key symbolic features. The landscape is measured and graded so that specific ascents might be thought of as 'acts' or 'scenes' in the unfolding drama. People get 'dressed' for performances so that boots, rucksacks, ropes, harnesses and trekking poles become props for use on the stage. Additionally, people attend to 'rehearsals' by training in more local settings than those they choose to visit in their adventure holidays. Moreover, as mountain spaces are developed through physical intervention such as footpath construction and signpost erection, the script becomes easier to follow because the space is rationalised and standardised, a manifestation of civilising processes. The following section examines the idea of the guide as performance director and mountaineering expert in more detail. The purpose here is to argue that clients across the continuum are socialised into the identity of 'being a mountaineer'.

8.3 Guides as Experts

Experts (Giddens 1990) such as guides and instructors are gatekeepers to the field of mountaineering. Historically they have had an important role to play and today they believe their 'position' still commands respect as the following dialogue shows. Tim, an FMA guide, recognises the importance of demonstrating one's competence early in the client-guide relationship. This comment came after a particularly misty, wet and windy first day on the Cuillin ridge:

> I like getting up there and show them how it's done by sorting it out. It might be claggy [misty with limited visibility] but we'll still find our way around. It establishes our credentials.

Vaughn, an FMA client on the second Skye trip, added some credence to Tim's belief when he said:

> Instructors and guides are like gods, but it is a two way process, gods have to be worshipped.

As the focus of mountaineering shifted from an exploratory and scientific rationale to one of sport and recreation, it was hunters and farmers who emerged as the earliest guides. These people possessed local knowledge, and gradually, through physical engagement with walking and climbing, also developed a rudimentary technical expertise. The relationship between guiding and economy has a long history and goes back at least as far as Paccard and Balmat's ascent of Mont Blanc in 1786 (Frison-Roche 1996, Bernstein

1989a, 1989b, Bernbaum 1997, Johnson & Edwards 1994, Fleming 2000). The original Alpine guides based their credentials on detailed local knowledge, for example Balmat (b.1762) in Chamonix and Gaspard (b.1834) in the Oisans in the European Alps. However, over time, and particularly as more mountain areas were 'opened up' and the Greater Ranges of The Rocky Mountains, Andes and Himalayas became more accessible, technical competence and transferable skills became as important as local knowledge as guides began to operate internationally. Today, the U.I.A.G.M. system for gaining an international guiding carnet bases its assessment on specific technical competence rather than the successful completion of specific climbs. However, certain routes such as The Cuillin Traverse or Zero Gully on Ben Nevis, are so well known amongst mountaineers that they take on a special significance for aspirant guides in what has become a self regulating profession. The symbolic capital attached to such routes is high because of the 'value' allocated to them by established mountaineers. This is not to suggest that today's guides are completely footloose. The Ackroyd family has operated 'Cuillin Guides' from its base in Glen Brittle since 1972. Moreover, most contemporary guides have a 'home patch' which they know better than their less frequented but perhaps more international arenas; Alan Kimber, for example, operates throughout the climbing centres of Western Scotland. Thus, the original geographical affinities of the early guiding tradition are sustained to various degrees today. But, more significantly, guides reinforce the patterns of participation (routes ascended and climbing style for example) that they have absorbed through their own apprenticeships. Contemporary guides characteristically have expert knowledge in the form of mountain experience and local detail. They also have technical knowledge of equipment and rope choice and use, as well as knowledge related to map reading, route finding, general safety and survival, self-reliance and sufficiency. Additionally, guides have absorbed the traditions of mountains in terms of icons, myths and folklore. This is the cultural capital (Bourdieu, 1986) guides exchange, as professionals, for financial reward so that clients, who may be more or less dependent on this expertise, can acquire the symbolic and physical capital they desire through their purchased experiences.

The connection between guiding and economy, therefore, has a long tradition. Motivations for people as 'guides to be', who ventured into mountains in the pre-modern era were varied but usually essentially economic: chamois hunting and crystal collecting (Diemberger 1983) are two examples. When the sport of mountaineering was 'invented'

(Bernstein 1989a, Frison-Roche 1996) it was local people who had knowledge to sell. Arrangements were struck up between visitors with aspirations to climb and local 'guides' that were mutually beneficial. Social barriers between upper class sporting amateurs and working class professional guides were transcended through the 'kinship of the rope' (Meier 1976). The principle of paying to achieve the symbolic capital of mountain ascents, therefore, has a history as old as the sport itself: adventure tourism is the rational and ordered consequence of such activity.

In the nineteenth century when class distinctions were based on social position, inherited wealth and education, mountaineering was unique in the way it brought two classes together and, on the mountain, reversed the leader-dependent roles of normal social life. This observation, it has already been suggested, demonstrates a limitation of Bourdieu's (1986) theory of social distinction. Bourdieu places a high premium on class taste and distinction in his theory but he has little to say about extraordinary spaces. He mentions mountains as locations that provide opportunities for exercise and austere recreations commensurate with bourgeois taste but does not explore ways that such spaces might undermine class structures. Today, adventure tourism is exclusive only in the capacity potential clients have to pay. The extent to which such capacity relates to class remains a point of ambivalence. Class distinctions no longer operate in the way they did in the nineteenth century. Wealth defines one's capacity to accumulate symbolic capital, and, because of the investment equation implicit in any such arrangements, guides, and the companies they might work for, are under more pressure than ever before to deliver the experience. One guide used the following examples to illustrate the tension that can be generated when a 'tourist-client', from close to one end of my continuum, has money but limited mountaineering experience. Here the client has not fully grasped the script, which, as an experienced actor-mountaineer knows, can not always produce the desired outcome at the time it is desired. Tim the guide explains:

> When a client is paying to achieve a specific aim in the mountains, and the weather is good, they never experience the down side of the mountains - like bad weather - that prevents you getting up. So they don't appreciate it in the same way we do. They have no real experience as a yardstick. They don't understand why you can't just go and do anything in the mountains.

'Knowing' about what can be 'done in the mountains' is a reflection of experience and, therefore, part of the cultural capital integral to 'being a mountaineer'. Sometimes, as Tim observes, social pressure for mountaineering achievement may not match the aspirations of the client. Again, the guide takes the position that demonstrates an understanding of a script that requires close relationships between experience, aspirations and challenge. Tim goes on to provide some further insights that include the way gender differences might emerge:

> The year before we had three very different characters on the Picos trip...And then there was the couple from Cleveland who were almost disillusioned from the word go. The lady said to me that she would rather be trekking in the Himalayas but that he'd forced her to come on this climbing trip. It went downhill from there for them and spiralled down for me too. Because his wife was having a bad time the chap started having a bad time. I think to begin with she was quite frightened. She hadn't yet decided if climbing was for her and the Naranjo trip is clearly for climbers.

Part of the expertise of guides requires operating the softer skills of dealing with emotions generated by the mountain setting, particularly among those clients who lack existing experience. Clients bring degrees of dependency to the mountains. In the example above the woman referred to appears to have made the wrong choice about the holiday, illustrating that there are limits to what may be achievable through client dependency. This is an example of the different level of responsibility a mountain guide has in comparison to a tour guide – client 'well being' (physically, mentally and emotionally) is paramount. This female client was moved into a frame (climbing) of which she had limited experience. Client 'dependency' therefore becomes an important element of 'freedom' in the mountains. Conversations with two guides from an Exodus holiday suggested that some clients were 'good' and some were 'bad'. Henry said:

> Some groups gel and some don't.

John said:

All groups are hard work. You have to be a leader all the time, in the mountains and in the bar. You are there to answer questions and to guide, that's what they want.

Henry tried to give himself a break from a group he worked with as an employee of Exodus by suggesting that, as a gentler alternative to a big mountain day, the group could walk a sign-posted valley walk of the 'nature trail' variety. But, apparently, the group refused to do this without their guide even though there was no technical difficulty to such an undertaking in the perception of the guide. Jim drew the following conclusion from this:

It's as if they have paid for a service and they expect value for money.

My interpretation of this example is that the Exodus clients are operating within the boundaries of a script that they have not yet fully grasped and were, therefore, still dependent upon their guides to act it out.

Guides are mountaineers who, because of their position of trust and responsibility to their clients, are obliged to operate in a legislative capacity (Bauman 1987). Guides, then, are in a position to influence the behaviour of clients through writing and directing 'scripts'. This happens in a number of ways. First, there are contributions to articles in the magazines, video representations and brochure design. Guides take photographs for example, and the best of these, in the sense of conveying a feeling for the sublime or aesthetically pleasing projections of wildness, appear in brochures and at company slide show presentations. Bennet's guide to the Munros (1985) is a good example, as are the series of climbing and walking books edited by Ken Wilson (1974, 1978a, 1978b) and discussed in the previous chapter. Second, again as the previous chapter has shown, a form of control over clientele is exerted through setting up grading criteria for walks, treks, climbs and expeditions. Third, out in the mountains, guides direct operations. The guide is thus both choreographer, or script writer, and stage director, controlling the mountain experience by selecting where to walk, when to stop to admire the view and how the group are positioned on and off the rope. The role of the guide is closely related to the performance necessary for gaining recognition as a mountaineer. To pursue such a line of analysis demonstrates the limitations of the 'enclavic-heterogeneous' model when it is applied to mountain spaces. Mountains are, in theory, wild and undeveloped areas of rugged terrain full of objective elemental dangers created by volatile weather, distant from civilisation and requiring skill and experience to explore. Heterogeneous space demands unbounded or improvised performances (Edensor 2000). However, my argument suggests that, in mountains, because of these objective variables, a limit can be reached. Thus, some clients are likely to become more dependent and be forced consciously to adhere to the script and performance because their safety, and ultimately, therefore, their pleasure, (that is what they take from the experience) depends upon it. In other words, clients have less, not more opportunity, to improvise on a *mountain* stage. The next section explores ways that scripts are written and the performance choreographed by mountain guides. The aim here is to explore the legislative position of guides, particularly the 'rules' that they enforce, and client responses to assess their level of adherence to rules, resistance and / or improvisation within this 'production'.

8.4 Writing Scripts & Directing Performances

To begin with, guides are instrumental in directing clients towards mountaineering objectives. Tim (the guide) suggests that:

People are looking for new experiences and new places to go. We are finding those places and bringing the two together.

When asked whether clients were directed in their choices by his recommendations and FMA's brochure, he replied:

I think it's largely our recommendation, I don't think the brochure yet adequately reflects what we can do. We are learning as we go along but I think it's fair to say that most people have come because I've suggested the idea to them. But I think it fits the bill for what they have described they want to do. Tom more so than Hugh wanted to do a long rock route somewhere and his enthusiasm rubbed off on Hugh – that's why they went [on the Picos de Europa course]. On the Cuillin trip, Tom connected with us through the brochure because it was something he wanted to do. Anthony came, I believe, because I'd spoken to him about the Cuillin and Leanne came because she knew me...The first contact is with me, the website or the brochure. Second is gathering information by measuring themselves against the things we are describing.

So, clients book a place on the course / holiday of their choice following an initial contact with the company by telephone, fax or e-mail. It is Tim who, in this example, 'suggested the idea to them'. This is the guide promoting the symbolic value of certain places. Unless the clients have undertaken a course with that company before, which many have, the initial gathering of a group, at a car park or hostel, is the first time that clients meet the guide(s). Thus, relationships start between guides and clients, and between the clients themselves, based on ongoing dramatic interchanges. Such social intercourse is not without social risks, particularly as the stage moves from the controllable familiarity of hostel and pub to the activity zone of the mountains. Vaughn, a client, had this to say when the group for the second Skye course first gathered:

> There are great social risks involved in coming on a trip like this, you might not get on and there might be some 'mardy buggers'. On a trip to the mountains like this, at some point over the week you're going to fall over on your bum and look silly; you've got to accept that.

Such potential for dramatic failings is tacit acceptance of the existence of a script. Thus, for most clients, there is little attempt to 'blow one's trumpet', as Vaughn would say, because it is generally recognised that to do so, particularly from the relative safety of the pub or hostel, could be setting oneself up for a fall, or 'looking silly'. A process of social constraint was thus observed to be operating even in the liminal zones peripheral to the main stage of the mountains themselves. The strategy I most commonly observed operating at the initial gatherings of clients for a trip was summarised in my field notes as 'hedging one's bets' or 'say little – nod and smile lots'. I noted such mannerisms had emerged from guides such as Tim, Chris, Henry and John and were practised by clients who had some experiences of mountains and, therefore, had grasped nuances of the script. Alternatively, inexperienced clients rarely presented any evidence to suggest they might know what they were doing – a strategy that suggested an awareness of Vaughn's point concerning 'looking silly'. Lee, for example, told us he was on the Skye trip because he was dared by his brother Robert to challenge his fear of heights. But Lee made no pretensions of being a mountaineer despite having some hill walking experience. Instead he said:

Being a footballer I am OK for the first ninety minutes of the day and then I'm expecting the final whistle. Unfortunately we are usually still going uphill at that point.

Lee walked very well on reasonably flat ground, he was fast and balanced. He carried a plastic water bottle at all times in his hand and squirted water into his mouth like footballers do when an injury stops play. He also wore his England football shirt to the pub one night.

The existence of a script is, therefore, acknowledged and a strategic performance enacted by guides and clients. It is possible that Lee was operating an anti-distinction role to avoid any connotations of 'being a mountaineer'. His pub dress code certainly suggested a frame drawing upon alternative recreation, in this case football. Impression management is particularly important at initial gatherings when a person's behaviour is likely to 'set the scene' for the social positioning of that person as the course / holiday progresses. Guides do not need to work hard at impression management because their position is taken for granted as they are qualified professionals, and, as Vaughn has suggested, they may be allocated a revered status. Manoeuvres among clients may be subtle but are generally a reflection of the experience each may already have. When the mountaineering frame is limited, as in Lee's case, so alternative frames are utilised and transfer is likely. Lee's use of a footballer's water bottle rather than the specialist containers used by mountaineers (in which the metal 'Sigg' bottle commonly appears) may influence the use of such 'props' amongst clients (and perhaps guides) in the future. However, Lee was not 'allowed' to wear his football shirt in the mountains as nylon has poor insulation and limited 'breathability'. Similarly, by using his water-bottle regularly Lee was only conforming to the 'drink little and often' rule set out by the guides. Such rules are enforced by guides and are part of the legislation process (Bauman 1987).

The guide, it is suggested, becomes a choreographer, stage manager and a director. The client's investment is accommodated by the roles the guide performs. These include safety officer (kit checks), entertainer (Tim's handstand on top of the Inaccessible Pinnacle is an example), entrepreneur (giving value for money and touting for new business) and teacher (how to be a mountaineer). Early guiding was something of a shared adventure between guide and clients. That idea remains central to adventure tourism today. However, the script of 'being a mountaineer' requires adherence to certain rational forms of behaviour. A blanket of 'safe practice' operates which generates rules. Adherence to these rules is paramount and people are warned of the consequences of not doing so when deaths are reported in the media[46]. The mountaineer's script is strongly influenced by this safety agenda which serves a purpose of investing guides with a powerful rationale to support their actions in directing clients. It also, in turn, limits opportunities for other interpretations of a setting. To take an extreme example, a client would not be allowed to wander into the mountains carrying a suitcase.

In mountains, guides choreograph the detail of each adventure by, for example, selecting where to walk, when to stop to admire the view, how the group are positioned, how to walk and conserve energy and how to move around obstacles. A guide must set a pace that is sustainable for a long period of time, and, therefore, will usually lead from the front at the beginning of the day when the route will almost certainly be uphill to some extent. In most mountains leaving the valley at the start of the day usually means following a path of some description. A guide will follow the easiest line up a slope, perhaps zig-zagging to find grass amidst scree slopes, walking round marshy sections and stopping at places that command good views or interesting focal points as in rock formations or the first sight of the objective of the day. An example occurred on a walk to Coire na Banachdich on Skye. The walk passes a hidden valley called Eas Mor. Although not far from the main valley this gorge-like feature is notable for a steep waterfall that empties into the upper end and a range of vegetation, including deciduous trees, that cling to its steep walls. One client, Anthony, a forester by profession, became very animated, and several others reached for their cameras. Leanne said it was *"beautiful, beautiful, beautiful"* and Jim likened the scene to Rider-Haggard's 'Lost World', illustrating the point that we make sense of our empirical experiences through frames of reference. Photographic activity is usually frenzied at such places and at such times. This did happen as I watched, but the opportunity has been created by the guide through route choice and 'allowing' the stop.

---

[46] A recent example has been reported in The Observer by David Rose (2001:24). In his editorial entitled 'A rock and a hard place' he draws upon two recent adventure tourism deaths, one on Mount Kinabalu in Borneo and the other on a small crag in South Africa. In both cases teenage girls were being 'guided' in their respective activities when the accidents happened. Rose draws upon opinion from Mike Rosser (of the Mountain Leader Training Board) and Doug Scott (famous mountaineer and director of his own trekking company) to suggest safety standards are too lax because people 'fast track' established mountaineering protocol. Scott says: "but there is a real danger that people just aren't serving what used to be regarded as a normal apprenticeship".

Possibly the best example of a guide using local knowledge to maximise the spectacular impact of a mountain occurred on the walk into Naranjo de Bulnes in the Picos de Europa. The walk began so early that it was still pitch black, a fact that disguised details of the landscape obvious by day. The leading guide, Tim, stayed in front and would not allow any stops, despite several clients finding the going very tough, until finally, coming round a corner just as dawn was breaking, he said: *"we can rest here for a few minutes"*. Above, bathed blood red in the early morning sun was the mountain. It looked steep and formidable. Out came the cameras. This particular sight and moment was referred to, without solicitation, by all four clients in subsequent interviews. Tom, for example, added:

> And I hadn't realised what a spectacular and beautiful valley we had approached the mountain through until we walked back down again in daylight.

So, one rule is to follow the guide who knows the safest route in hazardous terrain. Guides can find their way in the dark, taking clients into the adventure of a perceived unknown through their unique grasp of where to go. It is part of the guide's job to point out spectacular views. Setting up an extraordinary aesthetic experience, like sunrise over the mountains, can be consciously accomplished by the guide insisting on a pace that will enable arrival at a certain point for that particular experience. Framing of the visual in this way supports a romantic view of mountains. Taking one's own photographs as a record of the real experience is likely to conform to the visual composition of unity of form and composition set out in books magazines and brochures. The picture of Naranjo de Bulnes as viewed by the group that morning appears in the FMA brochure. Tim directed the route ostensibly for safety purposes but movement was specifiable and timing important to provide space for contemplation. The performance of the guide does try to communicate meaning and identity dependent on the audience understanding the social message. The mountain is a stage for the rehearsal of performances of patterns of locomotion derived from following and observing the guide. It also involves witnessing and capturing first hand the aesthetic experience rehearsed second hand through brochures and other media.

Tourist-clients who follow unquestioningly do replicate patterns of behaviour and language that guides exhibit. But, they do so in a reactive way because it is required for the situation they are in. Clients who want to learn and progress across the continuum as mountaineers are more proactive in their interaction with guides and actually imitate more closely guides' behaviours. To illustrate this difference, Jim said, after he had been untied from the rope:

> I hope you're not expecting me to re-tie that knot.

Jim did not see himself as a climber but Anthony, who has some climbing experience, clearly wanted to further this. Anthony was prepared to tie himself into his harness provided it was checked by the guide. Further along the continuum, Dave, who did see himself as a climber, not only tied himself in to his harness but was also prepared to discuss the merits of different ways of tying in with me.

Working from the premise that to understand and perform the rules is a 'statement' of cultural capital, distinction will emerge for those clients who most closely replicate the guide's script. For some clients, their desire to deploy their cultural capital in ways showing distinction was shown by a conscious replication of the behaviour of a guide. But more importantly, because those who have physical co-ordination, balance and poise appear to move more effortlessly through mountainous country than others, positions such as 'aspirant mountaineer' become socially acceptable. Moreover, part of this is expressed in a desire to 'look the part' and therefore, as chapter six has shown, the clothing and equipment used by guides, who are by definition mountaineers, become an important reference point. This is one reason why famous guides can gain lucrative sponsorship deals with equipment manufacturers. Following guides through the nuances of their performances is a way of 'becoming' a mountaineer. There are many ways of following the guides, and hence gaining social status, that I noted operating in the field. Examples include, telling anecdotes about trekking and climbing experiences at home and abroad; sitting in the front of the minibus with the guides or sitting at the 'instructors' table in the centre; buying drinks for guides; organising personal mountain routes on the recommendations of guides, (assuming that you haven't already done the route, if you have then your status is assured) and taking on specific responsibilities such as carrying some group emergency kit or carrying and uncoiling the rope when it is needed.

The following example illustrates the point about replicating behaviour. Peter, a young male client from the Lake District course, was enthusiastic and keen to impress. In more reflective times the group walked without talking. At these times Peter would often take a tangent, as if locating himself outside the group. Peter had clearly learnt elements of the script such as postures, gestures, group positioning and language and was experimenting with these. In the course of an hour he had enthusiastically drawn attention to, caterpillars (twice), fungi (three times), and several soaring birds. He alternated between animated excitement (for example finding some ruined huts that were marked on the map) and being aloof, 'cool' and detached, with a far off look in his eye. Additionally, although he may have learnt such behaviour from any one of the guides he had been with over the week, or any significant other in the mountains, he did two things in direct imitation of me. First, he took every opportunity to take up a position at the rear of the group, a position that I was increasingly occupying because the visibility had improved thus 'becoming the guide' through positioning. Second, he began to walk with his hands in his pockets, something that I do because it keeps my hands warm, it 'locates' my hands when walking and, because I have always done this, it has become part of my own mountaineering habitus. Peter had not walked with his hands in his pockets at the beginning of the course. It is likely that I discovered this 'style' many years ago when I was, like Peter, experimenting with different ways of being seen to be a mountaineer. Peter was not leading the group but he was putting in a credible performance of 'aspirant mountaineer'.

So the role of the guide as choreographer comes down to minute detail of being a leader or a follower or taking up a position at the back of the walking party. Group positioning is one point. Another is attitude, gaining autonomy in decision-making or not, learning the confidence to lead a route, to wean oneself to independence from the guide, by imitating his or her behaviour and picking up his or her expert knowledge. Further, beyond dress and equipment, posture and gesture can signify 'credible and knowledgeable mountaineer'. Mountaineering guides have characteristically been the ones who have written guidebooks. These in turn set out scripts. These may be interpreted by clients in ways unintended by the position adopted by established mountaineers. Far from this context offering opportunities for "more amorphous and open-ended" performances (Edensor 1998:66), there is an agenda linked to the traditional apprenticeship system of becoming a credible mountaineer. So, mountaineering performances in an adventure tourist context are imitative for some clients who emulate the guide: a broad, take all weathers and conditions learning experience. Others do not want to acknowledge or do not realise that mountaineering has a seriousness which is much deeper than for pleasure. These latter clients are the tourists, from the guides' perspective. The playfulness of a self-conscious "negotiated form of tourism" (Edensor 1998:66) which parodies the role of the tourist appears to have no place on a mountaineering stage directed by guides. However, although clients wedded to the idea of becoming a guide themselves have little room to manoeuvre, the 'dependency factor' of clients on guides continues to be an important aspect of adventure tourism. This means that those clients who are inexperienced, and, therefore, highly dependent, and who actively promote a non-mountaineering position (Lee the footballer for example) paradoxically have greater opportunities to interpret the scripts through their own frames. Nevertheless, in contrast to other tourist guiding scenarios a tacit purpose of the mountain guide's performance is a didactic one constrained through the rules of mountaineering.

The Lake District course provided some interesting data, partly because the group was big and there were four guides, and partly because the weather was not good and this tested the resolve of guides and clients alike. One aim of this course was to improve clients' mountain navigation and rope-work skills. The role(s) of the guide are well illustrated by the following description. The evening before rock scrambling skills were to be taught was taken up with an indoor rope-work session. I organised and delivered this session and became very conscious of my teaching role. I felt like a magician, as I drew gasps from the audience with slick demonstrations of rope coiling and knot tying. The intention was to demonstrate some simple techniques involving the rope which are useful in certain situations in the mountains. This aim was achieved but I was aware that the performance also gave my credentials a public airing. The rope is a symbol of the mountaineer. The following morning, when sorting out kit for the scrambling day Peter strapped the rope to his rucksack, the action first described in chapter three. This was not an act negotiated with others in the group. To Peter, the hardship of carrying the extra weight up the mountain was obviously outweighed by the symbolic identification with the status of mountaineer. Improvisation of performance (Edensor 1998) in this context is experimentation with the script written by the guide.

The didactic nature of the lead actor's role operates at two levels. At one level, clients have to be able to perform simple tasks in order to complete routes. Thus, the guide will teach a client to keep his heels down when walking up steep ground because this takes the strain off the calf muscles and so preserves energy, an important requirement in the unpredictable mountains. Or, the guide will make sure that a client knows how to adjust the strapping systems of modern rucksacks for the most comfortable and efficient use of this piece of equipment. Energy preservation and comfort can make an important contribution to the successful completion of a route. At another level, however, the guide can teach skills that are transferable to non-guided mountain recreation. The correct way to use and tie into a harness is an example, as is an understanding of appropriate mountaineering footwear. The intricacies of foot and finger work on rock climbs is another. How to use a map and compass is yet another example. Some clients will be content to let the guide tie them in and to do the navigation, however experienced they are. Some will want to progress in their own level of skill by learning from the guide and putting this into practice. Practical engagement with mountains demands the use of certain practical skills. It is part of the guide's role to teach these. There is, therefore, an educational element to mountain recreation. The 'lessons' are not formal as they are in schools but the mountain does become a 'classroom' from this perspective and the guide a teacher. A further example of this is moving over rocky ground. In the valley this is not usually a problem although the guide will probably find the best route, meaning the most efficient in terms of time and energy expenditure. However, in positions of exposure the mind controls motility in different ways, usually, in the inexperienced, by increasing the level of conscious movement. Conscious of the exposure, fear makes movements become awkward and jittery, security is felt to be found close to the rock. A nervous client, Brendan, was told to: "*stop making love to the rock*" by one of the 'aspirant-mountaineer' clients, Vaughn, on a section of the ridge to the summit of Sgurr nan Gillean on Skye. Here Vaughn is articulating a 'safe practice' procedure probably absorbed from the didactic role of the guide. However, the more subconscious and habitual movements of experienced mountaineers, particularly guides but also some clients, may create a real gap between experienced and inexperienced performers. Another client, Michael from the Lake District course, talking of a course in Snowdonia, recounts how he was left to his own devices to scramble nervously round:

A huge boulder in a precarious and exposed place by a guide who simply did not see this feature as an impediment to progress!

Goffman's (1959) work suggests that it is common for actors to work together. Guides often work in small teams, and do discuss their clients' performances. Such dialogues commonly occur towards the end of mountain days. One such sharing of observations occurred as Tim and myself descended the well worn path to the Sligachen hotel on Skye well behind the clients who were racing ahead to reach the bar. For a short while we had a rare opportunity to take a backstage (Goffman 1959) position in that performance in front of our clients was dropped. But the role of guide is not entirely relinquished. The day's objectives, the summits of two Munros reached via some exposed rocky passages high on each mountain, had been achieved. As the first mountain day on this particular course, tourist performance (Edensor 1998) had been a useful indicator of the clients' capacity to achieve comparable objectives over the following days. The more experienced clients moved with a sense of rhythm and did not appear to be put out by some of the exposed positions. This sense of composure in exposed positions is an important part of the script. Clients such as Bruce, Vaughn and to a certain extent Anthony (who was on his second Cuillin course and had 'learnt' a great deal from his experiences on this particular ridge first time round) demonstrated composure. They did this by contrasting their stance and motility to the performances of Robert, Lee and Brendan, for example, all of whom looked far from composed at times. The case of these less experienced clients was discussed in detail. Tim explained how he had found Brendan, *"sprawled on the rock like a jelly"* despite suggestions, and demonstrations, that it is safer and more efficient to walk or climb as upright as possible keeping weight over the feet. This may have been what Brendan knew he was supposed to do but he clearly *felt* much safer with as much of his body in contact with the rock as possible. I concurred with this, and explained that I had had a similar experience with Lee. Tim went on to say, of Brendan:

> He was a liability because his technique was bad but this didn't stop him jumping and lunging for holds. He took a lot of controlling, particularly where the holds aren't big anyway - he's a very big man, and he was leaping around like a man possessed. He was very keen to get to the top.

In these examples the guide is teaching the client because it will make the ascent safer for them both. Brendan was using the 'safety net' of being guided as a way of exploring the 'edge' of what he felt he was capable of doing.

8.5 Guides at Work.

Once the group is assembled part of the first meeting will be about details of what to expect on the course they have opted for. There will, therefore, always be a briefing of some kind to discuss practicalities for the day or days ahead. At this gathering details of kit will be checked and, if appropriate and possible, sometimes basic skills will be taught to help matters as the course progresses. It is the guide that makes the decisions about what to take and how to use certain kit. Clients are also advised what food to carry and how much water to drink. This occurs at the beginning of activity in the mountains and assumptions are made that initial guidance given via kit lists issued at the time of booking will be adhered to. Chris and Dave, my two clients for the ascent of Naranjo de Bulnes, knew the basics of what to carry for this climb, although Chris still managed *"to carry spare underpants and socks up the route by mistake, and I didn't carry enough water"*. Tom and Hugh, who were being guided by Tim on the ascent, were ignorant of almost anything to do with kit. Hugh said: *"I had thought that the climb would be close to the car park so I would have brought my suitcase if Tim hadn't given me a rucksack"*. At the hotel in Arenas de Cabrales Tim made a thorough investigation of Tom and Hugh's rucksacks in the early hours before setting off for the drive up the valley to walk in to the mountain, an event first mentioned in chapter six. Dave and Chris, in contrast, had both purchased all-terrain shoes for the walk-in and knew this was the only footwear they would need in the mountains except for their specialist rock shoes.

There is also an opportunity for a guide to demonstrate a technical knowledge and expertise. Two days after our initial ascent of Naranjo de Bulnes, Tim, the guide, had completed an ascent of Merciana a route up the impressive west face of the mountain and he shared details of this with two American climbers who were about to attempt the route. The technical detail was considerable, and the audience was attentive in the way a group might listen to a master story-teller. When describing the passage up a steep and featureless wall, the crux of the climb, Tim held up a small number one wire stopper and explained how he had slid the 'nut' up the wire to create a loop at both ends, hooked the top end over a 'copperhead'[47], clipped a sling to the lower loop and carefully stood in the sling to make upward progress to the next holds. Tim's audience was impressed and all eyes were focussed on the pieces of equipment used to illustrate the narrative. As Tim swung round to point at the mountain, the eyes followed Tim's. One of the audience picked up the small wire and practised sliding the tiny nut up and down whilst looking up at the section of the climb where Tim had suggested the technique was required. The guide at work here is acting out the role of teacher and, more broadly, entertainer, complete with props.

Having briefed the clients about what to wear, what to carry and about the objectives for the day and how the logistics might unfold given the prevalent weather conditions, guide and clients emerge from the bothy, hostel or car and begin the day in the mountains. Here, the role of guide transforms from words to action. The guide becomes the director of operations. Leanne said to Tim:

> I wouldn't hire a female guide because she wouldn't have the strength to haul me over the tricky bits if it was necessary.

Tim's response to this defended female mountain guides and he went on to say:

> The whole skill of guiding clients in the mountains is to use route choice and rope-work in ways that hopefully eliminate the need to haul anyone up anything. Skill and experience are always more important than strength.

Thus, 'skill and experience' are points of distinction for guides. The implication here is that anyone can have or gain 'strength' (for example by going regularly to a gym), but not everyone has the expertise to ascend tricky mountain terrain. The guide's performance therefore appears to exude confidence based on good route choice and sensible use of 'tools' such as rope and carabiners: the performance is consistent and professional

---

[47] Nuts, wires and copperheads are all specialist pieces of mountaineering hardwear. Mountaineering manuals readily describe such equipment although to have experience of using them is a mark of distinction.

because if it were otherwise a guide would get no business. Danny for example through his work as a guide for Wilderness Expertise said:

> You need to portray a professional image. Impressions are important so a guide must look the part in order to inspire confidence.

Thus, part of the work of the guide is giving clients satisfaction for money. Part of client expectation is of being looked after. However, the commercial characteristics of adventure tourism will contribute to the construction of 'value' in mountaineering so that symbolic capital may become re-defined around criteria drawn from clients at the 'tourist' end of my continuum. The following section examines the relationship between guides, clients and the business of adventure tourism.

Guides use business terminology concerning profit margins, cutting edge technology and forms of advertising. Thus, the Picos de Europa mountains are described in the FMA brochure (2000) in terms of their value to adventure tourism. Tim, the guide, summarises:

> The Picos is still a developing area for the British. High and Climber have both run articles on it. People have gone there either through word of mouth, or from me, or from the kind of things we write about it in the brochure: we are advertising Naranjo de Bulnes. I think the way it will go in the future is four times at the beginning of the season and twice at the end, June and September. And in this way Naranjo and that area will become a goal that people go and do with FMA. Exodus have doubled the number of people they take walking there. This indicates a lot of growth already.

Here the entrepreneurial side of guiding work comes to the surface and the guide has a chance to use his knowledge of the mountains to sustain business opportunities, and even to 'develop' these before other companies do likewise in this area. The Picos is 'a developing area' and, given the right level of promotion 'Naranjo...will become a goal that people go and do'. They will want to climb it because it looks precipitous and spectacular and fits the idealised shape of a mountain. Hugh, a tourist-client said that he would have taken a helicopter to the foot of Naranjo. I asked Tim if he was tempted by such short cuts and he said:

Currently no. The walk in and self sufficiency is part of the experience. I actually like the effort involved. It's a journey and, providing you've got the time to do it, it will have its pay-offs. The sights, the views, doing it self sufficiently. Having said that, if I was a local guide and someone offered me a lift because I was doing it everyday I'd probably take it. But for Hugh and Tom and people who are out there for the first time, I think it's a lovely walk with superb views and it builds you up for the ascent.

Tim is careful to convey the right responses here; the 'pay-offs' are seen in the physical capital created by the walk in and the heightened aesthetic awareness such a walk stimulates as it 'is a lovely walk with superb views'. He is also concerned to be seen to be giving a holistic experience as close to the approach he would use as a mountaineer. Helicopters are not in the code and the walk in 'builds you up for the ascent'. He is aware that the clients want to climb the mountain but they also want to 'be mountaineers', at least for the period of the holiday. This is why Hugh so candidly said that he did not enjoy the walk up to the hut but he did "enjoy being among like minded people once we were up there". There is no helicopter ride to the foot of the mountain available so everyone in and around the hut had had to walk up there, and Hugh had shared that experience. There may be a tension generated between mountaineer and businessman. However, Tim is absolutely clear about why his clients are employing him:

> I think that the reason they are buying in to the experience is that they want to be organised by someone. If they researched the trip, trained, planned it, made the contacts and sorted out travel for themselves then they wouldn't come to FMA, they'd go by themselves. What they need is some indication of when they should be getting up, what they should pack and what they should do in order to get to the top. I had to take a pair of leather casual shoes out of Hugh's rucksack for example. It's our job to get that balance right, so that it is happening in the background without being too up-front. Because if you are going to take a military approach to it then it wouldn't be a holiday. But it needs to be sufficiently thought through and controlled that the background activity is maximising a client's chances of achieving the objective. And having a good time along the way. But they've got the ultimate call: they can say 'this is too fast' or 'I want to slow down' or 'I'm not enjoying this route I want to ab[48] off' or 'I can push myself more than this, let's go on a harder route. A lot of people today are working very hard and putting in long hours. Living in

---

[48] Climbing slang for abseil, that is, to retreat off a mountain by sliding down and then recovering one's doubled ropes. Abseils are technical manoeuvres requiring skill and knowledge. Mountaineers generally understand abseiling to be more dangerous than climbing itself. As an adventure activity it has been lifted from its mountaineering context and deployed as an end in itself by some adventure tourist companies and activity centres.

London, say, people don't have time to join a mountaineering club or to go out and gain mountain skills. So they short circuit it and go straight in with people who have been around the mountains a bit and know what's out there to be done.

The guide's position is clearly set out here through Tim's articulation of his business or work. The language of the market place emerges very strongly as clients are 'buying' in to an experience. Client 'needs' are assumed to be the responsibility of the guide, these being to 'match' objective to client and to sustain a 'holiday' atmosphere. The 'needs' however, must be 'thought through and controlled' to maximise enjoyment. Needs, then, are socially constructed from the guide's legislative position. The desire to achieve the symbolic capital of a successful ascent facilitates a 'short circuit' of traditional approaches to mountaineering. The notion of an apprenticeship leading a novice towards greater independence and, therefore, greater 'freedom' is challenged as clients do not construct their own needs in the first instance. For some clients, Lee and Hugh are examples, their inexperience leaves them unaffected by a desire to progress towards greater freedom and independent activity in the mountains. For others, such as Paul, there is an awareness of the potential tension that exists between 'freedom' and constraint and the implications this may have for identity and distinction. Paul, who has taken adventure holidays with Exodus and HKE and JG, has also clearly thought through why, as a client, he is prepared to buy adventure tourist holidays. Paul said:

> Unlike a few years ago I now have the earning power not to worry so much about the difference in cost between someone else organising it and me. I'm paying to avoid the hassle factor. Also, HK, from my own experience and from talking to others that have travelled with them, have a deserved reputation for safety and quality. There is also a social aspect and, not having to look after myself the whole time I am there - where am I going to sleep tonight? If there isn't room then where will I go instead?, -that sort of thing. Not having to worry about such things makes it more of a holiday. And I am with kindred spirits. I do use organised trips to do things I wouldn't do myself, like climbing Nelion and Batian on Mount Kenya. But also I find it harder to come to terms with the danger imposed by visiting places that are dangerous for social, economic or political reasons. To be in a group and to be looked after by local guides and agents takes some of these concerns away.

The capital exchange equation is emphasised by Paul's 'earning power'. By paying to avoid the 'hassle factor' Paul is maximising his 'investment'. He clearly sees a benefit in 'safety' through the others taking responsibility, particularly in places that are 'dangerous for social, economic or political reasons', but he links this idea to 'quality'. There is a tacit acknowledgement here that the guides know what 'quality' is. So, for Paul, the adventure holiday may be about greater enjoyment because other people take on the more onerous aspects of the experience, but it simultaneously accepts the constraints of fixed itineraries and, therefore, the construction of 'needs'. The investment trade-off for Paul is that he can 'use organised trips to do things I wouldn't do myself'. He cites the example of climbing Mount Kenya, a mountain conveying considerable symbolic capital.

Viewed from this perspective the opportunities presented through adventure tourism in mountains purport to offer 'freedom' but actually constrain. Moreover, the stronger the link between economic capital invested and the 'ease' of achieving symbolic capital in mountaineering, the more rigidly socially constrained people are likely to become in their 'choice' of objectives. Paul's stock of cultural capital in mountaineering is far from insignificant, yet there seems to be an acceptance, at least tacitly, of the investment equation discussed above. Paul points out that 'packages' are more readily available now than in the past. Also, he has gained a lot of experience as an independent traveller and met a lot of people in the mountains, particularly the Alps. He refers to these as 'kindred spirits' and expects the people he will travel with on an adventure tourist package to be the same. Understanding the mechanisms that 'short circuit' the accumulation of mountaineering capital does not seem to alter the sense of identity suggested among his 'kindred spirits'. However, the significance of the cultural capital of mountaineering is its deployment to engender distinction. Adventure tourism appears to have emphasised successful completion of a climb or walk, that is the achievement, at the expense of the quality of the experience. It is the style or mode of ascent that has been thought to be an expression of freedom that is being compromised. It is not the element of competition within the field that is new, competition has always existed in establishing distinction, but the subtle changing emphasis towards a more general acceptance of the value of 'conquering' the mountain as being greater than how it was 'conquered'. Such a line of analysis is consistent with the suggestion that adventure tourism has made the boundaries of the field of mountaineering more porous because the 'distinction' emerging from accumulating cultural capital may be used to establish status outside the field. If this is the case then the value a mountain may have must be generally accessible and understood and this, in turn, means greater constraint upon which mountains to climb.

However, such an argument does not give credit to the outcomes of the work guides undertake to create an identity of mountaineer for their clients. The point is that clients do indeed assume the identity of mountaineer, partly because they have to in order to perform mountaineering activities and partly because that is a requirement of being in the field – it is legislated for. Moreover, the market mechanisms that operate to create commodities out of mountains are ongoing. One result of this is that competition between adventure holiday companies will mean that new mountain areas will be opened up. For example, the war in Afghanistan, fought in the autumn of 2001 and into 2002, politically destabilised substantial areas of the Himalayan and Karakoram mountains. JG and many other companies responded to the reduced bookings in this part of Asia by opening up 'new' possibilities in the Andes of South America. Choices continue to become available to climb and trek all over the world. It is now easier to exchange economic capital for symbolic capital leading to cultural capital, to use Paul's phrase, 'to do things I couldn't do by myself', that is, to move beyond the ordinary. To be a mountaineer is partly about living close to 'the edge' and clients across the continuum from 'tourist' to 'aspirant-mountaineer' do so every time they go in to mountains. The idea of 'edgework' has been theorised by Stephen Lyng (1990) and it is this concept that can usefully contribute to further understanding 'being a mountaineer' in the context of adventure tourism.

8.6 Performance as Edgework

It has been suggested that mountaineering has espoused Romantic values because these have a central concern with re-discovering a more 'natural' way of life, including the sense of community generated through 'being with mountaineers'. Mountaineering offers the possibilities of Rojek's (2000:172) "symbolic continuity in fixed horizons and stable spaces". Finlay (2001:15) suggests that walking and climbing endeavour re-create a sense of community lost in an increasingly secular world. Writing of the contributions to his anthology of literature made by mountaineer-authors he says:

> Mountains are implacable realities and powerful motifs. From Ben Lawers to Hozomeen or Mount Analogue, they are our most enduring images of completeness. It will come as no surprise that many of the contributions to this anthology echo the Romantic tradition, portraying the individual in extremis. Less widely noted by critics of this literature is the underlying sense of community

concealed within much writing about mountains. There is perhaps a nostalgia at work here, deriving from an archetypal memory of a mountain dwelling people...The climbing fraternity can be seen as a latterday reflection of this community – a clannish brotherhood, adapted to the austerities of the wilderness and bonded by a sense of mutual-aid and courage in adversity. Climbing is the return to an environment that we now find alien and inhospitable.

So, according to Finlay, there is a 'nostalgia' at work here drawing upon a collective 'memory' and creating a 'clannish brotherhood' bonded by 'courage in adversity'. To engage with mountains, it is suggested, is to valorise effort in adversity and engage those more elemental aspects of being such that we come closer to 'completeness'. It has been noted in chapter five (Lewis 2000) that the 'metropolitan body' is desensitised and passive when set against the engaged and sensitised 'climbing body'. Rojek (2000) argues that desensitisation caused by civilising processes is a characteristic of city life and that 'wild leisure' is a response to such emotional constraints. He argues that wild leisure allows for physical engagement and emotional expression and can take a number of forms of which 'limit experience' and 'edgework' are examples. Limit experience is about pushing boundaries. So that when Light (1995), for example, suggests inner city disturbances following the Rodney King trial in Los Angeles lead us to think of cities as 'urban wilderness', the behaviour of the rioters might be seen as a 'normal' street culture extending its remit to an extreme. In this case limit experience crosses the boundaries of what is acceptable whereas edgework is generally located at, but within, those limits. Edgework, because it is concerned with risk taking, has a close fit with mountaineering and is the more useful of the two examples for that reason.

Stephen Lyng (1990) originated the concept of edgework as a classifying category for voluntary risk taking. He says: "activities that can be subsumed under the edgework concept...all involve a clearly observable threat to one's physical or mental well being or one's sense of an ordered existence" (1990:857). Edgeworkers engage in high risk sports such as mountaineering. Lyng (1990) suggests edgeworking is a measured response to emotional suppression. Drawing upon the work of Goffman (1959, 1971) he suggests people become more self consciously engaged in games and play that offer uncertainty of outcome and / or a sanctioned display of one's abilities. Thus, "people often seek a substitute for spontaneous action in pursuits that offer some of the phenomenological characteristics of such action" (Lyng 1990:871). He goes on to suggest edgeworkers are not typically interested in thrill seeking or gambling as they like to remain in control.

Moreover, the use of technology does not diminish the potential for edgework, rather individuals will use the situation (e.g. hot air ballooning and cave diving) to explore the outer limits of human performance through the technology (balloon design and breathing apparatus for example). Previous chapters of this study have established what it means to be a mountaineer, namely, a measured and informed approach to planning for and climbing mountains, an awareness of objective dangers and the application of experience to decision making to minimise risks such as using specially developed equipment and clothing. From this perspective mountaineers might be seen as edgeworkers. Following this argument it is likely that part of the attraction of mountains to adventure tourists is an opportunity to explore their 'edge'.

Edgework does, however, require knowledge of the activity and good judgement in order for the participant(s) to stay in control. In mountaineering as in many other high risk activities there is also a technical interface (boots, clothing and other equipment) which mediates the experience (Urry 2000, Michael 2000). But, as has been noted in chapter six, such objects are actants, whereby physical and human entities combine, and define the role the human plays in mountaineering. Using technology does not necessarily reduce the edgework characteristics of mountaineering. Tejada-Flores (1978) has shown how the use of technology changes the rules of mountaineering. To climb the highest and remotest mountains multiple technologies such as air lifts, bolts, fixed ropes and even ladders are 'allowed' but none of these can be used in the 'bouldering game' whereby the challenge is between climber and rock. To use a ladder would make climbing a boulder meaningless. As the technology improves in mountaineering so edgeworking-mountaineers can simply apply the rules of a more rigorously defined climbing 'game' to a more exacting mountaineering challenge. For example, Everest was climbed in 1953 by using a huge team of porters and climbers, fixed ropes, oxygen, ladders and a series of temporary camps were systematically established up the mountain. Subsequent ascents of Everest have applied more rules. Examples of these rules include, ascend by a different route, do not use intermediate camps, reduce the size of the climbing team and climb without using supplementary oxygen. In 1978 Reinhold Messener and Peter Habeler climbed Everest without using supplementary oxygen and in 1980 Messener re-climbed the mountain solo, without oxygen and via a new route on the north face. The rules, therefore, become important in defining what constitutes mountaineering and mountaineers, the people who set out the rules, are edgeworkers who may artificially increase risks to remain close to 'the edge'. To operate as an edgeworker, that is, to voluntarily engage with risk, requires an understanding and an acceptance of that risk – taking responsibility for one's actions in the knowledge of the potential consequences. This in turn requires an understanding of the mountaineering frame outlined in chapter two of which specialist knowledge (concerning training, planning, grading, equipment, and specialist techniques for example) and specific experience (of walking, climbing and navigation for example) are important elements. Edgeworking is more about controlled testing than thrill seeking and requires a knowledge base to operate from. Such analysis raises questions about the relationship between adventure tourism and mountaineering as edgework.

Clients buying adventure holidays may be attracted by the potential for emotional release (the adventure) but may not necessarily be mountaineers because they lack an understanding and experience of the mountaineering frame – one has to know the risks in order to appreciate that they are risks. But it does not necessarily follow that clients can not be edgeworkers. Clients who are inexperienced mountaineers might be thought of as edgeworkers because, for example, they will have made a conscious decision to undertake a mountaineering adventure holiday rather than taking a package to a Mediterranean beach resort. The very act of engaging with a performance-script-stage that they are not familiar with leaves tourist-clients in the realm of edgeworking. There are risks involved in buying mountaineering holidays. These risks are of the mountain environment, that is physical, but are also social because of the relationship between cultural capital accumulation, exchange and transfer in the field of mountaineering. Edgeworking becomes a conceptual tool for illuminating tourist-client performance in mountaineering.

Client capacity and / or inclination to absorb the characteristics of edgeworking appears to vary. The findings from my fieldwork suggest adventure tourist clients can be located (though not necessarily fixed) on a continuum from 'tourist' to 'aspirant-mountaineer'. Mountaineering is a 'broad' adventure experience (Rubens 1999) encompassing sustained endeavour (for example walking to the mountain, enduring hardship and learning appropriate skills). 'Aspirant-mountaineers' identify closely with the codes that define such endeavour. Clients who are closer to tourists appear to identify more closely with Ruben's (1999) narrow view of adventure, which emphasises thrill and excitement (in relatively concentrated bursts) at the expense of sustained endeavour. Tom illustrates adherence to this latter interpretation of mountaineering when he suggests of his ascent of Naranjo de Bulnes with FMA:

> I was quite impressed by how easy it was to get there. I enjoyed the fact that we did it so quickly. I find it an odd thing in the brochures that trips seem to take a long period of time, six to ten days say. It was much more of a challenge because we went from the valley to the summit and back down to the hut all in one long day....I've only got five weeks holiday a year...so inevitably you try and build these things around work and other commitments...in Peru in a two week period we managed to do three summits...I much prefer just getting on with it.

Tom locates himself at the 'tourist' end of the continuum by suggesting the centrality of work to his life (lawyer in London) placing his mountaineering ambitions around 'work and other commitments'. However, he also understands and articulates the 'challenge' created by the ascent, an element enhanced by going from 'the valley to the summit and back down to the hut all in one long day'. Here, then, is evidence of edgeworking in operation. The satisfaction Tom felt through his efforts was enhanced by the additional challenge of the time-scale over which the ascent took place, an idea fully understood by Tom. Dave and Chris, at the 'aspirant-mountaineer' end of the continuum, talk of their frustration of being in the city and their need for extended periods away in the mountains. These two clients do climb independently as often as they can and have both expressed a desire to gain mountaineering qualifications. They have already undertaken some preliminary training courses in mountaineering instruction. Dave even described his own tendency to speed up the intensity of his outdoor experience over short periods of time (week-end trips away in the UK for example) by sleeping outside the tent on each first night. One motivation for this behaviour was to replicate his Picos de Europa experience when we all spent time outside the hut gazing up at the stars one night. As a client's cultural capital increases, so more rules are brought into operation to sustain the edgeworking characteristics of the experience.

8.7 Summary

Client performance is strongly influenced by the legislative position, here epitomised by mountain guides. The metaphor of tourist performance has indicated the influence a guide may have at several levels of the adventure tourist industry. Mountain guides script their own performances and keep tight control of the drama on a circumscribed stage leaving little scope for improvisation. The essentially didactic nature of the guide's performance has been illustrated through the identification of rules patterning the tourist experience, namely the governing concern for safety in the choice of equipment and ways of moving. Posture and gesture are also governed by rules of display. This is related to identity because some adventure tourists begin to negotiate credibility as mountaineers. Part of this credibility comes from a capacity to correctly identify appropriate aesthetic rules within walking and climbing activities. Perhaps a greater part, however, comes through the degree of engagement with the physical demands of achieving mountaineering objectives. The analysis suggests that guides hold a powerful, perhaps hegemonic, position that works to sustain legislative agenda. The reproduction of this agenda continues through clients learning to perform like mountaineers. The challenge comes from adventure tourists who now have access to the previously select mountaineering culture. Adventure tourists by-pass, or at least fast-track the traditional mountaineering apprenticeship which has hitherto generated an ethos of independence based on self reliance. The rapid growth of adventure tourism has accelerated the process by which mountains are commodified and, thereby, given 'value' in ways that offer possibilities for identity both within and outside the field of mountaineering. Almost anyone who has determination, a reasonable degree of physical co-ordination and the right income can 'buy' into mountaineering. The more tenuous a person's connection to the field the more likely that person's 'needs' will be constrained to well known mountains. Arguably, on the one hand, this by-passes the usual introductions required by a mountaineering apprenticeship. On the other hand, the performances analysed in this chapter offer a contribution to mountaineering self reliance for those who seek it.

Chapter nine: Conclusions

The aim of this book has been to illuminate the relationship between identity, capital and social distinction in mountaineering in the context of consumer culture and adventure tourism. The originality of the study is the synthesis of tourism literature, mountaineering literature and research into adventure tourism. I started with an interest in uncovering the extent to which adventure tourism might be making it 'easier' to become a mountaineer. Drawing upon my own experience as a mountaineer, which has included an extensive time spent reading about and doing mountaineering, I was able to present my pre-fieldwork ideas as a set of claims that could be investigated. These were, that mountaineering is defined through its own tradition, that clients have to be mountaineers to some extent and that clients who buy mountain based adventure tourist holidays are socially malleable in that they relinquish independence at the expense of being guided.

Each chapter from four through to eight has added to an understanding of the relationship between identity, capital and social distinction and has utilised evidence to support the conclusions set out below. Chapter four explored cultural constructions of mountains and mountaineering. It was found that being a mountaineer involves understanding a set of rules constructed around a number of discursive strands that have been heavily influenced by the values of Romanticism. Understanding and acting upon these rules conveys cultural capital and builds a frame of reference through which people make sense of mountaineering. The extent to which a participant has grasped these rules becomes a manifestation of distinction. It was at this point that the idea of a continuum of clients first arose, although this was not fully articulated until the following chapter. Romanticism was found to be a major constituent of a mountaineering frame for clients but there is a tension between what is 'natural' and what is socially constructed. Adventure tourism enhances the 'value' of mountains that are well known, which offer opportunities for capital 'exchanges' within, but also outside the field of mountaineering. As certain mountains are popularised and 'taken over' so mountaineers have to retain distinction by generating a discourse of 'tourism' (as in the 'tourist route' of ascent) for people who are not mountaineers.

Chapter five found that being a mountaineer means following the rules of physical preparation and performance. In mountains, the adventure setting transcends ordinary habitual practices. The rules are part of the way that being a mountaineer is legislated for. It became evident, for reasons of safety, that interpretation of the rules was restricted to the non-serious spaces of mountaineering. The efficiency of the body to 'mountaineer' is a function of training and preparation. Mountaineers develop a 'mountaineering habitus' based upon body techniques that can only be fully developed through independent operation in mountains. This is partly because developing a habitual pattern of behaviour takes many years, and adventure tourism acts to concentrate time so that experiences become 'narrower'. The continuum outlined in chapter five suggests a scale of distinction from 'tourist' at the left end to 'aspirant-mountaineer' at the right end.

Chapter six found that clothing and equipment offer symbolic representations of identity as a mountaineer. Clothing in particular has become a symbol of inclusion. Knowledge of clothing and equipment, particularly when this is combined with personal ownership, conveys cultural capital. Clothing and equipment appears to contribute to the creation of social hierarchies. These are a reflection of cultural capital. Being a climber requires knowledge and understanding of harnesses, ropes and carabiners; this becomes a point of distinction between walkers and climbers for example. Image management as a part of identity construction is not straight forward. At the 'tourist' end of the continuum, the left, clients are told what to wear, and may even be lent (or hired) specialist clothing. At the 'aspirant-mountaineer' end of the continuum, the right, retaining distinction becomes more problematic because of consumer culture. Mountain clothing appears as fashion clothing in cities and, developing technologies constantly improve clothing and equipment for mountaineering, so that one can never be quite sure just how up to date one is. Buying a rucksack with a 'lifetime guarantee' may be problematic because rucksack design (and colour) does change. Retaining distinction, therefore, becomes more difficult. Conversely, wearing faded and tattered clothing that conveys a 'lived in' and comfortable image can become a point of distinction as it suggests experience as a mountaineer. Clients who are 'aspirant-mountaineers' wear their clothing and equipment more 'comfortably'. By this I mean image is not just about what one wears, it is about *how* one wears it, in other words it is about deportment, gait, posture and familiarity with the garment or equipment. Contrary to my original assumption that clothing is a facilitator that brings urban levels of comfort to mountains, which it arguably does, I have discovered that a mountaineering habitus requires body and clothing-equipment to merge. Tourist-clients might wear all the 'right' clothes and carry the 'right' equipment, but this does not make them mountaineers.

Chapter seven showed how the science of mountaineering has emerged as measuring and grading systems. Following the idea explored in chapter four, that certain mountains are given a symbolic value because of their shape, height or location, this is their distinctiveness, an important connection between mountains and commodification was explored. It was found that 'freedom' in mountains is influenced by a reduction to measurable indices. Guide-books purport to open up the 'freedom of the hills' to people interested in mountaineering but actually operate as signposts to indicate the most 'valued' objectives. Alternative forms of 'measuring' mountaineering do exist amongst clients, for example through weight loss and / or physique development, but such indices are still linked to socially constructed ideals of body shape. The result is constraint rather than freedom to be 'oneself'.

Chapter eight considered the role of the mountain guide and developed the metaphor of performance to show that clients across the continuum are subjected to legislative constraints. Having reached this point it is now possible for the discussion to offer an appraisal of the claims I made in the early chapters. First, mountaineering is defined through its tradition but this is subject to change. Attempts have been made to stabilise the tradition, through heritage centres for example, but mountaineering is fragmenting. As 'interpretations' of mountaineering emerge, being 'distinctive' becomes more difficult. Climbers, for example, are now divided into 'adventure climbers' and 'sport climbers' or 'wall climbers' and 'real climbers'. Walkers are 'non-serious' or 'serious' and may use props such as poles to suggest an identity of 'trekker'. Second, clients have to be mountaineers to 'do' mountaineering, that is, to do what I do in mountains. There is undoubtedly a strong legislative agenda of safety operating, directed by guides, which effectively moves all clients across the continuum from the left towards the right relative to their starting position. This means that clients have to perform like mountaineers in order to undertake the activities, but it does not mean that clients are mountaineers. Whilst 'aspirant-mountaineer' clients might well develop some of the body techniques of being a mountaineer, a mountaineering habitus can only be developed following a long immersion in mountains, whereby these body techniques are honed to the point of sub-conscious operation. Third, clients do relinquish independence and appear to become socially malleable. The legislative agenda of a rational, rule bound approach to mountaineering is strong, whereby 'distinction' is gauged in terms of cultural capital accumulated. However, as it has been established that clients can not be mountaineers because they opt for a context of dependence. Such a position needs a re-assessment because of the difficulties of independent operation in general.

The continuum from 'tourist' to 'aspirant' is useful because it shows the nuances that exist within adventure tourists. Most notable in this respect are those clients that appear to adopt a subordinate role and perform as 'tourists', albeit in a somewhat more demanding and dangerous setting to that of more conventional tourism. But equally important are those clients who do not see themselves as tourists, and who take umbrage at the very suggestion that they are. The continuum is not fixed. Broader changes in social access to mountaineering and the transformation of some mountain space from predominantly heterogeneous to increasingly enclavic have combined to make it more difficult to operate independently in mountains. It is evident that a client does not remain in one position on the continuum. Each client has to move across the continuum from left to right because this is the only way that clients can accomplish the objectives of their chosen holidays / courses. This progression towards 'aspirant' becomes a freedom of sorts. One of the consequences of an emerging 'industry' of adventure tourism, has been a proliferation of guides, books, brochures and companies, all of which have eroded the possibilities of genuinely exploratory and independent mountaineering. The whole continuum may well be moving from the right towards the left so that 'independent' is being re-defined. The reasons for this include the invasion of mountains by some enclavic characteristics, but a consequence of this has been to intensify mountaineering experiences so that the time required to complete an objective is often reduced and the mountain experience concentrated so it becomes less 'broad' and more 'narrow'.

It is the relationship between mountaineering and capital that is making a significant contribution towards the re-positioning of the continuum. The social practices of mountaineering have become increasingly defined by commodity production. Mountains are becoming increasingly differentiated in terms of capital. Social distinction in mountaineering is defined in relation to capital accumulated. Cultural capital resides predominantly with experienced mountaineers who operate a legislative control over people who aspire to be mountaineers. Legislators formulate and apply the rules of mountaineering in ways that align the most difficult and demanding ascents with the greatest capital. However, in doing so, they are restricting the currency of their cultural capital to the field of mountaineering. Tourist-clients are interested in the transferability of their capital to normal life. In this respect the nuances of the style of an ascent, or the details of the route itself are less important than achieving the objective. For mountaineers, ascending a mountain means physical effort without resorting to mechanical assistance, so the 'style' does matter. As mountains become more actively 'consumed' by non-mountaineers, so mountaineers have to 'retreat' into their field, because it is here that their cultural capital is recognised, and can be translated into status.

Adventure tourism costs money, and, the greater the symbolic capital invested in the mountaineering objective, then the more it is likely to cost. This is the commodification of mountaineering in operation. Countries such as Nepal contain mountains that command high 'peak fees' for access so that its mountains can make a contribution to the national economy. Adventure tourist companies pass such costs on to their clients. This, together with the requirement for companies to employ experienced and qualified professional guides to 'look after' their clients, places considerable investment pressure on clients. Clients exchange economic capital for cultural capital, particularly symbolic capital. The cost of adventure tourism in mountains is socially exclusive of those who can not afford to pay. This is not reflective of a class based distinctiveness per se, but it does strongly align adventure tourism to people who can afford to pay for it. Social distinction is, therefore, seen to be operating but not necessarily though the 'taste' of different social classes. Instead 'taste' is being overridden by market forces. These emphasise the capital element of distinction across class boundaries to create a different relationship between 'taste' and social distinction. It is possible, therefore, that the future will see a 'class' of adventure tourists who exchange economic capital for social distinction through buying the cultural capital of mountaineering.

The continuum is a useful tool if one wants to illuminate the extent to which clients might 'be' mountaineers. However, empirical data suggests the framework needs adjustment. I have argued, for example, that a mountaineering frame is essential to constructing an identity as 'mountaineer'. However, this 'measures' clients in relation to my understanding of being a mountaineer, that is, a person with significant cultural capital in mountaineering. Clients can not be mountaineers because they do not operate independently. Acquiring cultural capital opens up potential for future independent mountaineering, but not all clients want to follow that direction, that is, they like the idea of being guided because they see themselves primarily as being on holiday. However, all clients can be edgeworkers. Edgeworking offers a useful conceptual framework because adventure tourists will 'frame' their understanding of mountaineering more closely to their 'ordinary', urban experiences. By purchasing mountaineering holidays, adventure tourists are exploring the edge of their experiences.

The issue of terminology has emerged as important. From chapter three onwards I have suggested that using the term 'holiday' as a descriptor of adventure tourism in mountains does not adequately identify the social processes occurring in this setting. The term 'holiday' is rarely found in brochures and other company literature. Its substitute seems to be 'course' or 'expedition', descriptors that convey a very different set of ideas to that of holiday. A course is a learning experience and perhaps an investment for the future. An expedition is a journey with purpose. In mountaineering this will mean the traverse of a mountain range, as in an extended walk or trek, or the ascent of a specific mountain or a route on that mountain. The way the terminology is used creates a tension between freedom and constraint. Holidays are about freedom from quotidian regimes and offer opportunities to explore, relax and play. Courses are about learning skills and acquiring knowledge and experience. In this respect mountaineering is located as 'serious' leisure, a nomenclature that has connotations of 'distinction', particularly in relation to the idea of a 'course' as education. This is a finding that could be usefully further explored because, to do so might illuminate the future of mountaineering in relation to adventure tourism, or indeed as a realm of serious leisure in its own right.

A strength of my study is that I have been able to let the voice of the clients come through, and I have offered an argument to suggest mountaineering remains defined by independent endeavour in the light of such evidence. However, this study remains a small window upon the world of mountaineering. I have connected identity and capital in ways that assume everyone wants 'recognition' for who they are, or might be, given the currency of the cultural capital they have accumulated. However, there may well be lots of people who consider themselves mountaineers but who do not feel the need to publicise the fact. It is possible that, if Eric Shipton had not needed to make a living from his expeditions, he might have been such a person. But people must live, and this generally means being productive in some way. Lots of possibilities exist for future research as I have only just begun to scratch the surface of investigating mountain based adventure tourism. I have provided an analysis based on my experienced perspective of 'being a mountaineer'. The concept of edgework could be further explored as it offers a useful conceptual tool for exploring adventure tourism because it is relative to a person's experience of a setting. It thus offers the potential to explore interpretations of adventure. The concept of a field needs further investigation because it may well be that mountaineering does not exist as one field but as several overlapping fields.

Twenty-two years ago I wrote an essay based on the following quotation from Eric Shipton. I was inspired by his book 'Upon That Mountain' to become a mountaineer, but that essay, essentially a reflective account of my own existing experiences, also began a parallel journey of inquiry that has led me to this book. I have arrived at a staging post in my academic journey and the possibilities for further illumination of the world of adventure tourism in mountains are only just beginning. Shipton's words seem as relevant now as they did when I first read them and my admiration for his vision is considerable. Clients may not see their holiday choices as a 'philosophy' for life but the vision of freedom through mountaineering, which may include a freedom from material constraints, is essential to his world view. Mountains are stable and enduring and, to explore them is to experience adventure. Adventure offers emotional engagement and, in turn, contrasts the desensitising proclivity of city life. This is Shipton's (1944:221-222) vision:

> He is lucky who, in the full tide of life, has experienced a measure of the active environment that he most desires. In these days of upheaval and violent change, when the basic values of today are the vain and shattered dreams of tomorrow, there is much to be said for a philosophy which aims at living a full life while the opportunity offers. There are few treasures of more lasting worth than the experience of a way of life that is in itself wholly satisfying. Such, after all, are the only possessions of which no fate, no cosmic catastrophe can deprive us; nothing can alter the fact if for one moment in eternity we have really lived.

References

Aitchison, C, MaCleod, N & Shaw, S. (2000) *Leisure and Tourism Landscapes.* London: Routledge.

Allison, M, Duda, J & Beuter,A. (1991) Group Dynamics in the Himalayas. *The International Review for the Sociology of Sport*, (26) 3:175-190.

Anderson, J. (1970) *The Ulysses Factor: The Exploring Instinct in Man.* London: Hodder & Stoughton.

Appleton, J. (1996) *The Experience of Landscape.* Chichester: Wiley.

Ashton, S. (1995). *Scrambles in Snowdonia.* Leicester: Cicerone Press.

Baddeley, M. (1884) *The English Lake District.* London: Bartholomew.

Barron, A. (1875) *Foot Notes: Walking As A Fine Art.* Wallingford, Connecticut: Wallingford Printing Co.

Barthes, R. (1973) *Mythologies.* St. Albans: Paladin.

Bartlett, P. (1993) *The Undiscovered Country.* Leicester: Ernest Press.

Baudrillard, J. (1985) The Ecstasy of Communication. pp. 126-134. In: Foster, H. (ed.) (1985) *Postmodern Culture.* London: Pluto.

Bauman, Z. (1987) *Legislators and Interpreters.* Cambridge: Polity Press.

Bauman, Z. (1991) *Modernity and Ambivalence.* Cambridge: Polity Press.

Beaumont, P. (2002) *The Great Outdoors*: supplement to The Observer, March 10th:8-10.

Bender, B. (ed.) (1995) *Landscape: Politics and Perspectives*. Oxford: Berg.

Bennet D. (1985) *The Munros*. Leicester: Cordee.

Bernbaum, E. (1997) *Sacred Mountains of the World*. London: University of California Press.

Bernstein, J. (1989a) [1965] *Ascent: The Invention of Mountain Climbing and Its Practice*. New York: Simon & Schuster.

Bernstein, J. (1989b) [1978] *Mountain Passages*. New York: Simon & Schuster.

Binkhurst, E & van der Duim, V. (1995*) Lost in the Jungle of Northern Thailand: the reproduction of hill-tribe trekking*. In: Ashworth, G & Dietvorst, A. (eds.) (1995) *Tourism and Spatial Transformations*. Wallingford: Cab International.

Birds Magazine (2000) *Publication of the RSPB*. Summer.

Birkett, B. (1983) *Lakeland's Greatest Pioneers*. London: Robert Hale.

BMC (1997) *Tread Lightly*. Manchester. BMC.

BMC (1999a) *Annual Report: Climbing Participation Statistics*. Manchester: BMC.

BMC (1999b) *Climbing Wall Directory*. Manchester: BMC.

BMC (2001) *Annual Report.* Manchester. BMC.

Bollen, S. (1994) *Training for Rock Climbing.* London: Pelham.

Bonnington, C. (1975) *I Chose To Climb.* London: Arrow.

Bonnington, C. (1978) *The Next Horizon.* London: Arrow.

Bonington, C. (1987) *The Everest Years.* London: Coronet Books.

Boorstin, D. (1963) *The Image.* Harmondsworth: Penguin.

Bourdieu, P. (1977) *Outline of a Theory of Practice.* Cambridge: Cambridge University Press.

Bourdieu, P. (1986) *Distinction.* London: Routledge.

Bourdieu, P. (1993) *The Field of Cultural Production.* Oxford: Polity Press.

Bragg, M. (1983) *Land of The Lakes.* London: Secker & Warburg.

Brendon, P. (1991) *Thomas Cook: 150 Years of Popular Tourism.* London: Secker & Warburg.

Brody, H. (1986) *Maps and Dreams.* London: Faber & Faber.

Bryman, A. (1988) *Quality and Quantity in Social Research.* London: Unwin-Hyman.

Bryson, B. (1990) *Travels in Small Town America.* London: Abacus.

Buck, R. (1977) The Ubiquitous Tourist Brochure. *Annals of Tourism Research*, 4(4): 195-207.

Bull, S. (1980) *Black Cuillin Ridge Scramblers Guide*. Edinburgh: Scottish Mountaineering Trust.

Burgess, R. (1984) *In the Field: An Introduction to Field Research*. London: Unwin-Hyman.

Buzard, J. (1993) *The Beaten Track*. Oxford: Clarendon Press.

Cannon, A. (1998) The Cultural and Historical Contexts of Fashion. In: Bryden, A & Niessen, S. (eds.) (1998) *Consuming Fashion*. Oxford: Berg.

Chaney, D. (1996) *Lifestyles*. London: Routledge.

Choegyal, L. (1997) *Nepal: Insight Guides*. Basingstoke: APA Publications.

Christiansen, D. (1990) *Adventure Tourism*. In Miles, J & Priest, S (1990) *Adventure Education*. State College, PA: Venture Publishing.

Classic Nepal (2000) *Mountaineering Brochure*. Alfreton.

Cloke, P & Perkins, H (1998a) *Pushing the Limits: Place, Promotion and Adventure Tourism in the South Island of New Zealand*. In: Perkins, H & Cushman, G. (1998) *Time Out: Leisure, Recreation and Tourism in New Zealand and Australia*. Auckland: Longman.

Cloke, P & Perkins, H. (1998b) 'Cracking the Canyon with the Awesome Foursome': representations of adventure tourism in New Zealand. *Environment & Planning D: Society and Space*, 16: 185-218.

Cohen, E. (1988) Authenticity and Commoditisation in Tourism. *Annals of Tourism Research*, 15:371-386.

Cohen, E. (1989) Primitive and Remote: Hill Tribe Trekking in Thailand. *Annals of Tourism Research*. 16:30-61.

Cohen, S & Taylor, L. (1992 2nd. ed.) *Escape Attempts: The Theory and Practice of Resistance to Everyday Life*. London: Routledge.

Collister, R. (1984) Adventure Versus The Mountain. *The Alpine Journal* 89:123-125.

Connor, J. (1999) *Creagh Dhu Climber: The Life and Times of John Cunningham*. Hong Kong: Ernest Press.

Cosgrove, D & Daniels, S. (eds.) (1988) *The Iconography of Landscape*. Cambridge: Cambridge University Press.

Craig, D. (1995) *Landmarks: An Exploration of Great Rocks*. London: Jonathan Cape.

Craik, J. (1994) *The Face of Fashion*. London: Routledge.

Crang, M. (1998) *Cultural Geography*. London: Routledge.

Creswell, J. (1994) *Research Design: Qualitative and Quantitative Approaches*. London: Sage.

Crick, M. (1989) Representations of International Tourism in the Social Sciences: Sun, Sex, Sights, Savings and Serenity. *Annual Review of Anthropology*, 18:307-344.

Curry, N. (1994) *Countryside Recreation, Access & Land Use Planning*. London: E & FN Spon.

Dann, G. (1996) Images of Destination people in Travelogues, pp. 349-375. In: Butler, R & Hinch, T. (eds.) (1996) *Tourism and Indigenous Peoples*. London: International Thomson Business Press.

Dempster, A. (1995) *The Munro Phenomenon*. Edinburgh: Mainstream Publishing.

De Selincourt, E. ([1835] 1977) *Wordsworth's Guide To The Lakes* (5th Ed.) Oxford: Oxford University Press.

Diemberger, K. (1983) *Summits and Secrets*. London: Hodder & Stoughton.

Dilley, R. (1986) Tourist Brochures and Tourist Images. *The Canadian Geographer*, 30(1): 59-65.

Donnelly, P. (1986) The Paradox of Parks: politics of recreational landuse before and after the mass trespass. *Leisure Studies* 5(2).

Donnelly, P. (1993) The Right To Wander: Issues In The Leisure Use of Countryside and Wilderness Areas. *International Review For The Sociology of Sport*, 28(2): 187-200.

Douglas, E. (1997) *Chomolungma Sings the Blues*. London: Constable.

Drasdo, H. (1997) *The Ordinary Route*. St. Edmundsbury: The Ernest Press.

Dunning, E. (1996) On Problems of the Emotions in Sport and Leisure: Critical and Counter Critical Comments on the Conventional and Configurational Sociologies of Sport and Leisure. *Leisure Studies*. 15(1) 185-207.

Edensor, T. (1998) *Tourists at the Taj*. London: Routledge.

Edensor, T. (1999) *Walking In The Countryside*. Draft paper.

Edensor, T. (2000) Walking in the British Countryside: Reflexivity, Embodied Practices and Ways to Escape. *Body & Society*, 6(3-4): 81-106.

Edensor, T. (2000a) *Landscapes and Topographies: Backpacking*. Unpublished paper.

Edensor, T. (2000b) Staging Tourism: Tourists as Performers. *Annals of Tourism Research*, 27(2): 322-344.

Edensor, T. (2001) Performing Tourism, Staging Tourism. *Tourist Studies*, 1(1): 59-81.

Elias, N. & Dunning, E. (1986) *The Quest for Excitement: Sport and Leisure in the Civilising Process*. Oxford: Basil Blackwell.

Exodus (2000) *Walking & Trekking Brochure*. London.

Explore Worldwide (1999) *Brochure*. London.

Finlay, A. (2001) *The Way To Cold Mountain*. Edinburgh: Pocket Books.

Fleming, F. (2000) *Killing Dragons: The Conquest of the Alps*. London: Granta Books.

Fletcher, C. (1967) *The Man Who Walked Through Time*. New York: Vintage Books.

Foundry Mountain Activities (2000) *Brochure*. Sheffield.

Foundry mountain Activities (2001) *Brochure*. Sheffield.

Frison-Roche, R & Jouty, S. (1996) *A History of Mountain Climbing*. New York: Flammarion.

Furedi, F. (1997) *Culture of Fear*. London: Cassell.

Fyffe, A & Peter, I. (1990) *The Handbook of Climbing*. London: Pelham.

Gair, N. (1997) *Outdoor Education:Theory and Practice*. London: Cassell.

Giddens, A. (1990) *The Consequences of Modernity*. Cambridge: Polity Press.

Giddens, A. (1991) *Modernity and Self Identity*. Cambridge: Polity Press.

Gifford, T. (1999) *Pastoral*. London: Routledge.

Gifford, T. & Smith, R. (1994) *Orogenic Zones*. Leeds: Bretton Hall.

Goffman, E. (1959) *The Presentation of Self in Everyday Life*. Harmondsworth: Penguin.

Goffman, E. (1971) *Relations in Public*. Harmondsworth: Penguin.

Gray, D. (1979) *Rope Boy*. London: Gollancz.

Greenway, R. (1995) Healing by the Wilderness Experience. pp. 182-193. In: Rothenberg, D. (Ed.) (1995) *Wild Ideas*. Minnesota: University of Minnesota Press.

Hammersley, M & Atkinson, P. (1983) *Ethnography: Principles in Practice*. London: Routledge.

Hammersley, M. (1992) *What's Wrong With Ethnography?* London: Routledge.

Harrison, C. (1991) *Countryside Recreation in a Changing Society.* London: TMS.

Hart, R. (1968) *The Inviolable Hills.* London: Stuart & Watkins.

Harvey, D. (1989) *The Condition of Postmodernity.* Oxford: Basil Blackwell.

Harvey, D. (1993) From Space To Place and Back Again: Reflections on the Condition of Postmodernity, pp. 3-29. In: Bird, J, Curtis, B, Putnam, T, Robertson, G, & Tickner, L. (eds.) (1993) *Mapping The Futures: Local Cultures, Global Change.* London: Routledge.

Henderson, J. (2001) *Pique Amid The Peaks.* The Observer, November 25th.

Henderson, K. (1991) *Dimensions of Choice: A Qualitative Approach to Recreation, Parks, and Leisure Research.* State College PA: Venture Publishing.

Hetherington, K. (1996) Identity Formation, Space and Social Centrality. *Theory, Culture & Society.* 13(4) 33-52.

Hewitt, D. (1996) Greene and Pleasence Land. *The Great Outdoors*, February:44-45.

Heywood, I. (1994) Urgent Dreams: Climbing, Rationalisation and Ambivalence. *Leisure Studies*, 13: 179-194.

High (1999a) *High Mountain Sports.* September, 202.

High (1999b) *High Mountain Sports.* October, 203.

High (2000) *High Mountain Sports.* January, 206.

High Places (2000) *Mountaineering Brochure*. Sheffield.

Hillaby, J. (1981) Forward: The Winding Trail. pp. 13-16. In: Smith, R. (1981) *The Winding Trail*. London: Diadem.

Himalayan Kingdoms (1998) *Winter Newsletter*. Bristol.

Himalayan Kingdoms Trekking (2000) *Brochure*. Bristol.

Hoskins, W. [1955] (1970) *The Making of The English Landscape*. Harmondsworth: Penguin.

Hubank, R. (2001) *Hazard's Way*. St. Edmundsbury: The Ernest Press.

Hudson, S. (ed.) (Forthcoming 2002) *Sport & Adventure Tourism*. London: Hawarth Press.

Hughson, J. (1996) *A Feel for the Game: An Ethnographic Study of Soccer Support and Social Identity*. Unpublished PhD. University of New South Wales.

Humble, B. (1986) [1952] *The Cuillin of Skye*. Edinburgh: Ernest Press.

Jagged Globe (2000) *Brochure*. Sheffield.

Jarvie, G & Maguire, J. (1994) *Sport and Leisure in Social Thought*. London: Routledge.

Jenkins, R. (1983) *Lads, Citizens and Ordinary Kids: Working -class Youth Life-styles in Belfast*. London: Routledge & Kegan Paul.

Jenkins, R. (1996) *Social Identity*. London: Routledge.

Jerome, J. (1979) *On Mountains: Thinking About Terrain*. London: Gollancz.

Johnson, B & Edwards, T. (1994) The Commodification of Mountaineering. *Annals of Tourism Research*, 21(3): 459-478.

Kellehear, A. (1993) *The Unobtrusive Researcher*. St. Leonards, Australia: Allen & Unwin.

Krakauer, J. (1996) *Into The Wild*. London: Macmillan.

Langmuir, E. (1995) *Mountaincraft and Leadership*. Manchester: The Mountain Leader Training Board.

Lay, P. (1999) Climb Every Munro. *The Times Weekend* p.21: July 24.

Le Sage, J. (2000) *An Exploration Into The Factors That Affect The participation of Asian and Afro-Caribbean Individuals In Countryside Recreation*. Unpublished under-graduate dissertation.

Lewis, N. (2000) The Climbing Body, Nature and the Experience of Modernity. *Body & Society*, 6(3-4): 58-80.

Light, A. (1995) Urban Wilderness, pp. 195-211. In: Rothenberg, D. (ed.) (1995) *Wild Ideas*. Minneapolis: University of Minnesota Press.

Loker-Murphy, L & Pearce, P. (1995) Young Budget Travelers [sic] : Backpackers in Australia. *Annals of Tourism Research*, 22(4): 819-843.

Lorimer, H. (2000) De-bagging The Munros: The Promotion and Commodification of Scotland's Mountains. Glasgow: *LSA Conference Paper*.

Lyng, S. (1990) Edgework: A Social psychological Analysis of Voluntary Risk Taking. *American Journal of Sociology*, 95(4): 851-886.

Lyotard, J. (1984) *The Postmodern Condition*. London: Routledge.

MacCannell, D. (1976) *The Tourist: A New Theory of The Leisure Class*. London: Macmillan.

MacDonald, J. (no date) *Discovering Skye*. Kilmuir, Skye: Beric Tempest.

Macnaghten, P & Urry, J. (1998) *Contested Natures*. London: Sage.

Maeder, H. (ed.) (1975) *The Lure of The Mountains*. London: Phaidon.

Marriot, M. (1983) *The Uplands of Britain*. London: Willow-Collins.

McLuhan, T. (1996) *Cathedrals of The Spirit*. London: Thorsons.

McNeill, P. (1990) *Research Methods*. London: Routledge.

Meier, K. (1976) The Kinship of the Rope and The Loving Struggle. *Journal of The Philosophy of Sport* 3(1): 52-64.

Meinig, D. (ed.) (1979) *The Interpretation of Ordinary Landscapes*. Oxford: Oxford University Press.

Melucci, A. (1996) *The Playing Self: Person and Meaning in the Planetary Society*. Cambridge: Cambridge University Press.

Miah, A. (1999) *Climbing Upwards or Climbing Backwards: The Technological Metamorphoses of Climbing & Mountaineering*. Paper for Ist. International Conference on Science & Technology in Climbing & Mountaineering. Leeds University.

Michael, M. (2000) These Boots Are Made For Walking: Mundane Technology, The Body & Human-Environment Relations. *Body & Society*, 6(3-4): 107-126.

Milburn, G. (1997) *The First Fifty Years of The British Mountaineering Council*. Manchester: BMC.

Miles, J & Priest, S. (1999) *Adventure Programming*. PA: Venture Publishing Inc.

Mills, J. (1961) *Airborne to the Mountains*. London: Herbert Jenkins.

Mitchell, R. (1983) *Mountain Experience: The Psychology and Sociology of Adventure*. Chicago: University of Chicago Press.

Moore, A. (1939) [1867] *The Alps in 1864*. Oxford: Blackwell.

Mortlock, C. (1973) *The Philosophy of Adventure Education*. pp. 656-659. In: Wilson, K. (Ed.) (1978) *The Games Climbers Play*. London: Diadem.

Mortlock, C. (1984) *The Adventure Alternative*. Milnthorpe: Cicerone Press.

Mortlock, C. (2001) *Beyond Adventure*. Milnthorpe: Cicerone Press.

Muir, J. (1992) *The Eight Wilderness-Discovery Books*. London: Diadem.

Neil, S. (2001) Preparing for the Alps. *Summit Magazine*, 23, Autumn.

Noyce, W. (1958) *The Springs of Adventure*. London: John Murray.

Observer Magazine (2000) *The Cost of Climbing Everest*. September 1st.

Oelschlaeger, M. (1991) *The Idea Of Wilderness*. London: Yale University Press.

Perrin, J. (ed.) (1983) *Mirrors in the Cliffs*. London: Diadem.

Perrin, J. (1986) *On and Off The Rocks*. London: Gollancz.

Poucher, W. (1964) *The Scottish Peaks*. London: Constable.

Poucher, W. (1983) *The Alps*. London: Constable.

Price, T. (2000) *Travail So Gladly Spent*. St. Edmundsbury: Ernest Press.

Reid, R. (1992) *The Great Blue Dream: Inside the Mind of The Mountaineer*. London: Hutchinson.

Ritzer, G. & Liska, A. (1997) *McDisneyization and Post-Tourism*. In: Rojek, C. & Urry, J. (1997) *Touring Cultures: Transformations of Travel and Theory*. London: Routledge.

Rojek, C & Urry, J. (1997) *Touring Cultures: Transformations in Travel and Theory*. London: Routledge.

Rojek, C. (1993) *Ways of Escape*. London: Macmillan Press.

Rojek, C. (1995) *Decentring Leisure*. London: Sage.

Rojek, C. (2000) *Leisure and Culture*. London: Macmillan Press.

Rothenberg, D. (ed.) (1995) *Wild Ideas*. London: University of Minnesota Press.

Rubens, D. (1999) Effort or Performance: Keys to Motivated Learners in the Outdoors. *Horizons*, 4:26-28.

Sands, R. (1999) Experiential Ethnography: Playing With The Boys. In: Sands, R. (ed.) (1999) *Anthropology, Sport and Culture*. London: Bergin & Garvey.

Sarup, M. (1996) *Identity, Culture & The Postmodern World*. Edinburgh: Edinburgh University Press.

Selwyn, T. (ed.) (1996) *The Tourist Image*. Chichester: John Wiley.

Sharpley, R. (1994) *Tourism, Tourists and Society*. Huntingdon: Elm Publications.

Shields, R. (1991) *Places on the Margin*. London: Routledge.

Shilling, C. (1993) *The Body and Social Theory*. London: Sage.

Shipton, E. (1944) *Upon That Mountain*. London: Hodder & Stoughton.

Short, J. (1991) *Imagined Country: Environment, Culture and Society*. London: Routledge.

Smith, C. (2001) Comfort Zone. *Summit Magazine*, 23, Autumn.

Smith, R. (ed.) (1981) *The Winding Trail*. London: Diadem.

Smythe, F. (1941) *The Mountain Vision*. London: Hodder & Stoughton.

Smythe, F. (1946) *The Spirit of The Hills*. London: Hodder & Stoughton.

Solnit, R. (2001) *Wanderlust: A History of Walking*. London: Verso.

Sparkes, A. (1992) *Research in Physical Education and Sport*. London: Falmer Press.

Spradley, J & Mann, B. (1975) *The Cocktail Waitress*. London: John Wiley & Sons.

Stainforth, G. (1994) *The Cuillin*. London: Constable.

Stainforth, G. (1998) *The Peak: Past and Present*. London: Constable.

Stephen, L. [1894] (1936) *The Playground of Europe*. Oxford: Blackwell.

Suits, B. (1980) *The Grasshopper: Games, Life & Utopia*. Toronto: University of Toronto Press.

Summit (1999) *Summit Magazine*, 15, Autumn.

Summit (2002) *Summit Magazine*, 25, Spring.

Swire, O. (1961) *Skye: The Island and Its Legends*. London: Blackie & Son.

Tejada-Flores, L. (1978) [1967] *Games Climbers Play*. In: Wilson, K. (ed.) (1978) *The Games Climbers Play*. London: Diadem.

Terra Firma (1997) *Trekking Brochure*. London.

The Great Outdoors (1995) April.

The Outdoor Shop (1998) *Newsletter*. Stony Stratford. Winter:1.

Thomas, K. (1983) *Man and The Natural World*. Harmondsworth: Penguin.

Trail (1998a) *Trail Magazine*, May.

Trail (1998b) *Trail Magazine*, December.

Trail (1999) *Trail magazine*, February.

Trauer, B. (1999) *Conceptualising Adventure Tourism and Travel Placed in the Australian Context*. Unpublished paper. University of Lancaster.

Urry, J & Macnaghten, P. (2000) Bodies of Nature: Introduction. *Body & Society*, 6(3-4): 1-11.

Urry, J. (1990) *The Tourist Gaze*. London: Sage.

Urry, J. (1995) *Consuming Places*. London: Routledge.

Urry, J. (2000) *Sociology Beyond Societies*. London: Routledge.

Visser, M. (1997) *The Way We Are*. Harmondsworth: Penguin.

Wainwright, A. (1958) *The Central Fells*. Kendal: Wilson & Son.

Walker, R. (1989) *Walks and Climbs In The Picos De Europa*. Milnthorpe: Cicerone Press.

Wallace, A. (1993) *Walking, Literature and English Culture*. Oxford: Clarendon Press.

Walter, J. (1982) Social Limits to Tourism. *Leisure Studies*, 1:295-304.

Walter, J. (1984) Death As Recreation: Armchair Mountaineering. *Leisure Studies*, 3(1): 67-76.

Weber, K. (2001) Outdoor Adventure Tourism: A Review of Research Approaches. *Annals of Tourism Research*, 28(2):360-377.

Weiler, B. & Hall, C. (eds.) (1993) *Special Interest Tourism*. London: Belhaven Press.

Wells, C. (2001) *A Brief History of British Mountaineering*. Manchester: The Mountain Heritage Trust.

Whillans, D & Omerod, A. (1971) *Don Whillans: Portrait of A Mountaineer*. London: Heinemann.

Whitehead, M. (1990) Meaningful Existence, Embodiment and Physical Education. *Journal of Philosophy of Education* 24(1):3-13.

Whyte, W,F. [1943] (1955) *Street Corner Society*. Chicago: The University of Chicago Press.

Williams, S & Bendelow, G. (1998) *The Lived Body: Sociological Themes, Embodied Issues*. London: Routledge.

Wilson, K & Gilbert, R. (eds.) (1984) *Classic Walks*. London: Diadem.

Wilson, K & Gilbert, R. (eds.) (1988) *Wild Walks*. London: Baton-Wicks.

Wilson, K & Gilbert, R. (eds.) (1980) *The Big Walks*. London: Diadem.

Wilson, K. (ed.) (1974) *Hard Rock*. London: Granada.

Wilson, K. (ed.) (1978a) *The Games Climbers Play*. London: Diadem.

Wilson, K. (ed.) (1978b) *Classic Rock*. London: Granada.

Winthrop-Young, G. (1933) *On High Hills*. London: Methuen.

Wolcott, H. (1990) *Writing Up Qualitative Research*. London: Sage.

Worldwide Journeys & Expeditions (2000) *Brochure*. London.